C000257677

TWIN ROCK'N RIOT SHOW!

ROCK 'N ROLL FROM OVERSEAS - DELINQUENT GIRLS

MIGHTIEST DOUBLE BILL IN THE UNIVERSE!

DOUBLE-DARE DOUBLE FEATURE

CAUTION THE MOST GRUESOME HORROR EVER SHOWN!

NOT FOR THE SQUEAMISH!

FREE FIRST-AID AND SMELLING-SALTS!

PRIMITIVE PASSIONS UNLEASHED!

WHITE WOMAN vs. DEADLY PYTHON!

FROM TOWERING WILD ADVENTURE... TO THE DEPTHS OF HELLISH HORROR!

THE DOUBLE SHOCK SHOW OF THE YEAR!

DOUBLE SOCK...ROCK...and THRILL SHOW!

Together on one program!

TWO TOP THRILLER-CHILLERS!

HE FIRST TIME! TWO Top Science-Horror Shows on ONE Program!

DOUBLE!! DYNAMITE! ACTION! THRILLS!

INCREDIBLY FANTASTIC! YOU WON'T BELIEVE YOUR EYES!

UNCENSORED

"THE SLEAZE-FILLED SAGA OF AN EXPLOITATION DOUBLE FEATURE"

GRINDHOUSE

WITH CONTRIBUTIONS BY
ROBERT RODRIGUEZ & QUENTIN TARANTINO
AND THE CAST AND CREW OF "GRINDHOUSE"

EDITED & DESIGNED BY **KURT VOLK**
PHOTOGRAPHY BY **RICO TORRES & ANDREW COOPER**

TITAN BOOKS

Copyright © 2007 Weinstein Books

Published in the United Kingdom by Titan Books
www.titanbooks.com

No part of this publication may be reproduced, stored in a retrieval
system, or transmitted, in any form or by any means without the prior
written permission of the publisher, nor be otherwise circulated in any
form of binding or cover other than that in which it is published and
without a similar condition being imposed on the subsequent purchaser.

A CIP catalogue record for this title is available from the British Library.

ISBN-13: 9781845763596
ISBN-10: 1 84576 359 9

First Edition
10 9 8 7 6 5 4 3 2 1

Edited and Designed by Kurt Volk
Color-Correction by Sean K. Lackey

Manufactured in the United States of America

CONTENTS

INTRODUCTION BY ROBERT RODRIGUEZ

BEFORE I DID SIN CITY, I was fooling around with this idea of making a double feature. Each story being between fifty and sixty minutes in length, but not at all like a *segment* or a *short story* but full feature stories that have been truncated and tightened, with all the boring stuff taken out, with a fifteen to twenty minute first act, twenty minute second act, and fifteen to twenty minute finale. Balls to the wall, and there'd be two of these back to back.

I was tired of traditional movie formats and wanted to do something new and different.

I ended up putting it on hold and making *Sin City* instead. But coming off the success of that, I presented this idea of the double feature to Quentin one day and he loved it. He came up with his own story idea, and I decided to do a story I've been working on over the years called *Planet Terror*.

One reason I chose that is because it had the best title, suggesting a whole other world. (But in classic exploitation movie tradition, it's actually set on Earth. Earth itself has become *Planet Terror*.) What excites me the most about this project is not just its bold nature of having two movies in one, made by two filmmakers who love to entertain their audiences, but that my story features the best action character I've ever come up with. So that has me salivating at getting this thing up on screens for people.

Overall, mine and Quentin's excitement level for this movie is so high, that at times we have to calm ourselves down. It feels like we have truly gotten ourselves into the mindset of making this pact with our audiences that they are going to see things they just would not get in regular movies today, and that we are going to give them *exploitable elements*. But the difference between our movie and the grindhouse movies of yesteryear is that we can actually afford to make a really great movie that is full of great characters, dialogue and story. We're taking this classic, forgotten genre and turning it into something big, exciting and new.

Welcome to our *Grindhouse*.

-Robert Rodriguez

INTRODUCTION BY QUENTIN TARANTINO

I'M A HUGE FAN OF SLASHER FILMS OF THE LATE '70S, EARLY '80S. It's one of my favorite genres and I've been falling in love with them all over again recently. And I decided I wanted to do a slasher film. But it's such a rich genre that everything I thought of doing couldn't help but come across looking self-reflective. And I wanted to make the movie I would have made if I hadn't gotten lucky with *Reservoir Dogs*, getting to make exactly what I wanted to do, artistically, right out of the gate. I always wished I would have had to make like two or three great exploitation movies until I got the chance to make *Reservoir Dogs*.

So now I'm going back. And now I want to make the exploitation movie I would have made if I could have done anything I wanted and at least have it play the grindhouse circuit. So my story, *Death Proof*, is in the vein of a slasher film, but instead of the slasher using his knife, he uses a car.

Funny thing is, when Robert and I came up with this idea of the double feature, we knew that our first movie should be in the horror genre. But then we started coming up with Kung Fu film ideas, Spaghetti Western ideas, Mexican action film and Italian crime film ideas and all this stuff and then we thought, "Well, wait a minute. Let's do it where those will be the trailers. Those will be the trailers that we'll have in between our two movies." And then we even thought of the idea of bringing a couple of our friends into it to let them do a couple of trailers. And our hope is that the trailers will be so cool, and people will like them so much, that for *Grindhouse 2*, they'll demand that we actually make one of those movies. And I love the idea of doing more *Grindhouse* movies. You know, that would literally be a great life. Life wouldn't get much better than that.

Robert and I have these great posters, but for the first time in grindhouse history, our movie is going to be *better* than the poster. We're going to deliver! We're going to deliver on each adjective we put on those ads!

-Quentin Tarantino

ROBERT RODRIGUEZ, Director: What is grindhouse cinema in the traditional sense?

QUENTIN TARANTINO, Director: All the big cities had their ghetto movie theaters. Either they were old theaters in areas that had become dilapidated—just playing for the people in those big city neighborhoods. Or they were all-night theaters that would play, one, three, four movies. It would be a place for the bums to go and sleep. Or, if you were hiding out from the law, you'd go there for the night. Then at six in the morning they'd wake you up and send you out, so you'd walk around for ninety minutes and come right back in again. So that's actually what the grindhouse theaters were. That's if you're talking about theaters. Grindhouse theaters were in urban areas in the bigger cities. Dallas would have grindhouses, and Houston would have grindhouses, but in the outer regions of Texas, it'd be more about the drive-ins. If you're talking about drive-ins, they had the same shows but they were a whole different setting. Mostly those were throughout the South.

ROBERT RODRIGUEZ: They weren't studio movies; they were all independently made.

QUENTIN TARANTINO: Well it's funny because they primarily played exploitation films, but it's actually a misconception that they never played studio fare. One of the things that was so wild about the grindhouses was how completely eclectic their double or triple bills were. They knew that if they played a kung fu movie or a blaxploitation movie, it didn't even matter what the hell it was. It could be any movie. Just call it *Black Jim* or *Kung Fu Fist of Death*. Make up your own titles, put them on the marquee, and people would

BELOW: New York's 42nd Street circa 1968. • **OPPOSITE:** Original window card for *I Was A Teenage Frankenstein* (1958) & *Blood of Dracula* (1957). Poster courtesy of the Benton Card Company.

EXPLOITABLE ELEMENTS

RODRIGUEZ AND TARANTINO DEFINE THE GRINDHOUSE EXPERIENCE

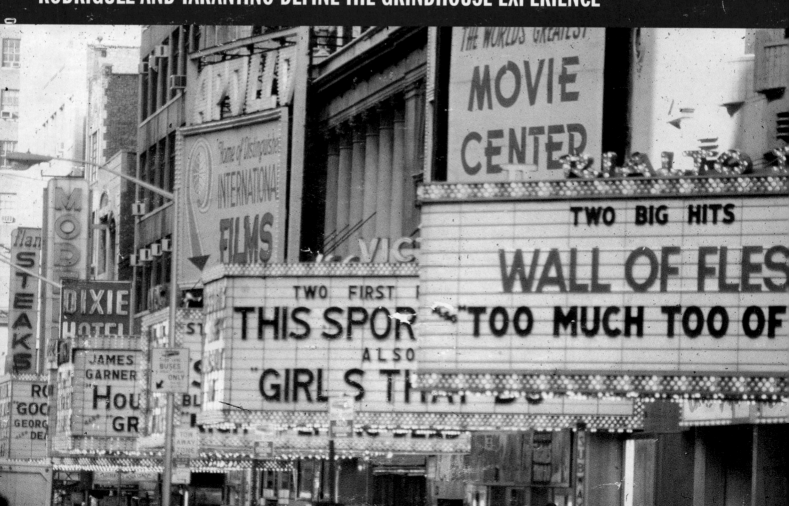

FIENDISH   FRENZIED   BLOOD-CHILLING!

NOTHING LIKE THIS IN ALL THE HISTORY OF HORROR!

BODY OF A BOY!
MIND OF A MONSTER!
SOUL OF AN
UNEARTHLY THING!

BOTH ALL NEW

in her eyes DESIRE!   in her veins
...the blood of a MONSTER!

I WAS A TEENAGE FRANKENSTEIN

BLOOD of DRACULA
WILL GIVE YOU NIGHTMARES FOREVER

starring
WHIT BISSELL · PHYLLIS COATES · ROBERT BURTON · GARY CONWAY
Produced by **HERMAN COHEN** · Directed by **HERBERT L. STROCK** · Screenplay by **KENNETH LANGTRY**
A JAMES H. NICHOLSON-SAMUEL Z. ARKOFF PRODUCTION · AN AMERICAN INTERNATIONAL PICTURE

starring
Sandra HARRISON · Louise LEWIS · Gail GANLEY · Jerry BLAINE
Produced by **HERMAN COHEN** · Directed by **HERBERT L. STROCK** · Screenplay by **RALPH THORNTON**
A JAMES H. NICHOLSON-SAMUEL Z. ARKOFF PRODUCTION · AN AMERICAN INTERNATIONAL PICTURE

CAUTION THE MOST GRUESOME HORROR EVER SHOWN!

NOT FOR THE SQUEAMISH!

FREE FIRST-AID AND SMELLING-SALTS!

DON'T COME BEFORE DINNER!

WARNING FOR PEOPLE WHO FAINT EASILY!

SEE FRANKENSTEIN'S MONSTER IN **COLOR**

675

BENTON CARD COMPANY, BENSON, N. C.

show up. Back in the day when movies played for six months, they also showed the big budget films that had been playing. They would get those films on their way out of town. *A Star Is Born* came out in '76, but, at a grindhouse in the middle of '77, you could easily see it playing with a kung fu movie.

Also you have to remember that when exploitation movies came in, it wasn't like the way movies are now where they open up on three thousand theaters playing everywhere at once. Exploitation companies would consider making twenty prints a big release. And they would take those twenty prints to Houston or Los Angeles or Atlanta. They'd just schlep them around the country, one city at a time. They usually only played for a week.

ROBERT RODRIGUEZ: A lot of the prints were so scratched up and worn out by the time anybody saw them because they made so few prints.

QUENTIN TARANTINO: Yeah, if you were lucky enough to get an exploitation movie at the beginning of its run, the prints could be okay. But after it played at the El Paso Drive-In Theater, *God fucking knows* what the conditions would be. How good the prints were going to be depended on what part of the daisy chain you lived in.

ROBERT RODRIGUEZ: How long ago was it that you started collecting film prints?

QUENTIN TARANTINO: That was about '96, just before *Jackie Brown*.

ROBERT RODRIGUEZ: I remember I went to your old apartment and you had a sixteen millimeter projector strung up. We were supposed to be working on *Dusk till Dawn* and instead we played hooky and watched *White Lightning*—sitting at home, watching movies on our own sixteen millimeter projector. Now your theater's grown.

QUENTIN TARANTINO: Yeah, now I have a theater alright.

ROBERT RODRIGUEZ: That's when we got the idea to do our own grindhouse movie.

When I came over to Quentin's house, he would show trailers, features, some more trailers—all vintage stuff—and then a second feature. All different types of movies, different types of film prints, some of them really worn out, some of them really nice—depending on what you could get from the collector. We thought, 'Let's recreate this experience that we have when we come over to Quentin's house. But for audiences all over the world. Fake trailers, two features, and make it a night at the movies.'

QUENTIN TARANTINO: Robert came up with his zombie idea a while ago. So he kind of knew where he was going to go with it. But when we first started off, the bigger idea was the idea of this whole package— that it would be two movies surrounded by trailers, surrounded by all the accoutrements—the candy ads that you see in the 70s, the ratings warning, all that stuff that I've collected. We wanted to put it all together as a show to kind of give the whole audience the exact experience. Almost like a grindhouse ride. You get to go into a safe multiplex and watch this instead of a dangerous grindhouse where you take your life in your hands.

ROBERT RODRIGUEZ: This idea built up over a period of about a year. It kept growing. I had come up with the idea of doing a double feature back and forth. I was really crazy about this idea because I had these scripts that were kind of half completed and thought, 'I'll never finish all of them. I'm going to have to start doubling up. Maybe I should start doing double features, three in a row.'

But after *Sin City*, I went over to Quentin's house to show him his scene and I stepped over this *Rock All Night/Drag Strip Girl* double bill poster—the same one I had at my house.

QUENTIN TARANTINO: He stepped over it because all my shit is all over the fuckin' floor.

ROBERT RODRIGUEZ: I have that same poster on the floor at my house, and I remembered I had an idea for a double bill. I was going to direct two movies, but I said, "You should do one and I'll do the other one." He said, "Oh I love double features. We gotta call it *Grindhouse*." This all came out in like five minutes. That's where the whole idea of doing the two movies together came from. He said if we do them together, we should do a horror movie first. A few days later, he was already talking about it to the press and I think I read it in one of the trades or something. By then he had already added the idea of trailers which I hadn't heard yet. I read about it and thought, 'Oh and we're doing fake trailers. We are? That's actually a great idea.'

QUENTIN TARANTINO: I grew up watching the regular, popular movies. I saw *Rocky* when it came out. I loved *Rocky*. I saw all that stuff when it came out. As I got older and could actually start to drive to theaters outside of my area, I'd even go see the foreign films. But concurrently, through my entire pre-teen years, I went to these exploitation movies.

These films existed outside the mainstream of Hollywood. It was similar to the way punk rock was. That shit was raw. Shit was off the hook. Sexuality was wild. You almost can't even believe some of the sexuality and gore and brutality that they got away with in these movies. You literally had to pinch yourself and say, 'Am I even watching what I'm watching?' When regular audiences watched that weird scene in *Blue Velvet* where Dean Stockwell sings the Roy Orbison song, there was this collective gasp in the theater. Shit like that was often in grindhouse movies. Weird non sequitur scenes that have you thinking you can not believe you're seeing what you're seeing. In the movie *Don't Go In The House* when you actually see the guy create an inferno room to burn women. Or in *Blood-Spattered Bride* where two lesbian lovers cut off the member of one of their husbands. It's just wild, wild stuff. And we saw that all the time.

That's always been where cinema can go for me. That is, cinema is not just Hollywood. Cinema is grindhouse; it can go there. So I grow up, I make *Reservoir Dogs* and at the time it's actually treated as one of the most violent movies ever made, and—I didn't get that at all. I mean I was really proud of the response, but to me the violence in that movie wasn't shit. I've seen the most violent movies ever made—*Reservoir Dogs* is not it. It might be one of the most violent movies you've ever seen, but, with the shit I grew up with, I have a huge tolerance. That's just moviemaking as far as I'm concerned.

I live to pay that money and sit in a movie theater and not believe what I'm seeing. And I don't mean in an incredulous I-can't-believe-it's-so-bad kind of way, but in like, 'Am I even watching this?' You look around at the rest of the audience and think, 'Well, yeah, they're watching it too. This is some shit. I'm going to remember this for the rest of my fucking life.' Well those moments happened in grindhouse cinema.

I could single out each sub-distributor and distributor; they all had their own little personality. But I think the biggest connection that we have to the old grindhouse days was Roger Corman's New World Pictures. Even though the Roger Corman movies were done fairly cheap, ultimately he was the auteur because no matter what you did on the set, he'd like re-shoot ten minutes of it, add more action, more car chases. Maybe if you had a more satirical bent, he'd take that shit out and keep it more grim. But having said that, the thing that was actually really cool about New World Pictures as opposed to AIP, the Italians, Crown International, or any of these other companies like Dimension Pictures, was that Roger Corman loved mixing up different sub-genres inside of one movie. It literally came out of the idea that if the audience doesn't like this ten minutes, all they have to do is hang on, and then they're going to have something wholly different coming in about ten minutes time. And if that doesn't grab them, they can just hang on a little bit longer and there'll be another ten minutes of something different. One of these things was sure to grab you. They kind of made the movies work ten minutes at a time. There's nudity, there's a car crash, and all the sudden a black stud

walks in; now it's a blaxploitation movie, now it's a car chase movie, now it's a women-in-prison movie. That happened a lot. Even with great writers like John Sayles. *The Lady In Red* is an exploitation movie of his that kind of mirrors both of ours in that it's so many different movies inside of one. It's one of the best scripts he ever wrote—the Dillinger story told from the prostitute's point-of-view. It's a prostitute movie, then it turns a corner and it's a women-in-prison movie for about twenty minutes. Then it becomes a gangster movie—with John Dillinger in it no less.

Actually, my dream back when I was like eighteen, nineteen was to approach Roger Corman in his parking lot and get him to hire me as the assistant editor on trailers and literally work my way up the way Joe Dante and Allan Arkush and Jonathan Kaplan did— all those guys who worked for Corman in the 70s. It never happened but that literally would have been my dream in life. And one time I actually tried to call Roger Corman at New World Pictures and I ended up just talking to his assistant. I told her my little story. You know what was really cool? She didn't put me in to Roger Corman, but she said, "You keep working at it, you keep working at it." She said, "You're on—you got the right idea. Keep it up. Don't give up. You'll be a director." She actually stopped to give me a ten minute pep talk, to say that I had the right idea and that I should just keep going on. That I shouldn't wait for Roger Corman to make my dreams come true, but make them come true myself. Just keep at it and don't give up. That was her number one thing. Just keep at it. Roger Corman's fuckin' assistant saying this to me, and I'm just a boy from the telephone. I could have been a phone freak for all she knew.

ROBERT RODRIGUEZ: Sometimes you'd see a double feature where Pam Grier was in both movies. She was like a prisoner in one, and then she's the warden in the other one. I told Quentin "Wow, we could make that work. When I finish casting, you should use my actors for parts in yours to play different characters. That would be great if some of them crossed over." And some of them did. Rose McGowan's in both. She's the lead in mine and supporting in his. Marley Shelton is in both too.

QUENTIN TARANTINO: Yeah, Nicky Katt's in both. Nicky Katt is our Dick Miller.

ROBERT RODRIGUEZ: He totally is. So we actually ended up with four people that did cross over.

QUENTIN TARANTINO: The twins are in mine too. That's actually one of the fun features of watching New World Pictures—Dick Miller was in every one of them for a long time. This happened a lot in films made in the Philippines. The Philippines was a great place for grindhouse films. We call them grindhouse films here, but there they were big movies. The thing that was funny is when Filipino directors like Eddie Romero or Cirio H. Santiago worked for New World Pictures, their budgets and the quality actually went *up*. When they did their own Filipino movies—it went way down dollar-wise.

And they would work with these amazing actors. People like Vic Diaz, Joe Mari Avelana, Leo Martinez, Ken Metcalf, John Ashley and, of course, Sid Haig. So Sid Haig would go to the Philippines to do one movie, Pam Grier's there to do one, Roberta Collins is there to do another. So the producers would think, 'Well fuck, we already paid their first-class plane ticket, and the hotel room isn't much. We might as well shoot another movie with them.' So with the cast of someone like Pam Grier, and say Judy Brown, they would do *The Big Doll House*, directed by Jack Hill—which has a very satirical bent to it, by the way. Then they turn around and do *Women in Chains*. They do *Women in Chains* directed by Eddie Romero, who was a huge director in the Philippines. And that movie is fucking grim. I mean totally grim. But it was funny, too, because you could still see it was the same trip as *The Big Doll House*. They took the same trip, and they did like three movies while they were there. If I ever came up with the right script, I would actually like to make a movie about making an exploitation movie in Philippines in the 70s about women in prison because Pam Grier told me a lot of stories about it. It was pretty cool.

We actually really liked that idea that Nicky Katt was in both of ours, Rose is sort of like our Pam Grier character. I think I'm like the Sid Haig character.

ROBERT RODRIGUEZ: Yeah, that's right.

QUENTIN TARANTINO: I'm definitely Sid Haig in your movie. That would definitely be the role Sid Haig would be playing if this was the 70s.

Most of the women in the grindhouse films married rich husbands. They almost all married millionaires at some point down the line, and they're now big house wives. Margaret Markov, who was the white mama on *Black Mama, White Mama* and *Pretty Maids All In A Row* and *The Hot Box* married Mark Damon who ran the company that made *Short Circuit*. I met them together. White mama. I even said, "I have your gorgeous poster for *Pretty Maids All In A Row*." And Mark Damon—her husband—said, "I have that poster too."

Part of the reason a movie was called an exploitation movie was because it couldn't afford a Barbra Streisand or Paul Newman to sell it. So they had to have *exploitable elements* like sex, action, violence, horror, blood. So the posters were these really graphically drawn, very exciting images of mayhem. Like a sexy girl with a shotgun, in a bikini, with incredibly long legs and all this mayhem going on around her. And

the poster was filled with these great tag lines that just screamed out all these sensationalistic adjectives describing everything.

Well then you would go see the movie and it was made for so cheap they couldn't afford to do any of that crap from the poster. Those adjectives don't usually really live up to most of the movies that I paid money to go see back in those days. With those films, you never knew what you were gonna see. Make no mistake, though, seventy percent of the time they let you down, alright. Seventy percent of the time. But every once in a while they *didn't* and that made them like the greatest movies ever.

ROBERT RODRIGUEZ: And that's what our movie is. Our movie's not a trick. We're not going to trick you in with the idea that it's going to be something it's not—it delivers. The posters say it and then we deliver.

QUENTIN TARANTINO: Exactly. We were just joking the other day that because mine fuses two different sub-genres together. It fuses the slasher film with high-octane car chase action, which was also a big staple. And fuses it so much so that they literally—the genres switch hands at some point in the movie. There is some point in the film when you're not watching what came before. You have actually switched genres now and you're into a different movie. You're involved with the characters so you don't notice it, but you're actually in a different movie now. We were talking about the idea if we could take existing movies and actually do a double feature that would duplicate more or less what our double features do in *Grindhouse*, it would have to be a triple feature.

ROBERT RODRIGUEZ: People are excited that they're going to get a deal. They're going to see something that was made with a lot of showmanship and something that's really intended to please the audience. That's the essence of *Grindhouse*—we are grinding out this experience and truncating it down to its vital parts. People will feel ripped off when they go see a normal movie after this. They'll think, 'You mean that you only see *one* movie for this price?'

OPPOSITE: Original window card for *Dragstrip Girl* (1957) & *Rock All Night* (1957). Poster courtesy of the Benton Card Company.

ROBERT RODRIGUEZ'S

PLANET
TERROR

TITLES: GRINDHOUSE: PLANET TERROR

INT. SKIP's GO-GO-GO DANCE CLUB – STAGE – NIGHT

Over titles, we are close on a pair of red go-go boots as the woman wearing them strides confidently onto the well worn stage.

This is CHERRY, a go go dancer. She's too good at what she does, meaning she should think about doing something else.

Oddly, tears run down her face throughout her dance.

Side note: The next time Cherry does this dance, people will die.

INT. SKIP'S GO-GO-GO DANCE CLUB – BACKSTAGE – NIGHT

We follow her boss, SKIP, as he walks through the backstage dressing area.

Girl's are getting dressed/ undressed. He stops at two girls making out.

SKIP
Come on girls, if you're gonna do that shit, do it onstage.

He shakes his head as the girls move on. He continues through the room.

SKIP (cont'd)
(to himself)
Smoking hot...

He walks over to Cherry who is wiping her self down, cleaning the invisible layer of scum off her skin.

We can see Skip in the mirror reflection.

SKIP (cont'd)
Cherry, darling. I've told you too many fucking times, you can't be up there crying and all that shit. People don't wanna see that. They just don't wanna see it.

Cherry puts her hair in a pony tail and slips on a guy's motor-cycle jacket.

SKIP (cont'd)
You know what a go-go dance is?

CHERRY
(nods)
Useless talent #12.

SKIP
No. It's a happy dance. You get up there, you dance happy. It's Go-Go. Not cry cry.

CHERRY
I'm quitting.

SKIP
(takes out money)
You say that at least one night a week.

CHERRY
This time I mean it. I need a
dramatic change in my life.

Skip counts out her money.

SKIP
That's funny, cause...
        (holds up her the money)
I'm the one who could do that for
you.

CHERRY
If you could do that, I'd work for
free.

She takes her money.

*She tears off the paper and
turns to him, shooting the
finger.*

CHERRY (cont'd)
Here's my finger... here's my bye
bye slip.

*She tosses the crumbled paper to
him and exits.*

Skip finds that odd.

SKIP
Never did that before.

EXT. HIGHWAY - NIGHT

Cherry is walking along the

*She tumbles to the side of the
road, falling onto a broken bottle.*

CHERRY
Assbag!

*We follow the trucks past a worn
sign that reads: "Military Base
2 miles."*

EXT. OLD ARMY BASE - TARMAC
- NIGHT

*ROMEY is wheeling a military
style holder with chemical tanks
attached out in front of an
abandoned biochemical division's
hangar. He shields himself from
the blinding headlights screech-*

SKIP
I've always said you're funny. Like
that Chris Rock. Only prettier.
But if you don't stop that crying
I'll have to fire your ass, and I
don't want to fire your ass, cause
I like looking at your ass.

*As Skip rambles on, Cherry stares
at her reflection in the mirror.
She reads a sign that's pasted next
to it while grabbing her things.*

CHERRY
Any girl leaving early must
check out with their finger and
have a bye bye slip.

highway. Her heels click against
the asphalt. She carries the
paper bag of gear.

*Closer on Cherry as she hears
something. She scans the
darkness behind her. Everything's quiet.*

*She walks. Suddenly a thunder-
ous convoy of military vehicles
brushes by her, splashing muddy
water. She looks up and sees a
bandana on one of the passengers.*

*Her foot hits a pothole and she
falls over. Hitting the ground.*

*ing his way. The army vehicles
squeal to a halt around Romey.*

*ABBY, wearing a tan suit and
bandana, steps out of the first
vehicle. He speaks to an unseen
person in the front seat. This
person is MULDOON and right
now he wears a gas mask. His
eyes seem to glow a sick pale
color. He takes a breath from his
breather and his eyes go back to
normal.*

ABBY
Wait here, Lt.

Abby steps out of the shadows

to face Romey, his partner and
the one in charge of tonight's
exchange.

An empty cage is torn open nearby.

Romey's men are around him, but we
sense their loyalty is with ABBY.

                    ROMEY
     Hey, Abby.

                    ABBY
     I see you had some trouble,
     Romey. I just wanted to make
     sure you were alright.

Romey eyes the situation suspiciously. His own henchmen have
already surrounded him.

Abby just watches. If his face
were a clock it'd read ZERO.

                    ABBY (cont'd)
     You gonna tell me what happened?

                    ROMEY
     They escaped.

                    ABBY
     All three...

Abby sees the torn open cage.

                    ROMEY
     I don't know how, Abby, I'm
     serious They got out before I
     could do anything. I couldn't do
     anything.

Abby's still on zero.

                    ABBY
     Sorry, Romey. But I just don't
     trust you anymore. And you know
     the rules. Hell, you wrote 'em.

A Henchman hands Abby a strange
clear GLASS JUG. It's full of
SPHERICAL OBJECTS floating in a
MURKY LIQUID.

Looks like pickled eggs.

                    ABBY (cont'd)
     I want you out of the business.

                    ROMEY
     I'm gone, Abby. You'll never see
     me again.

                    ABBY
     Not so fast.

Romey stops.

                    ABBY (cont'd)
     I also want your balls...

Romey's men turn on him. Backing
away.

                    ROMEY
     No, Abby, there was nothing I
     could do!

                    ABBY
     I want 'em now, Romey!

Romey looks at the FLOATING
SPHERICALS in the jar. TEARS
stream down his face. He now
knows those aren't pickled eggs.

He starts crying.

                    ROMEY
          (looking at his groin)
     I'm really kind of attached to em,
     Abby...

                    ABBY
     I was attached to my specimens,
     Romey. And now they're out
     there. In the night. Doing God
     knows what.

Abby is handed two mean looking
blades.

                    ABBY (cont'd)
     Take the boys out of the
     barracks.

Abby tosses a mean looking blade
at Romey.

Romey catches it.

                    ABBY (cont'd)
          (lifting the lid off jar)
     Chop 'em off and...toss 'em over.

Romey looks at the sharp bladed
thing in his hand.

                    ROMEY
     I can't Abby...

Abby NODS to the henchmen. They
move in.

                    ROMEY (cont'd)
     Abby NO!!!!
          (to the men in the vehicles)
     You don't need him! There's more!
     A LOT MORE! I can get you all
     you'll ever want!

The henchmen take Romey down.
Hard.

Push in on Abby as he impassively watches Romey get cut
from the team.

We hear the sounds of FLESH
RIPPING, a pile of wet cut ball
his the ground. But it is suddenly
drowned out by a screeching
sound.

Abby turns.

We see the soldiers in the
vehicles. They have masks on
their faces. Their tanks turn
red. They shut off their tanks,
cutting off the sound. They
remove their masks.

The main one steps forward...
into the light.

This is LT. MULDOON.

                    MULDOON
          (long beat)
     Where's the shit?

                    ABBY
          (points to the tanks)
     The shit's right there. The deal is
     still good.

                    MULDOON
     No, it's not. I want ALL of it, now.
     And fuck you very much for holding
     out on me.

Abby pulls his popper and starts
firing.

Muldoon does a ridiculous but
very effective 'cartwheel' type
move, taking out several of
Abby's flankmen, who didn't even
know where to look as Muldoon
made his move.

The military vehicles advance
on Abby and his men. One of the
vehicles hits Abby and sends
him crashing into the henchman
holding the goodie jar.

The Jar BREAKS wide open,
SPILLING THE BALLS all over the
asphalt. Abby tumbles into the
mess on the ground. FACE DOWN.

Balls spread all around him in
a pool. A few plump ones DANGLE
from Abby's face.

Muldoon walks up, as his men kill
more of Abby's henchmen.

MULDOON (cont'd)
Looks like I got you by the balls, Abby.

Abby coughs blood and struggles with the pain.

MULDOON (cont'd)
So I'll ask you one more time.
            (leaning down)
Where's... the... shit...

We see Muldoon's face start to bubble and distort.

Abby pulls out his gun and fires at Romey's supply rack... exploding it and sending a wave of gases everywhere.

Some of Abby's men are standing near it and immediately are affected. Becoming strange fleshy masses before falling over in a pile of blood and pus.

A few others run off like mutant freaks into the night. Screeching and hollering.

Muldoon's soldiers stop what they're doing and walk in front of the emitting gas. Like junkies they stand in front of it. Breathing it all in. As much as their lungs will hold.

Muldoon follows them.

Abby sees this and sees the gas going into the air.

ABBY
Oh balls...

INT/EXT. MILITARY VEHICLE/ HIGHWAY - NIGHT

Abby grabs a vehicle and drives away. Fast. Abby looks in his rear view mirror. Making sure he left everything behind. One of his comrades, not looking so hot, is climbing up his car behind him. He reacts and swerves his car trying to knock him off the back.

He almost sideswipes a SILVER VOLVO which swerves and pulls into:

EXT. JT's BONE SHACK - NIGHT

The overheated silver and rust VOLVO clatters its way to the gas pumps of a gas station/BBQ joint called THE BONE SHACK.

JT, proprietor, stands outside watching while he stirs something in a white kitchen bucket. Smoking a cig.

TAMMY steps out of the ragged car. She pops the hood as steam billows out.

JT
Get that thing away from the pumps!

Tammy grabs a bucket from her car and heads over.

TAMMY
It's just overheated.

Tammy starts pumping a bucket full of water from the faucet next to JT.

TAMMY (cont'd)
(looking at her watch)
Need to get to town. It's just
a stripped radiator cap. Water
leaks as soon as it heats up.

No pressure.

*JT nods his head and goes inside
as Tammy finishes filling the
bucket.*

*Tammy fills the radiator to the rim.
She replaces the shoddy cap. Water
spurts out almost immediately.*

*Cherry is walking up from the
road. She passes Tammy at the
pumps.*

JT (cont'd)
Take this with ya.

TAMMY
Aw, not your good spring water?

JT
Ain't nothing good about it.
Bottle this myself, sell it right
here at the store. I get it out of
the hose, and if you can taste the
difference between this and the
toilet, you can eat my lunch.

*Tammy accepts the jug and shuts
the hood.*

TAMMY
Thanks...

JT
Saving lives, are you?

TAMMY
Now how did you know that?

*She gets in her car and pulls
away very fast. JT stares as he
pulls out a sloppy rib bone from
his mixing bucket and nibbles on
it.*

JT looks at his watch.

*CLOSE UP on a digital read-out as
it hits 8:00.*

*But it's not JT's watch. We are
now in....*

*Tammy eyes her, sees her wounded
leg.*

TAMMY (cont'd)
Are you okay?

CHERRY
Oh, I'm just Cherry.

JT
(to Cherry)
I'll be right in. Have a seat.
Wherever you want.

*Cherry goes into the building.
JT hands Tammy a gallon of
locally produced drinking water.*

(reading label on water jug)
JT.

JT
We're serving inside tonight.
(off Tammy's look)
Best BBQ in Texas. Round the
clock.

*She peers inside the white bucket
he's stirrin-g. Looks like blood.*

TAMMY
I gotta go.

*JT looks at her suspiciously.
Untrusting.... Puts his cigarette
out on the ground.*

INT. BLOCK AND DAKOTA's BEDROOM
– NIGHT

*The alarm clock blares. The
night stand light clicks on.*

*WILLIAM BLOCK lifts his head
from it's anchored position and
shuts the alarm off. Beside him,
his wife DAKOTA does the same.*

*He throws his feet over the side
of the bed. Her too.*

Their backs face each other.

BLOCK
Open the shades would ya? Get

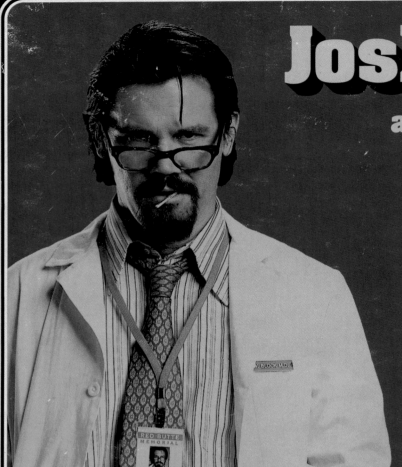

Josh Brolin
as Dr. William Block

JOSH BROLIN: I grew up in Central Coast California, where we had the drive-ins. So you'd go and you'd see a double feature. You'd see a Bruce Lee movie, and then a Charles Bronson movie. The great memories that I have are of my buddy's uncle bringing a twelve pack to the drive-in. He would get smashed drunk, so by the time the double feature was over he'd be passed out somewhere. So we would have to call somebody and have them come to the drive-in to pick us up. Seeing a double feature, that was the best thing, because you got two bangs for your buck. When Quentin and Robert started talking about doing this movie, started saying, "We're gonna watch *Zombie*, *Vanishing Point* and these great old exploitation films." We went to Quentin's house and saw a lot of movies with them. And it was great to have the experience I had of watching these movies as a kid, but in the Rodriguez/Tarantino way. It was cool.

Marley Shelton
as Dr. Dakota Block

MARLEY SHELTON: The funniest thing about my character is that I essentially lose the use of my hands early on. So for me the challenge was the physicality of playing a character who can't use her hands, and funnily enough I have hyper-flexible wrists, so I was like, "Robert, I was born to play this character" because I can actually move my wrists in a really bizarre way—stupid human tricks. That was really fun for me, playing with the frustration. She's a doctor who's rendered awkward. She's someone who's a hyper efficient, type "A" personality who is now out of control, who now can't use her hands which are the tools of her trade. She can't protect herself, she can't protect her son, she can't escape. So it helped me emotionally to get into the pure physicality of being helpless.

some some light in here.

DAKOTA

Yes. Light we need.

Dakota stumbles over to the heavy shades, the kind that keep all rays of light out. She whips them open.

The pale glow of the full moon bathes her face in light. She squints at it's brightness.

We realize it's 8pm, not 8am.

DAKOTA (cont'd)

Nice night.

Dakota stares out into the night. Her day is just beginning.

BLOCK

Coffee.

Dakota turns as we see the HAZE OF THE CHEMICAL drift across the MOON, as it sweeps through the town...

INT. DAKOTA KITCHEN - NIGHT

Dakota is in the kitchen on the phone talking to the babysitter and serving dinner to her son, TONY.

She's trying to make coffee and a bowl of cereal. Coffee grinds, spills, and mix ups abound.

DAKOTA

I couldn't get off work this week, But you only have to stay till ten.
(whispers)
A friend of mine will be here before ten to pick up Tony.

Tony, 6 years old, sits at the kitchen table playing with action figures: One alien, one human. The Alien bites the human's head.

TONY

"I'm gonna eat your brains and gain your knowledge..."

DAKOTA
(taking toys away)
What did I tell you? No playing with toys at the table. Didn't I tell you that?

While arguing with the babysitter, Dakota's typing into a PDA. (We're in macro).

DAKOTA (cont'd)
(into phone)
There's a packed suitcase under his bed. Give it to Tony to take with him when my friend picks him up.

Her message says, "PLEASE HURRY, BABY. I THINK HE KNOWS."

She lowers the PDA to reveal Block walking in.

DAKOTA (cont'd)
I'll leave him watching TV, but you need to be here in the next 20 minutes. Thank you.

She turns around from Block, hiding the PDA. Block locks eyes

...h it.

Block reaches for her hand and raises it. But instead of the PDA, it's his cup of coffee. He takes it.

TONY
Good evening, dada...

A tense moment passes between Dakota and Block.

BLOCK
Let's hope so, son.

He sits next to Tony.

BLOCK (cont'd)
Say a prayer for your old man. "No dead bodies for Dad tonight."

Tony clasps his hands together.

TONY
No dead bodies for Dad tonight. Amen.

BLOCK
Who was that you were talking to?

DAKOTA
Babysitter. She's on her way.

Block nods, then notices his wife slipping her Palm Pilot back into her purse.

She reaches over to turn on a sink faucet.

CUT TO:

INT. JT'S DINER – WOMEN'S ROOM – NIGHT

CLOSE on a faucet turning on.

Cherry is in the bathroom washing off her bloody leg. She pulls a shard of glass out of it.

CHERRY
(under breath)
Fucking catastrophe.

EXT. JT'S DINER – NIGHT

WRAY, early 30's, parks his WRAY'S WRECKAGE truck outside of JT's.

He walks up the stairs towards the Bone Shack.

He enters.

INT. JT'S DINER – NIGHT

WRAY
How's it going, JT? Still open I see.

JT
Oh yeah. All night.

Wray takes a seat at the counter. He's the only one there, it seems.

WRAY
(pointing behind JT)
Cup of coffee and some cigarettes.

JT tosses him his own pack.

JT
Free of charge. Tonight's a... special night.

The camera pushes in slowly on Wray. He doesn't know the weight of such words yet. Neither does JT.

WRAY
Yeah? What's so special about it.

JT
Been open 25 years.

WRAY
Good things usually die.

*JT passes Wray his coffee and
they toast each other with their
cups. JT's cup is filled with bbq
sauce.*

WRAY (cont'd)
Why didn't you throw a party?

JT
I did. See the balloons?
*Wray looks around. A few
misshapen balloons float above
the empty seats.*

JT (cont'd)
You're the second person to show
up.

WRAY
Who's the first.

JT points behind Wray.

*Wray turns around. Lights his
cigarette.*

*In the booth, and partially
obscured by the booth wall, sits
Cherry. Just the sight of her
hits Wray hard.*

JT
(shrugs)
Don't know. Must be passing
through. Seems only outsiders
eat here.

*Wray takes his cup and walks
over to the booth.*

WRAY
I eat here, JT.

JT
Yeah, you sure do.
(re: His single cup of coffee)
Don't go choke on all that food
you're eating.

*Wray studies the girl at the
booth. Puts out cig. Smiles.*

WRAY
Hello, Palomita...

*Cherry doesn't turn around.
She's staring out the window.*

CHERRY
I don't go by that name anymore.

WRAY
Why not?

She turns to him.

CHERRY
Cause it's the name you gave me.

WRAY
Ever become that...fancy doctor?

CHERRY
Never did.

WRAY
(disappointed)
Thought for sure you would.
Talked about it enough.

CHERRY
That's the problem with goals.
They become the thing you talk
about, instead of the thing you do.

Wray sits at her table.

WRAY
That's my jacket.

She shrugs.

WRAY (cont'd)
I looked for it 2 weeks.

CHERRY
How long did you look for me?

WRAY
So now what are you doing?

*There's no reason she should tell
him, which is probably why she does.*

CHERRY
I'm going to be a stand up comedian.

WRAY
Really?

She nods. It's the truth.

WRAY (cont'd)
(confused beat)
You're not funny.

CHERRY
That's what I've been trying to
tell everybody... they all say I'm
hysterical.

WRAY
But you're not.

CHERRY
(reminding herself)
You're such a fucking prick.

WRAY
I'm just the only one with the
balls to tell you the truth. (or,
it's a bad move)

CHERRY
Great, that's fantastic, what am
I going to do now. I believed
everybody else and I've already
booked shows in town.

WRAY
That sucks. Really.

CHERRY
There's a difference between
being frank...and being dick.

*She turns back to the window.
Wray nods. Stands.*

WRAY
It was really good seeing you...

*She FLIPS HIM THE BIRD without
looking at him. We can only see
her face in the window reflection now.*

WRAY (cont'd)
What name do you go by now? In
case... I want to catch that show.

CHERRY
Cherry. Cherry Darling.

WRAY
(nods)
Sounds like a stripper.

CHERRY
No, it sounds like a Go Go Dancer.
There's a difference.

WRAY
(smiling)
You'll always be Palomita to me.

*Wray goes to the counter to pay.
That name is a knife in her heart.*

CHERRY
I need a ride. What do you say, El
Wray...

*Wray can see the tears in her
eyes from the counter.*

WRAY
I'll give you a ride.

JT turns and reaches for the

kitchen door.

CUT TO:

INT. HOSPITAL INTRO – NIGHT

The auto doors open and Dr. Block and Dr. Dakota enter the hospital together.

DAKOTA
(kissing her husband)
Goodbye, Bill.

BLOCK
Don't you mean, 'see you later.'

DAKOTA
Of course.

Dakota.

BLOCK
She is, huh. What happened to your arm?

JOE
Got bit.

He lifts Joe's hand off the forearm revealing a gaping rip in the skin.

BLOCK
Bit? Bit by what?

JOE
You wouldn't believe me if I told you.

He examines it closer by pulling a second light over.

BLOCK (cont'd)
Only problem is... this one doesn't bleed.

Doc Felix is not finding a match, but we're getting an eyeful of some pretty fucked up DISEASES.

DOC FELIX
Oh shit, check this out. When this place was still a military hospital, this one guy came back from Iraq with this.

Doc Felix shows them the computer screen. A horrific

As they're greeted by staff, they go their separate ways.

Block walks over to the ER. JOE, an old friend, stands in the doorway, clutching his arm.

Block puts a classic glass thermometer in his mouth like a toothpick. A ritual.

BLOCK
Joe? What are you doing here?

JOE
Wife's looking good there, Block.

Block realizes he's talking about

CUT TO:

INT. HOSPITAL – JOE'S EXAM ROOM – NIGHT

Block is running a test on the bite. Thermometer still in his mouth. DOC FELIX is in the room as well, looking up diseases on a computer.

JOE
Can't you just sew it up?

BLOCK
Normally I would. I'd even be doing something to stop the bleeding.

melted DICK. Sores all over it.

DOC FELIX (cont'd)
Chronic herpetic leision. When he urinated, it came out through all these holes here, like a fountain.

Joe wants to pass out.

JOE
How did you treat it?

Block and Doc Felix make the dreaded CHOP motion at the same time.

JOE (cont'd)
Well, fuck that, I was never in Iraq.

DOC FELIX
Good for you. The shit they
spread around there... you
wouldn't believe.

Block examines it closer.

JOE
Well what is it?

BLOCK
It's fucked up, is what it is.

DOC FELIX
Can't find anything like it
in the system. It's almost an
accelerated combination of a
variety of viral infections. That
looks like gout.

*He clicks by a particularly
gnarly disease photo. Joe reacts
with disgust.*

*Block takes out Joe's electronic
thermometer. Reads it.*

BLOCK
(to Felix)
He's running a temperature of 105.

JOE
Is that bad?

BLOCK
It's high.

DOC FELIX
Bad is 108. You could go into
seizures, become psychotic....
finally keel over probably.

*Doc Block goes back to Joe with a
tongue stick.*

BLOCK
Say ahhh.

*Joe opens his mouth. An UGLY,
DISEASED, SERRATED TONGUE
sticks out. Block stumbles back
out of his chair at the sight.*

BLOCK (cont'd)
Ugh! Jesus!

DOC FELIX
Ooo, Black Tongue. Nice.

*Block tugs on it and touches it...
Then remembers his glove and*

puts his glove on.

DOC FELIX (cont'd)
All abcess's should be drained.
Period.

*Block presses around the pus
ball. His glasses fall over his
face.*

JOE
Blah blah blahth.

BLOCK
Shut up, Joe.

*Squeeze, pop, splat. The cyst hits
his glasses. Spattering across
the lens.*

*Block flinches, and then realizes
the glasses kept his eyes clean.
He calls Dakota.*

BLOCK (cont'd)
Bring your needles, baby. Right
now.

CONTINUED:

INT. HOSPITAL - DAKOTA's PREP
ROOM - NIGHT

Dakota stops what she was doing
and grabs her kit. She also puts
an extra, dangerous looking
silver metal syringe on a leg
strap under her skirt.

                    CONTINUED:

          DOC FELIX
We should quarantine the room.

Block nods. Joe can't believe his
ears.

Block notices the wound has
grown.

          BLOCK
It's spreading....When did you
say you got this bite?

          JOE
Just now.

          BLOCK
(pointing to charred edges of arm)
See this? It shows the advanced

stages of gangrene and
epidermal rot.

          JOE
What do you mean advanced...

          BLOCK
     (interrupting)
And this..over here...shows
swelling of the tissues and a
lack of any type of circulation.
See you're telling me that you
just got this bite...

          JOE
I did- 30 minutes ago.

          BLOCK
Yet what I'm seeing here is a deep
impact wound with several virals
and secondary bacterials, and that
by the accumulation of denuded
tissue around the incision marks,
indicates that you've had this bite
for over 14 days. Could that be
possible?

          JOE
14 days? No way. I mean.
     (confused)

What's today?

          BLOCK
Today's Wednesday.
     (beat)
The fifteenth.

Doc Felix is outside the door of
the exam room, pulling a curtain
across it.

Joe tries to put pieces together.
He's overwhelmed.

          BLOCK (cont'd)
Of April.

          JOE
Does this mean I'm gonna need a
tetanus shot?

Block looks to Doc Felix. Felix
gives the nod.

          BLOCK
We gotta lose the arm, Joe.

          JOE
What? What do you mean...lose...
the...arm?

BLOCK
I'm sorry but this thing is spreading all the way up to your shoulder. If we don't sever it now it'll take over your chest, and we can't very well cut that off.

Joe is perplexed. Dakota walks in and Doc Feliz whispers in her ear what they'll have to do to Joe.

BLOCK (cont'd)
Joe, you know my wife, Dakota.

DAKOTA
Hi, Joe. Now I'm going to give you a very strong anesthetic so you don't feel anything during the procedure.

Joe is barely listening. He's still mouthing pathetic protests to losing the arm.

Dakota sits and pets his hand.

She has a little pocket protector in her shirt, only instead of holding pens, it holds three different hypodermic needles. Yellow, Blue and Red.

DAKOTA (cont'd)
Now, these guys here-
          (re: needles)
Are my friends.

She pulls out the yellow one and stabs it into his arm.

DAKOTA (cont'd)
This bad boy is just to take the sting off... Feeling alright Joe?

Joe is so beyond this world he can't think.

Dakota tosses the needle in the red trash can and pulls out number two: Blue.

DAKOTA (cont'd)
This one here... you'll barely feel.
          (stab)
That means the first one's already taking hold. See how fast my friends work?

Joe nods slowly.

DAKOTA (cont'd)
It's a heavy dose of vitamin K. It'll clot your blood quickly so

when we take off the arm there's no messy cleanup afterwards.

She tosses that one aside and then pulls out the third one, RED.

DAKOTA (cont'd)
And after this one...

Stab. She looks to make sure Block isn't listening...

DAKOTA (cont'd)
          (whispered)
You'll never see me again.

Joe's eyes are starting to close against his will. We see his vision of Dakota blurring out and starting to spin and the image BRIGHTENS.

CUT TO:

EXT. HIGHWAY – TAMMY'S CAR/SIDE OF ROAD – NIGHT

A BRIGHT HEADLIGHT, dimming at every turn of the cranky key.

That same silver and rust VOLVO sits dead on the side of the road.

Its flickering headlights shining on a sign that says "Military Base – 2 miles"

The radio is still playing. JUNGLE JULIA on Austin Hot Wax 505. Her voice purrs over the speakers as Tammy struggles to get the car started.

Tammy is inside the car trying to turn it over. It answers with a pathetic "Click."

TAMMY
Well I'll be god fucking damned.

She shuts off the radio.

She checks her Palm Pilot. It says, "I THINK HE KNOWS. PLEASE HURRY, BABY." She breathes out a calming breath. Now what the fuck?

Shock cut to the POPPING HOOD. She checks the radiator. Cool to the touch.

Now her flashlight blinks on and off. On it's last legs.

TAMMY(cont'd)
Goddamn it...

The occasional passing car illuminates her world, then it's back to PITCH BLACK DEAD NIGHT.

She hits her flashlight again, then hears it's echo off in the woods. At least she thinks it's the echo.

She slams her door and walks hurriedly back up the highway, her dying flashlight barely a flicker as it lights the path for her feet.

She hears that echo again, only she didn't make a corresponding sound. She stops and listens.

Okay.

She walks a little faster.

Only now she's hearing mumblings.

Maybe voices.

She begins a nice easy jog. Nothing but the wind she tells herself.

She trips over a ditch and falls face down in the gravel shoulder.

Her flashlight lies dead somewhere.

Another echo.

Fuck this.

A car approaches and Tammy runs out onto the highway, waving her arms.

The car lights are so bright in this pitch black night that all we see is Tammy's silhouette as it passes her up.

Tammy. Alone in the middle of the dark highway. Just her and those sounds that seem to be growing behind her.

She runs.

Another car in the far distance rushes toward her. The headlights again silhouette Tammy as she waves her arms more frantically than before.

This time the passing light reveals something behind her. Tammy is running now. The next car's lights grow over her petrified and contorted face.

We SEE the SHAPES move in behind her as the car passes. Gone.

Pitch black screaming.

The next vehicle reveals nothing but the silhouette of several human looking shapes crouched over her prone body in the middle of the highway.

Now a TRUCK approaches. The headlights illuminate the SHAPES dragging the carcass off the highway.

We see this first in silhouette, then from the point of view of the passengers in the truck.

WRAY
Deer. We got a lot of them around here.

They pass several deer grazing at the side of the road.

WRAY (cont'd)
I read a statistic that said the eating of venison has risen 30 percent in the last few years. 60 percent of that, is from roadkill.

CHERRY
Fucking people eat roadkill?

WRAY
Hunting season opens up soon to get rid of the overpolulation,

darts out in front of you... if you blink or brake or swerve you'll just kill yourself.

CHERRY
So what do you do?

He accelerates.

WRAY
You take him out. By speeding up.
        *(takes his hands off the
         wheel to demonstrate)*
And you just pick him off, like this. Send it flying away from you. Might do a little damage to your front guard, but at least you're not spinning around out there on the shoulder.

INT/EXT. WRAY'S TRUCK - NIGHT

We cut inside the passing TRUCK to find that it's Wray and Cherry, riding in his wrecker truck down the highway toward town.

CHERRY
What the fuck was that?

WRAY
        (shrugs)
People picking up roadkill. Probably to eat it.

CHERRY
You mean like an armadillo?

otherwise they're just wandering out into the road and getting hit.

CHERRY
Unacceptable.

WRAY
Hey we are not talking Bambi here, these things are a fucking menace.

CHERRY
Have you ever... you know. Killed... one?

WRAY
A few. If you're driving out here at 70 miles an hour, and a deer

CHERRY
Unacceptable.

He takes his foot off the gas. The Truck slows a little.

WRAY
Not really, it's a clear case of you or him.

CHERRY
        (shaking head)
Just drop me off at the Ho Ho Ho Club.

WRAY
Look, I'm sorry about what I said earlier, I'm just the only one

with the balls to tell you the truth.

CHERRY
Yeah, sure, have a party, but I'm gonna be funny and that's that.

WRAY
Hey.

They look at each other.

Wray watches her instead of the road for a beat. That's all it takes.

A SHAPE darts out into the highway IN FRONT OF THEM.

Wray doesn't speed up or hit it. Instead he does EXACTLY what he just said he SHOULD NOT DO. He SWERVES. Violently.

They hit the shoulder and the tires eat gravel. He tries to control the wheel but he swerves back onto the highway. His wheels grab asphalt and they FLIP.

They spin and roll over and over, breaking through a deer crossing sign and finally coming to rest in a heap on the roadside.

INT/EXT. WRAY'S OVERTURNED TRUCK – NIGHT

Wray shakes himself. Blood streams down his brow. He has to rub it out of his eyes to check on Cherry.

She too is hanging upside down. Blood flowing down her face.

CHERRY
I thought if you saw a deer you shouldn't.. fucking... swerve!

WRAY
(struggling to get out)
That wasn't a deer...

He unsnaps his seatbelt and hits the ground. He tries to reach her belt.

Suddenly the glass SMASHES in on her side. Hands reach in and

GRAB HER! Yanking her out of the truck.

WRAY (cont'd)
Cherry!

He hears sounds of struggling and see's Cherry's body being dragged along the gravel shoulder.

We hear god awful SCREAMS of BLOODY MURDER.

Wray kicks open his seat (now over his seat) uncovering a rack of weapons. He snaps together a gun in the dark, expertly as he grabs a TUBE LIKE contraption and tumbles out of the truck.

Wray slaps the scope on his rifle and scans the area with his night scope and sees Cherry on the ground. Three Hideous SHAPES are huddled over her, ripping at her clothes it seems. Gnawing on something, he can't make it out.

Wray fires at the three shapes. A few direct hits and they

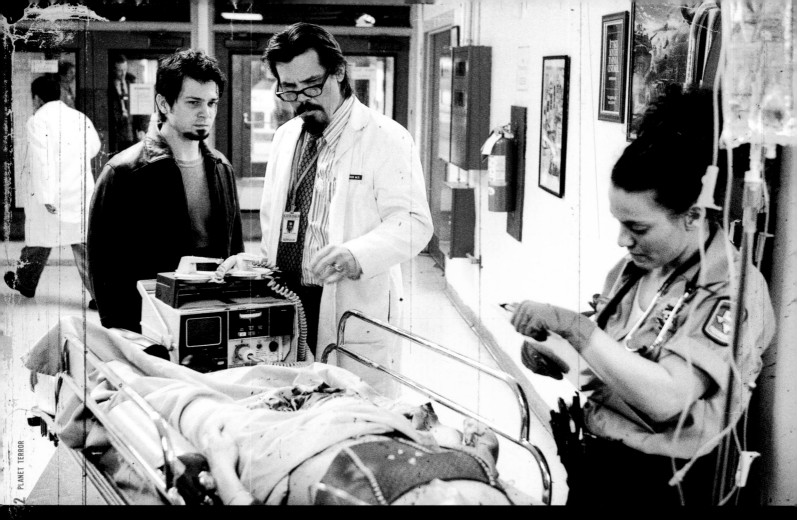

disappear into the night carrying something with them.

Cherry lies writhing and in shock on the ground.

He runs over to her with his flashlight.

                    WRAY (cont'd)
Palomita, are you alright...

He sees her bloody body and falls silent.

                    WRAY (cont'd)
Oh Jesus.

                              CUT TO:

INT. HOSPITAL - NIGHT

The outer hospital doors KICK IN as a gurney is shoved through.

Wray is walking beside the gurney that's bringing in what's left of Cherry. She's under heavy sedation.

Block is running in with an assistant.

                    WRAY
Don't let her die on me, Block.

                    BLOCK
Who do you got here, Wray?

                    WRAY
Cherry... Darling.

They follow the body through the ER, passing people with various ailments.

                    PARAMEDIC
Car accident, heavy contusions about the torso, possible spinal trauma...

Block examines her. The paramedic lifts the lower half of the sheet.

                    PARAMEDIC (cont'd)
One severed limb.

                    BLOCK
Where's the leg?

The paramedic shrugs.

                    BLOCK (cont'd)
You don't have the leg?

Wray just sweats it out as he walks.

                    BLOCK (cont'd)
What the hell's going on?

                    WRAY
Three..."psychos" attacked her. I shot at them. I never miss.

Block gives him a look.

                    WRAY (cont'd)
They took the leg with them.

SHERIFF HAGUE walks in, projecting confidence and control. His trusted deputy TOLO is at his side. Shotgun at the ready.

                    SHERIFF HAGUE
You have to come with us Wray, we need to talk about this, you know.

BLOCK
He has to sign her in.

Block holds up the clipboard.

SHERIFF HAGUE
Do what, now?

BLOCK
If he's with her, he's responsible
for her.

SHERIFF HAGUE
(grabs board)
He'll fill it out after we talk.
Let's go.

*Block reacts, then checks his
temperature.*

Crane shrugs.

DR. CRANE
Suit yourself.

*He whips the curtain closed.
We see him and Joe behind the
curtain in silhouette.*

*Block rejoins the legless Cherry
behind another curtain.*

CUT TO:

INT. HOSPITAL – GLASS CORNER
– NIGHT

Sheriff Hague talks to Wray at the
glass corner of the hospital wing.

stuff anymore.

WRAY
Not even hunting?

SHERIFF HAGUE
Not even hunting, and you know
that. Not with your history.

*He looks around, makes sure no
one's listening.*

SHERIFF HAGUE (cont'd)
Here I stick my neck out for you,
stick it out far... and now you've
got a girl in your wrecked truck,
missing a leg. Missing a leg that's
now missing, and here you're saying
in front of everybody that someone

DR. CRANE
Hey Block!

*Block turns around to DR. CRANE,
who has one hand on a curtain,
the other on an ELECTRICAL
SURGICAL SAW.*

DR. CRANE (cont'd)
You want to be here for this?
Taking your friend's arm off.

*Block peers over and sees Joe
asleep on the table.*

BLOCK
You do it.

SHERIFF HAGUE
What were you doing with a rifle,
Wray?

WRAY
Nothing, I was... thinking
about...
(shrugs)
Maybe doing some hunting when
the season breaks.

*Sheriff shakes his head like he's
been through this a thousand
times.*

SHERIFF HAGUE
Come on, Wray, you know you're
not supposed to be doing that

up and snatched it. That you shot
at em with a gun you shouldn't have
and that now they're gone.

*Wray has been watching a few
patients go by with different
ailments. Sores. Infections.
The sound design highlights
anytime someone touches or
scratches at one of their wounds.
The sound of infection spreading.*

WRAY
I know how it sounds, don't think
I don't know.

SHERIFF HAGUE
It doesn't look good for you this

time, Wray. You can see that, I hope.

Wray's got determination burning in his eyes.

WRAY
What if I find the leg?

Sheriff waits a beat.

SHERIFF HAGUE
So now you know where it is?
(beat)
You show us where it is and give us a full confession, you're saying?

Wray sees another person wheeled by, scratching at strange sores on their face. That sound again. Crawling under our skin.

WRAY
Sheriff, can we finish this somewhere else?

SHERIFF HAGUE
My thought exactly.

Close on CUFFS snapped onto his wrist.

INT/EXT. JT'S DINER - NIGHT

Close on JT slicing up meat in his meat slicer. (need for sound overlap from previous scene) He serves it to RUSTY as he talks on the phone while mixing up a new batch of sauce.

JT
I know it may be a little arrogant, putting up on the sign, "best BBQ in Texas Period. " But.. .who's gonna come in here and argue with that.

JT tastes it. Drops in another chunk of bone and some brisket trimmings.

JT glances up.

Standing outside by the gas pumps is a new body. Standing and staring.

JT (cont'd)
Yeah, Big BBQ contest coming up this week. I'm working on the perfect recipe. Winning that'll get me on the Food Channel. Put this place back on the map.

JT walks over to the door and opens it.

JT (cont'd)
Hey there.

The shape does nothing. Just stands.

JT (cont'd)
We're open. All night, we'll be open.

And stares.

JT (cont'd)
You feel like getting some food, you just holler.

JT goes back in all smiles.

Michael Biehn

as Sheriff Hague

MICHAEL BIEHN: I play Sheriff Hague. He's a small-town sheriff, kind of a tough guy. I have a brother played by Jeff Fahey, who has a barbeque stand, and we're always fighting. When our grandfather died, he left the barbeque recipe to my brother, and gave me ownership of the building. So I'm always fighting him, always raising the rent, always trying to get the recipe off of him. This is a guy who's just trying to survive, trying to make things right. He's a guy who is reacting to the situation, and trying to keep everybody safe. As the movie progresses, I learn that Wray [played by Freddie Rodriguez] has a secret. I learn what that is and, even though he's this punk kid who shouldn't be playing around with guns and stuff, I learn to respect him. All the characters are really well-defined... I mean, for a *zombie* movie. You think a zombie movie is just people running away from zombies. But we all have our relationships with the other people in the movie that are very strong, and the characters are really well written. That's what's going to make it all pull together. It's a pretty crazy movie.

Jeff Fahey

as J.T.

JEFF FAHEY: My character's name is J.T. and he's fortunate enough to be the owner and proprietor of the best damn barbeque joint in Texas period—in his mind. He's working on the perfect recipe as this whole story unfolds in this one night. He's concerned with getting the perfect recipe, and he's just about there. Then all hell breaks loose and this gets in the way of his dream to be on the Food Channel, which would put his barbeque place back on the map. So the wonderful thing for myself and this character is that in the midst of all this insanity and this wild ride, he's got one thing on his mind and that's that barbeque sauce. That's it for him. And he's not going to share the recipe with his brother, who is played by Michael Biehn. He owns the land and I have the recipe and I'm not going to give it to him. So that's what he's holding onto. He's going to fix that recipe, even if it means going down with the ship.

INT. HOSPITAL – CHERRY'S ROOM/
ER – NIGHT

*Block finishes the last stapled
touch on Cherry's leg. He pulls
off his goggles and his mask as
the assistant nurse cleans up.
He looks at Cherry's peaceful
sleeping face.*

He exits, wiping his tired brow.

    ATTENDANT
Dr. Block. Three fresh ones
rolling in!

    BLOCK
Christ, you're kidding.

    ATTENDANT
Automobile accident off Highway 18.

*Block reaches the bodies. One is
alive. The other two are getting
sheets lifted over them.*

    BLOCK
DOA's? Get Andy to pick em up.

    ATTENDANT
He's out on 620 picking up
another two. Won't be here for
another hour or so.

    BLOCK
Fucking Wednesday nights.

*Block lifts the first sheet.
Examines the dead man.*

*Attendant notices the thermom-
eter in Blocks mouth.*

    ATTENDANT
That's unsanitary.

*Block removes it. Looks at it,
sticks it back in between his
teeth.*

    BLOCK
Not if I'm the only one using it.
Helps me monitor my state of
calmness.

    ATTENDANT
If you get worked up enough to
crack it, could cut yourself
pretty good.

    BLOCK
Then I'd know I was not calm.

*Block lifts the sheet off the
second body. He stares at it,
studies it... can't quite make out
what he's even seeing. Until...*

*His thermometer SHATTERS
between his clenched teeth.*

    BLOCK (cont'd)
Somebody call my wife.

                   CUT TO:

EXT. SHERIFF STATION – NIGHT

*A truck passes by right in front
of camera on the cut. We see
Wray being escorted into the
police station.*

INT. SHERIFF STATION – NIGHT
CELL BLOCK

*Sheriff Hague walks Wray
through the prison cells. Filled
with assorted criminal men and
women. THEY HAVE FULL CUFFS on*

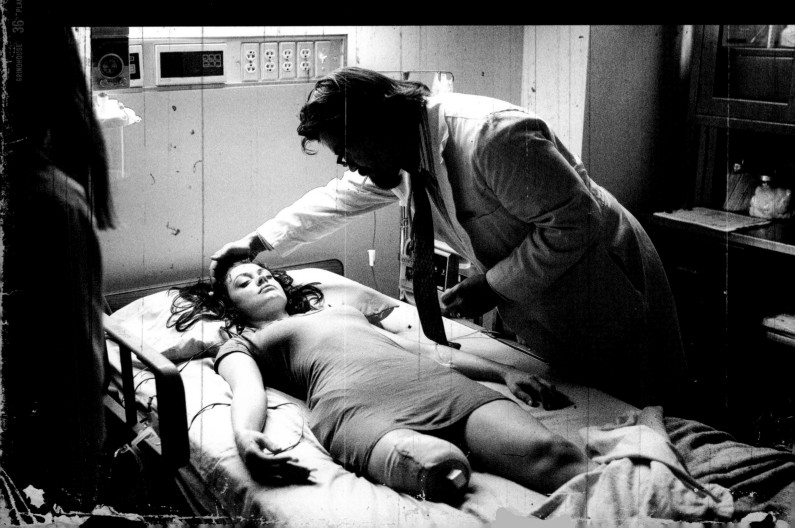

Wray. His ankles and wrists.

SHERIFF HAGUE
I remember the day when we'd take a hardnosed son of a bitch into a cell block like this and kick the truth out of him. And I'm feeling reeeaaal nostalgic right about now.

WRAY
I want my phone call.

They pass a sexy sheriff who slams the prison doors using the slammer.

CUT TO:

INT. SHERIFF STATION

Close on photos and memorabilia on Sheriff's desk as he rifles through his paperwork.

Wray is finishing his phone call. Must be speaking in some kind of code, cause he's talking right in front of the Sheriff and Sheriff can't make heads or tails of it.

WRAY
DC2... what about countering with atropine? Gotcha.

Sheriff pulls out a small notepad from his pocket and jots down DC2 and Atropine on his notepad.

As Wray talks, he glances over the shotgun rack, then peers over at a TEXAS RANGER pinning DEAD BRIDE crime scene fotos on the wall.

He turns to leave. It's EARL MCGRAW.

MCGRAW
I'll check on you all in the morning, I have to get back home, Sheriff.

SHERIFF HAGUE
Alright, then. Thanks for the extra help, Earl.

McGraw recognizes Wray.

MCGRAW
You in trouble again, Wray?

WRAY
Just passing through I hope.

WRAY (cont'd)
How's the wife?

Hague gives Wray a look, wondering why they get on so well.

MCGRAW
Not so good. But it's her own doin in a way. All those cigarettes, and now she don't want nothing to do with the chemo. It's taking it's time, I tell ya.
          (beat)
You don't smoke do ya, Wray?

Wray shakes his head "No."

MCGRAW (cont'd)
That's good. 'Night fellas.

McGraw is out the door.

Wray LIGHTS HIS CIGARETTE.

SHERIFF HAGUE
You're gonna start by telling me

when you first started carrying this gun, and then we'll make our way up to when you first saw this girl Cherry.

Wray reacts. That could take some time.

                                    CUT TO:

INT. HOSPITAL – CHERRY'S ROOM – NIGHT

She feels the stump where her knee should be. Tears start to pour down her face. A silent sufferer.

She touches the metal prong

The bodies outside don't move.

                    JT (cont'd)
You from Dinky's BBQ? You tell that sum bitch he thinks you're gonna come in here and get my recipes, well, I've got a double barrel answer to your query right here.

No movement. JT starts eating the food himself and fades back inside.

INT. SHERIFF'S OFFICE – NIGHT

Sheriff gets a call while he interviews Wray.

was something I could do.

                    JT
The last thing I want is to call you asking for anything. But I'm not calling my brother right now. I'm calling the sheriff.

JT is talking on a HOT DOG phone.

            SHERIFF HAGUE
What's the trouble.

                    JT
Well, it's not trouble really, not yet anyway. Might need you to send someone over. Two delinquents been hanging out here for over an hour. Won't

poking out of her bandaged stub. She holds back her tears. She closes her eyes. She fights it.

Maybe even accepts.

EXT. JT's DINER – LATER – NIGHT

Now there's TWO Bodies standing outside at the pumps.

JT opens the door with a plate of food.

                    JT
Can I interest you fellas in a plate of soon-to-be award winning BBQ?

            SHERIFF HAGUE
Sheriff Hague.

INT. JT'S DINER – NIGHT

                    JT
It's JT, Sheriff.

            SHERIFF HAGUE
How's the barbeque business.

                    JT
Well, ever since my bastard landlord raised the rent to the sky, it's been shit.

            SHERIFF HAGUE
Sorry to hear that. Wish there

leave, won't purchase. They're just...
                    (beat)
Oh never mind, here they come.

We see that JT is looking at the two delinquent shapes standing right outside the door. They just stand and stare.

            SHERIFF HAGUE
                (leaning forward)
You cook the meat at 250 degrees don't ya?

He's cooking up a sauce while he talks.

                    JT
I don't know. Set the heat by my
hand.

              SHERIFF HAGUE
                  (beat)
Give me that recipe, or I'll raise
your rent higher than a Georgia
pine.

                    JT
Brother, no Texan's ever gonna
tell you their BBQ recipe, that's
a fact. They take it to their
dying grave. I could be bleeding
like a stuck pig, I aint' gonna
tell ya... I could be dying in
your arms, I ain't gonna tell
ya...

JT hangs up.

*We see the two shapes still at
the door.*

                 JT (cont'd)
Well? You gonna look? Or you
gonna eat?

The shape pushes the door in.

                                                    CUT TO:

INT. HOSPITAL - TAMMY'S ROOM
- NIGHT

*Close on door opening and
Dakota stepping into operations
at a clip.*

*Dakota joins the paramedic and
Block.*

                  DAKOTA
You called for me?

                  BLOCK
Yes, I need you to see this.

*Block lifts the sheet off the body
and we see the face. It's Tammy.
Her face frozen in the shock of
death.*

                BLOCK (cont'd)
Prepare yourself.

*Dakota can't believe her eyes. She
can't breathe.*

*Block looks at her closely for
her reaction.*

              PARAMEDIC CECI
          (still talking to Block)
Looks like a no-brainer.

                  FELIX
What do you mean?

*Paramedic turns Tammy's head to
the side. We can see the brain is
missing.*

              PARAMEDIC NIXER
No brain. Scooped clean out of
her skull.

                 DOC FELIX
I know what that is...Liquifactive
necrosis.

*Dakota walks into another room.
Containing her composure.*

                  BLOCK
Thank you. That'll be all.

*Block removes something from
Tammy's pocket and then walks
over to Dakota. She embraces
him. He consoles her.*

Stacy Ferguson

as Tammy

STACY FERGUSON: The character I play, Tammy, fits into the world of *Grindhouse* in an element of surprise. You don't really know her story until the movie unravels. She's actually with Marley Shelton's character, Dakota, and they're planning to run away together, away from her abusing husband. Basically, I'm on the way to us leaving, the car breaks down, and the girly-girls get me. As you can tell, I lost my voice when I shot that scene. I just kind of wanted to go for it. I don't have a show tomorrow, so I could scream and sound like this at the end of the day. It's just the common horror film thing to have the big screams, and the damsels in distress. At the beginning of this picture, Robert and Quentin invited all of the actors to Quentin's house, and we got to watch all of these different types of period films—mostly horror and sci-fi—to get into the style of the film. I was trying to capture that. It's all a bit over-the-top at some points.

Tom Savini

as Deputy Tolo

TOM SAVINI: I'm Deputy Tolo. Michael Biehn is the sheriff and I'm sort of his second in command—his right-hand guy. In my actor's preparation, he's my brother-in-law, he married my sister. These things just evolve while you're shooting. I have three studs in my ear and I took them out right before the first day, and I guess the holes were still kind of prominent. He walked up to me and just whispered in my ear, "I would have never hired you if you had those earrings, you know." I said, "Well, the reason you hired me is because you married my sister." So that just evolved. Now when I look at him, I have more motivation. I care about him and I'm trying to protect him because he's my brother-in-law. And then he didn't believe me when my finger was cut off. There's a scene where I accidentally shoot some old guy carrying his I.V., and I'm mortified. [Sherrif Hague] walks up behind me and calls me a dumbass.

BLOCK (cont'd)
Did you know she was back in town?

DAKOTA
No. I didn't. What happened to her?

BLOCK
I don't know, baby.

*His arm moves to her back.
Squeezes. He's very calm. Too
calm.*

BLOCK (cont'd)
I thought you stopped seeing
each other.

DAKOTA
We have.

BLOCK
Yes, you have NOW. She's fucking
dead.

DAKOTA
I mean, we stopped before. I
haven't talked to her in a while.

*He moves his hand up to her
neck. He kisses her forehead.*

BLOCK
But you've written each other?

DAKOTA
Here and there, but nothing...

*Block has pulled her PDA out of her
pocket. She takes it away.*

DAKOTA (cont'd)
What are you doing?

BLOCK
I want to see your last three
messages.

DAKOTA
I can't.... You have no right to-

BLOCK
-I don't?

*He takes one of her needles out
of her pocket protector.*

BLOCK (cont'd)
I don't have a right?

*He bites off the protective top
and spits it at her. Hits her face.*

BLOCK (cont'd)
Let me see it.

*She holds up her hand to protect
herself.*

BLOCK (cont'd)
Show it to me.

DAKOTA
No.

*Block stabs her hand with the
needle. She pulls her hand back.
A small hole.*

BLOCK
That's just to take the sting
off....SHOW IT TO ME.

*She backs up into the wall.
Worried she won't scream loud
enough.*

DAKOTA
No, please... I...

BLOCK
(stab) SHOW IT... (stab) to (stab)
ME.

He's stabbing both her hands, as
she protects her face.

BLOCK (cont'd)
Now let's see how fast your
friends work.

Dakota's hand goes numb. The
pilot slides out of her hand and
into Block's. By the way her hand
is posed we realize they've been
numbed by the needles.

BLOCK (cont'd)
(impressed)
Pretty fast!

He picks up the pilot. Clicks at
it. A readout comes up:

"I THINK HE KNOWS. PLEASE HURRY
BABY."

BLOCK (cont'd)
What do I know, exactly, my love...
That you're a cheating, lying, sack?

DAKOTA
I....didn't want to hurt you.

BLOCK
No... But you did.

He takes out her other needle. The
BIG one.

DAKOTA
Because.. you're insane. And I'm
afraid of you. Afraid of what you
might do. To me...

He takes off the needle top
with his teeth. Spits it at her.
Bounces off her face.

DAKOTA (cont'd)
And to our son...

She tries to stop him, but her
hands are rubber.

BLOCK
And after this one...

A paramedic runs into the room.
Block hides the needle.

PARAMEDIC NIXER
Doctor Block!

BLOCK
What?

PARAMEDIC NIXER
You've gotta see this.

BLOCK
Be right there.

Paramedic Nixer leaves.

DAKOTA is shoved into a small
room. Block locks the door.

INT. HOSPITAL - ER - NIGHT

A curtain is pulled aside
revealing 3 empty gurneys...

BLOCK
WHERE ARE THE BODIES?

PARAMEDIC NIXER
That's what we wanted to show
you, they're gone.

BLOCK
Well they didn't just get up and
walk out, did they?

*Paramedic Nixer points to the
ground. Block sees bloody streaks
leading to under a closed door.
Follows them to the waiting room,
which is going nuts.*

He walks over and joins Doc Felix.

          DOC FELIX
Viral Infections. All of them.
They came pouring in.

*We see the full waiting room.
Patients scratching at their
infections. It's nasty.*

        DOC FELIX (cont'd)
Some are rapidly developing
coliform leisions...Highly

INT. HOSPITAL – ER HALLWAY – NIGHT

*Block heads back to the elevator.
He hears a BUZZ SAW start up. He
goes up to where Joe was getting
his arm removed. He hears the
blade grinding into something.*

*Odd. That procedure should be
done by now.*

*Blood can be seen spraying onto
the curtain from the other side.*

*Block tears open the curtain. ZOOM
IN ON:*

*An ARMLESS JOE is standing
above Doctor Crane. The saw is*

all over Block's face and eyes.

*Joe leaves him be. Block turns
around, thinking this is odd as well.*

*We see that Block has instantly
developed his own DISEASE ON HIS
FACE.*

EXT. SHERIFF STATION – NIGHT

*We see the sheriff station and a
few cops coming in and out of it.*

                    CUT TO:

INT. SHERIFF STATION – NIGHT

DEPUTY GUY comes tearing into

contagious. Especially if they
touch you.

          BLOCK
Self preservation comes to mind.

          FELIX
          (nods)
Let's get the hell out of here.

They SPLIT!

          BLOCK
Let me get my wife. (or, First let
me get my wife.)

[OMITTED]

*buried in the doctor's CHEST.
Joe turns to Block. His face is
unrecognizable. Joe lifts the
saw and starts towards Block.*

*Block closes the flimsy curtain
and backs up.*

*The blade slices through the
bloody curtain. Joe approaches
Block, with the blade held high...
The PLUG pulls out of the wall
socket and the blade dies by the
time it gets to Block's EYE.*

*Joe looks over Block and places
his diseased hand onto Block's
face. Squeezing it. Then rubs it*

the Sheriff Station screaming.

          GUY
Somebody take care of this perp
for me before I fucking kill him.

        SHERIFF HAGUE
What the hell's going on?

          GUY
Was causing a ruckus down
at Skip's, so I cuffed him and
the son of a bitch just bit my
goddamn finger off.

        SHERIFF HAGUE
So quit hollering and get
yourself a goddamn band-aid.

GUY
I'm not exaggerating, using
colorful speech, Sheriff, he bit
my finger clean OFF!
(holds up his hand)
Fucking... shit. Get out there
and book him cause I'll fucking
kill him If I have to do it. He's
in the squad car.

SHERIFF HAGUE
Carlos, go get him. Wray, you stay
put.

EXT. SHERIFF STATION - SQUAD
CAR - NIGHT

Carlos goes up to the vehicle.
The scene is shot from inside the
car... he's trying to see him.

CARLOS
You sure he's in there?

Unlocks it...

Looks inside. No one's there.
Looks to the other window.

The window is smashed...

CARLOS (cont'd)
Holy shit.

Carlos runs around to the other
side.

Picks up something on the
ground.

Looks around. Looks under the car.
Pops back up.

ARRGH!

Sheriff is there.

CARLOS (cont'd)
He's gone. Broke out the window.

GUY
Where's my finger.

CARLOS
Found your ring.

Wray is at the steps.

SHERIFF HAGUE
(sensing something is wrong)
Could it have been the same guy

as your leg snatcher?

WRAY
I didn't get a good look at mine.

They turn around at the sound of
rustling off camera.

SHERIFF HAGUE
(casual)
Is that him over there?

Several THINGS come leaping out
of the shadows.

Deputy Guy's entire ARM is torn from
his body!

Several others attack Carlos and
rip him to pieces! Blood flies!
Sheriff pulls his gun and starts
firing.

Tolo is lifted and thrown,
SMASHING into a squad car. Wray
is attacked by one of them, he
manages to kick his feet around
it's neck, the chain across his
ankles choking the creature.
The creature opens it's mouth

and some weird THING shit starts vomiting out towards Wray.

Wray grabs Deputy Guy's gun from his severed arm and shoots the creature in the face THROUGH his ankle cuffs. Killing two birds with one bullet.

Sheriff runs over to the downed creature. He tries to help the poor thing by checking his vitals.

WRAY
No! Don't touch him!

Sheriff pulls his hands away, watches the person/creature die.

Sheriff takes the gun.

SHERIFF HAGUE (cont'd)
Where the fuck you think you're going!?

WRAY
I gotta get Cherry.

Sheriff keeps the gun on Wray, but sees that the scene is hopeless.

SHERIFF HAGUE
Fine. But we'll be taking my car.

Just then his car EXPLODES behind him. Through the flames he sees several other shapes

rip Carlos' scalp off and they eat his brain.

CUT TO:

[OMITTED]

INT. EARL MCGRAW HOME - NIGHT

Earl McGraw is feeding his wife soup. She's not looking too good. Earl sweet talks her.

A photo is nearby. Earl Mcgraw on a motorcycle with his then young wife on back.

WRAY (cont'd)
He's infected...

SHERIFF HAGUE
With what?

WRAY
Everything.

Wray runs to his truck.

Sheriff levels his gun at Wray.

SHERIFF HAGUE
Drop the fuckin' gun, Wray.

Wray flips the gun upside down so the barrel is pointing at himself.

running around in the shadows. Not all look human.

SHERIFF HAGUE (cont'd)
I'll ride with you. Don't you fucking make any sudden moves.

A few other cops come aboard. Deputy Guy is dragged onto the back of Wray's truck. They take off. Some cops standing on the back like it's a fire engine.

They are firing at the shapes that keep coming after them.

We see the shapes gathering around Carlos' dead body. They

SHERIFF HAGUE
(over walkie talkie)
I hate to do this to you, Earl. But we need every man on the job. Shit's hit the fan and then some.

SHERIFF HAGUE (cont'd)
(riding in Truck with Wray)
Get us guns, ammo. Meet me at my brother's.

MCGRAW
Alright. I'm on my way. Ramona, you're gonna have to eat this kinda quick.

He turns to her. Her boil covered face causes him to stumble backwards. Soup bowl hits the floor and breaks.

Ramona's eyes are lifeless. She stands. Her face covered with boils and pulsating skin.

                    MCGRAW (cont'd)
Ramona...

He pulls his gun. Can't believe he's even doing it.

INT. HOSPITAL

Cherry tries to get out of bed, but can't. She rings the NURSE'S button. But no one answers. She rings it several times...

                    CHERRY
Hello? Someone? I need to pee!!

She looks through the open door into the hallway. A NURSE runs towards the room...

                    CHERRY (cont'd)
It's about time...

The nurse is tackled by a group of SHADOWED figures. They rip her to pieces.

Cherry pulls the sheets up over her head.

One of the FIGURES looks up from the feeding. Stares right at Cherry's room.

EXT. HOSPITAL - PARKING LOT - NIGHT

Dakota crashes out of the 2nd story window and onto the ground in a pile of glass and window frame. She runs through the parking lot.

Her hands are numb from the meds, so fumbling for her keys becomes a sick comedy routine. She gets the ignition key into her teeth, but her car is an old 70's model with a push button handle.

Her hands flop uselessly onto the door, unable to grip the handle.

She jams one of her hands all the way THROUGH the door handle for leverage and uses her foot to push in the button.

She gets the door open...

But slips on the wet pavement. Her hand still stuck in the loop of the handle.

The fall breaks her hand and wrist IN THE DOOR HANDLE with an ugly SNAP.

She screams.

She pulls her broken jelly hand out. It flops around on her wrist, and we realize it's too numb for her to really feel. She holds it lifelessly under her arm.

She puts the key in the ignition with her teeth and turns it in the ignition the same way. We hear a crack and she spits out a tooth with some blood.

She unsnaps her watch with her

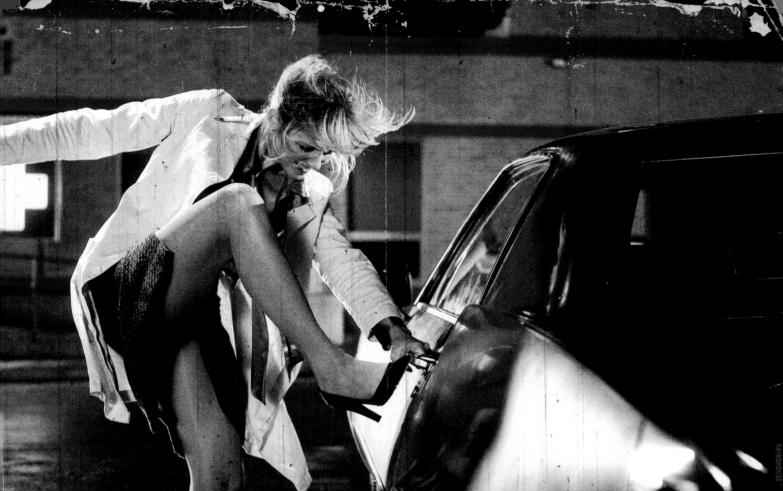

teeth and hooks the elongated band onto the stick shift and puts it in reverse. She tries to steer with her hands flopping like fish on the steering wheel.

High angle shot as she crashes into a couple of parked cars while she tears out of the parking lot, driving like a drunk.

She swerves, almost hitting WRAY'S WRECKER, which comes tearing INTO the hospital parking Lot.

INT. WRAY'S TRUCK - HOSPITAL - NIGHT

Sheriff rides bitch with his .357 still trained on Wray.

                SHERIFF HAGUE
What the hell is going on?

EXT. HOSPITAL - PARKING LOT - NIGHT

We reveal the hospital, in flames. Patients are flooding the

parking lot, most walking slow, some still attached to their hospital gear.

They're walking not unlike zombies, but most are just regular sick patients having to evacuate a burning building.

                WRAY
I'm going in.

Sheriff knows he can't stop him.

                WRAY (cont'd)
Are you gonna give me a gun?

                SHERIFF HAGUE
            (same voice pattern)
Are you fucking kidding?

Wray shakes his head and gets a scuba knife or cool switchblade or cool blade in general out of his glove compartment.

Wray takes off running.

As he does, Sheriff raises his gun, aims it at Wray's back. A FIGURE stumbles up behind,

reaches for Tolo. Tolo BLASTS him one. Looks down to see...

                PATIENT
Help me...

Tolo realizes he didn't shoot a zombie.. just an old man of a patient looking for help. Patient dies...

                SHERIFF
Goddamn it..
            (to his men)
Let's sort this shit out, boys!

Sheriff sees the old man is dead. Turns to Tolo...

                SHERIFF HAGUE
Dumb ass.

INT. HOSPITAL - NIGHT

Wray goes tearing into the hospital using his knife techniques on a few attacking zombie things.

Fire has spread everywhere.

INT. HOSPITAL – CHERRY'S ROOM/
ER – NIGHT

*He finds Cherry still in her
room. A sheet over her head. He
reaches for it.*

       WRAY
Cherry? Palomita?

*He slowly pulls it off her. She's
lying there crying in her own
private hell.*

       WRAY (cont'd)
Get up. We're leaving.

       CHERRY
I can't walk.

       WRAY
So what? Get up.

*He grabs her, pulling into a
sitting position. She yells in
pain.*

       CHERRY
Mother fucker, look at me! LOOK
AT ME.

She's showing him her stub.

       CHERRY (cont'd)
I was going to be a stand up
comedian. Who's gonna laugh now?

       WRAY
Some of the best jokes are about
cripples. Let's go.

       CHERRY
    (crying over leg)
It's not funny, it's pathetic.

       WRAY
Stop crying over fucking... spilt
milk.

       CHERRY
I have NO LEG!!

*Frustrated, Wray TEARS a leg
off of a table. He JAMS it onto
the metal stud in her stump. He
WHACKS it into place. Hard.*

       WRAY
Now you do. What do you think?

She holds her peg leg up in the

air and looks at it.

       WRAY (cont'd)
You could use it in your act..
Okay?

*Cherry stops crying. Examines the
leg. Holds the stub up in the air.*

       CHERRY
  (seeing the comic potential)
Maybe.

*He pulls her out of the bed. She
stumbles around on her new leg.*

*He's pulling her by the arm.
Making her walk awkwardly.*

       CHERRY (cont'd)
You could carry me, Wray.

       WRAY
You never wanted that before.
Why start now?

*He stabs a zombie-thing attacker
in a cool WRAY move where he's
finished and back up to support
Cherry before she falls over.*

EXT. HOSPITAL – PARKING LOT – NIGHT

They exit. Many cars are on fire
...the parking lamps flicker.
Most are out.

It's dark out here. Wray's truck
is empty. No sign of the cops.

         WRAY
Sheriff must have taken the
others to the rendevous point.
Get in.

INT/EXT. WRAY'S TRUCK – HOSPITAL
– NIGHT

       My stick leg is stuck in the door.

         WRAY
It's just wood.. Leave it alone.

         CHERRY
It's splintering.
    (getting worked up again)
Why is this happening to me?

         WRAY
Look, will you just do me a favor
right now? And just...

She's teary.

      WRAY (cont'd)
Stay... strong.

       paint each other's toenails red.

Little Tony's talking about his
tarantula and Scorpion pets as if
there's no tomorrow. (There isn't)

     BABYSITTER TWIN 1
    (on her cell phone)
I'm only taking two classes
this semester, and my BRAIN is
BURNING...

     BABYSITTER TWIN 2
  (Says something in Spanish
   in her own cell phone.)

Tony resumes talking about his pets.
Dakota enters the house.

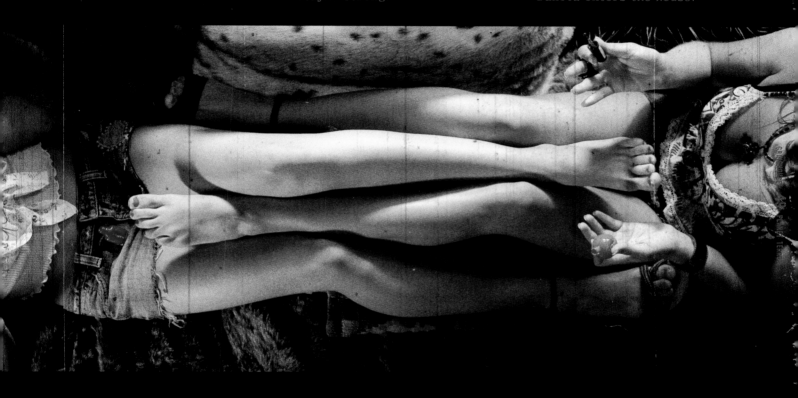

Wray gets in the truck. Doesn't
help Cherry into the passenger
seat. He starts the truck and hits
the gas. We see her trying to climb
in while limping on her peg leg.

She barely makes it into the truck
as he's already driving off.

He hits a few transformed
patients on the way out.

INT. TRUCK

Cherry can't get her leg all the
way inside.

        CHERRY
Stay?

Wray looks to her while driving.
Shakes his head.

         WRAY
Stay.

She smiles. Looks down at her leg.

INT. DAKOTA AND TONY HOME –
NIGHT

The BABYSITTER TWINS, both aged
17, are sitting with their bare
legs over the couch armrest,
chewing gum and looking tarty as

        DAKOTA
I'm... sorry... I'm...

      BABYSITTER
   (fuming, as usual)
Coño, chica.., you said 10pm! We
can't be watching your kid all
goddamn night.

Dakota's not in the mood, but
tries badly to apologize anyway.
Babysitter #2 is acting like a
bouncer, giving Dakota attitude,
glare, and a puffed out chest.

     BABYSITTER (cont'd)
Your friend never showed up, and
I got shit to do.

Dakota uses her arms to grab Babysitter by the hair and push her through the door.

DAKOTA
Then start doing it.

This takes Babysitter #2 by surprise, and she willingly leaves. Dakota kicks Babysitter #2 out into the sidewalk, then kicks the door closed.

DAKOTA (cont'd)
Tony, we're leaving.

Tony's carrying his bag.

TONY
(holding up container)
Wait! My turtle.

DAKOTA
Bring it, let's go.

TONY
And my scorpion. And my tarantula!

There's two more containers on the table.

DAKOTA
And we're not octopuses so we can't carry everything. Let's go, now!

INT/EXT. DAKOTA'S CAR - NIGHT

They get in the car. Tony is finishing dumping all his pets into the same container.

DAKOTA
Tony, what did I tell you? We're not bringing them all!

We see a close-up of the pets facing off with each other.

TONY
They can live in the same tank together. Wait, what about my pocket-bike?

DAKOTA
(trying to put car in gear)
It's in the trunk.

Shot on Dakota suddenly jumps to

SLO MO as WHACK!

Her window cracks, spiderwebbing across it from the impact of the pick axe.

BABYSITTER
Where you going, fucking bitch!?

The baby-sitters whack at the car with a shovel and pick axe, denting and cracking glass. Even on TONY'S side.

BABYSITTER (cont'd)
I'm gonna fucking kill you!

TONY
They're mad at you.

Dakota SLAMS ON THE GAS and RUNS OVER one of the BABYSITTERS.

But like a Venezuelan acrobat she leaps back to her feet and they both chase after Dakota while cursing. Dakota speeds away.

(By the way, these girls are not infected at all, they're just crazy.)

EXT. JT'S DINER – NIGHT

Cherry pulls up to JT's diner.
Wray leaps off the back. Sheriff
is there with a few of his
officers. They are staking out
JT's.

Some other civilians are with him.

                WRAY
What do we got.

            SHERIFF HAGUE
Something's wrong up there. JT
always comes out and greets.

Deputy Tolo brings Sheriff a
shoe box and guns. Sheriff dumps

Creeping around the sides...

            SHERIFF HAGUE (cont'd)
Try not to shoot yourselves...
don't shoot each other, but
especially...don't shoot me.

INT. JT'S DINER – NIGHT

They sneak into the diner...alert.
Searching. Nothing. They hear the
sounds of eating. They look behind
the counter and find JT on the
ground with his dog licking and
chewing on what looks like JT's
intestines.

Sheriff hauls the dog away.

JT holds up what we thought were
his intestines to Wray.

                JT
Barbecue?

Wray breaks off a link.

                WRAY
            (takes a bite)
Damn good link sausage.

                JT
Best in Texas.

JT stands.

            JT (cont'd)
I must have passed out after

out the box of badges onto the
car hood.

        SHERIFF HAGUE (cont'd)
Everybody grab a badge and a
gun! You're all deputies as of
this moment forth!

Wray is the first to move on it.

        SHERIFF HAGUE (cont'd)
 Except you, Wray.
            (to the others)
LET'S GO!

He waves and they climb up to
JT's Diner.

            SHERIFF HAGUE
Get the hell off him, Rusty!

Wray tends to JT.

Sheriff begins to react to his
dead brother...

        SHERIFF HAGUE (cont'd)
JT...

But JT sits up suddenly with his
shotgun aimed at Wray. He's in a
panic.

JT feels his intestines. A sigh of
relief. He takes a bite.

killing those things.

                CHERRY
Nice shooting!

We see the SHAPES from earlier
laying on the ground with their
heads blown off.

            SHERIFF HAGUE
Everyone... Get supplies. We're
heading out in twenty.

The others gathering things from
the store and putting them in boxes.

JT eats some of the sauce off his
shirt.

JT
I think I've nailed it. Holy shit. Finally cracked it. My award winning sauce...

Hague sees what he's licking...

SHERIFF HAGUE
There's blood in it.

JT notices...

JT
Well I'll be damned. There sure is, isn't there.

CHERRY
I think you'd be disqualified for that.

. JT
You raised the rent on me, bastard... a brother don't do that to his kin. Now you're planning on giving up the badge, and picking up the brisket. Open your own BBQ joint. Well... ain't gonna happen. Not with this recipe anyway. Grandad passed that onto me. ME.

SHERIFF HAGUE
And he passed me ownership of this building. Checks and balances sort of deal.

JT
Well, you fucked me, so you don't get shit.

Dakota looks at his bloody tooth.

DAKOTA
Put it in my pocket, we'll save it.

She smiles.

TONY
Hey...your tooth fell out, too.

She looks in the mirror. Sure enough. A big CHIP taken out of her tooth.

TONY (cont'd)
We're toothless buddies.

DAKOTA
We sure are, aren't we.

JT
That's funny.

CHERRY
(looking at Wray)
Thank you.

JT follows Sheriff around the store as Sheriff takes charge of the evacuation.

JT
So what, you call state of emergency and raid my place?

SHERIFF HAGUE
You catch on quick. Plus, it's half mine.

SHERIFF HAGUE
Right now, all I want are the supplies. Then we're out of here. And I'd advise you to come with us.

INT/EXT. DAKOTA'S CAR/MCGRAW'S HOUSE – NIGHT

Dakota pulls up to a house off the main highway.

She HITS the horn, several long bursts. No one comes out. Porch light is out.

TONY
My other tooth fell out.

She looks around frantically. Hits the horn again.

DAKOTA (cont'd)
Can you open that for Mommy?

She points to the glove compartment. He opens it. A gun is inside.

DAKOTA (cont'd)
Take it, carefully...and if anyone comes to the door that isn't me... You shoot them. Okay?

Tony isn't sure if she's joking.

DAKOTA (cont'd)
I'm not kidding, Tony. Nothing is

safe anymore. Shoot them. Just
like your video games. Shoot
them in the head.

                    TONY
What if it's Dada?

                    DAKOTA
Especially if it's your dada.

*She's crying as she cracks the
door open and peeks out. She
turns back and sees the gun
pointed at her head, Tony studying
it. Dakota lowers Tony's arm.*

                    DAKOTA (cont'd)
Be careful where you point it,
you'll blow your own face off!
Okay?

*She's looking around to make
sure there's no one out there.*

                    DAKOTA (cont'd)
 I'll be right back.

*She kisses him. She turns towards
the house.*

Takes a few steps... slow ones

*There's rustling out here. And
wind.*

*She hears something out in the
field. She starts towards the
house and hears screams coming
from inside. A man. Yelling. She
hears something crashing and
breaking. Then silence.*

*She hears a loud GUN SHOT. Turns
back around. No one's outside the
car.*

*She runs back to the car and
peers in the frosty window.
Tony is slumped in the front
seat. Shot.*

*A bloody mess where his face
used to be.*

*She reacts as a hand reaches in
from off camera and PULLS HER
HAIR.*

*She screams at the pain and it
turns her enough that we can see*

*it's Block. His face is more fucked
up now, but we can tell it's him.
He's got a giant needle in his
hand. His face is full of sores.*

                    DAKOTA (cont'd)
You bastard! Look what you did!!
Look what you did to our son!!!

*Dakota beats Block back with a
mother's fury. Pummels him to the
ground, but stops when...*

*Other INFECTED approach from
down the street.*

*Dakota stumbles around to the
passenger side of the car. She
opens Tony's door with her key.
He falls out into her arms.*

*BLOCK stands. Half his face is
CAVED-IN from Dakota's beating,
but this only makes him scarier...
especially when he stands... and
reaches for Dakota.*

*Dakota carries Tony to the house
as the other Infected fall in-
line behind Block.*

Carrying Tony, Dakota can't run as fast as she wants. The infected walk towards her as if possessing the knowledge that she won't get very far, so why rush.

[Alt] TONY realizes zombies are everywhere. Hitting the car...

DAKOTA (cont'd)
Tony....

Tony realizes he's in a shit situation.

TONY
Well this sucks!!

He splits, dodging zombies all the way to the door.

As she nears the front door, McGraw swings it open.

He's inside his house...holding a bloody axe. He can't believe his eyes.

MCGRAW
I told you I never wanted to

fucking see you again.

DAKOTA
Daddy, please...

He sees what's behind her and gets her inside. Slams the door.

INT. JT'S DINER/BACK ROOM AREA – NIGHT

JT leads them to the back to his living quarters by passing through the MEAT LOCKER. JT pokes at hanging slabs of beef as they pass through. Out of habit mostly.

JT
Escape vehicles you need? Escape vehicles I got. This way, please.

A tarp lays over a shape in the next room.

JT (cont'd)
Meet my wife.

JT pulls the tarp off.

We reveal his custom chopper in

all it's awesome glory.

Sexy. Long, lean... mean machine.

JT (cont'd)
Jesse James custom Dominator. I served Jesse a plate of BBQ so good he made me this bike free of fuckin charge.

WRAY
Got anything that can transport more people?

JT unveils a primer black '56 chevy.

JT
How bout this?

WRAY
Where's the top?

JT
(proud)
It's chopped. Permanent convertible. No roll bar, no chicken wire, non of that shit.

Rose McGowan
as Cherry

ROSE McGOWAN: *Planet Terror* is absolutely a wild ride. I wouldn't even really know how best to describe it. It's all these bizarre things happening to all these bizarre people. And my character, Cherry, starts out as this kind of normal girl whose life is a bit on the skids, and all the sudden I kind of have to save the universe. You know how that goes. Cherry has renamed herself. She likes to rename herself I think with each new job she has. She's kind of a wanderer/searcher, and things never really seem to pan out. I always ask Robert, how did you come up with the fact that I have a machine gun leg and every time he's like, "Well I was sitting in traffic," and that's where it stops. Okay, I sit in traffic a lot. I don't often have machine gun legs that pop into my head, but that's just me.

Freddy Rodriguez
as Wray

FREDDY RODRIGUEZ: I play Wray or *El Wray*. He's kind of a mysterious character. The film takes place in Texas, and by his appearance, the way he talks, and who he is, Wray is clearly not from Texas. We really don't know who he is or where he's from. He's kind of a loner. As the movie unfolds, you see the different layers of Wray being peeled away, and you see more and more of who he is until ultimately, in the other movie, it's revealed fully who he is.

Cherry is an old girlfriend of Wray's. And at the beginning of the movie he reconnects with her after a period of time so there's that sort of weird energy that goes on between a couple after they've not seen each other for a long time, a little sexual tension too. And when all hell breaks loose in the town, Wray does everything he can to save her.

WRAY
No protection.

JT
She's fast. Nitrous injected...
350 horsepower engine...

Wray brushes by Sheriff, who grips
his arm.

SHERIFF HAGUE
Who the hell are you Wray?
I mean... Really.... Wray's
Wreckage? That's what it says on
your truck. You a wrecker, Wray?

WRAY
I'm nobody. Easiest thing to
remember. So remember it.

Sheriff reveals a tattoo under
Wray's jacket sleeve. He then
reveals his own identical tattoo.
A dove.

Wray steps off.

INT. JT'S DINER – NIGHT

They're in the back, gathering
their supplies and making a

plan.

Cherry is watching a TV set
looking for the news update.

EXT. TRENCHES – NIGHT

GERALDO is on TV. He's on the
move... reporting from the
trenches. Doing what he does best.

GERALDO
We have exclusive confirmation
that terrorists have unleashed
a biological weapon here in a
remote part of Texas. The few
that are not affected by this
airborne plague... are killed by
the ones that are.

Just then, Geraldo is ATTACKED by
plague victims. His cameraman
goes next. The camera lands
in a way that we see Geraldo's
screaming as he tries to fight
off the cannibalistic marauders.'

He gets killed... Blood splatter-
ing the camera lens.

INT. JT'S DINER – NIGHT

Cherry shuts off the TV.

CHERRY
Tool.

JT sits beside her with a plate of
brisket.

JT
You eat meat?

CHERRY
Oh yeah. That's all I eat.

JT
Good girl.

CHERRY
And shit. I eat a lot of shit. See
this?

She smiles big, teethy.

JT
What's that?

CHERRY
Shit eating grin.

JT
You should be a comedienne.

CHERRY
(looking at Wray)
Thank you, I think I will. What do
you think of my leg?

JT
(walking out)
It's pretty funny.

CHERRY
Terrific.

*Someone asks where the tools
are. JT goes to show them. Wray
walks in the small bedroom and
closes the door behind him.*

INT. JT'S DINER - SMALL BEDROOM
- NIGHT

*Wray locks the door with the
latch.*

WRAY
How's your stump?

CHERRY
They knocked it out something
fierce. Still can't feel a thing.

*Wray lays on the waterbed with
Cherry.*

They bounce around a bit.

Wray takes off his jacket.

WRAY
This must be real Bone Shack...
(eyeing the beads and tassles)
Ol' JT knows how to live.

CHERRY
Like FUCK he does. I'm sure to
you this is a class setup, but...
no fucking way.

WRAY
You say fuck a lot. Do you like
fuck?

CHERRY
Fuck you.

*Wray takes off his shirt. Wray
is covered in tattoos and bullet
wounds and other assorted scars.
He's like Rambo times ten.*

WRAY
Fuck me?

Wray starts undoing his pants.

CHERRY
Oh, now you're the comedian?

Go ahead, drop your pants. I'll
laugh.

WRAY
I highly doubt that.

*He removes his belt and his
wallet.*

He starts taking off his watch.

WRAY (cont'd)
That's my jacket.

CHERRY
Yes. I know.

WRAY
(nods)
I looked for it 2 weeks.

CHERRY
Yeah... You said that. Look, You
were being an unbelievable dick. I
was walking out on you. I was cold.
I needed a jacket. I took yours.

*Wray isn't upset as much as he's
amused.*

CHERRY (cont'd)
So If you're gonna start your
fucking psycho-obsessive-
controlling rant over a fucking
jacket, then fucking TAKE
IT. Cause, I'd rather fucking
freeze...than hear your fucking
shit.   .

WRAY
Did you find what was in the pocket?

CHERRY
NO! Fuck...

WRAY
Find it.

*She searches a zippered compart-
ment. Nothing.*

WRAY (cont'd)
The other one.

*She turns the jacket over...there
in the back are 2 more zippered
compartments. She undoes one
and finds a small red box. She
opens it.*

WRAY (cont'd)
I was going to give it to you.
But...you left me...and you took
the jacket...and I
(speaking together)
looked for it for 2 weeks...

*She pulls out a ring. An engage-
ment ring.*

WRAY (cont'd)
Read it.

CHERRY
(reading inscription)
"Two against the world..."

WRAY
(whispered)
Remember that?

CHERRY
I never forgot it.

*They kiss. She lifts her shirt
up. The film print gets shaky
and grittier for a reel change. A
few jump cuts and we can almost
barely see what looks like it
was originally a really hot
love scene. It's so hot the film
literally sizzles.*

WRAY
Why did you leave?

CHERRY
You didn't believe in us...or me...

*Her answer is practically
inaudible for the film print is so
screwed up it finally BURNS.*

TITLE CARD reads: MISSING REEL.

(plays for 10 seconds)

EXT. JT'S DINER - ALL HELL
BREAKS LOOSE

*We start the reel with a stinger,
over an exterior shot of the
diner. IN FLAMES*

*HUNDREDS of zombie thing
creatures are out here, walking
up towards the now BURNING
BUILDING...*

*We must have missed a good 20
minutes, so as an audience we're
playing CATCH UP to the story...
but basically..*

*ALL HELL HAS BROKEN LOOSE.
Those that were infected before
with skin diseases are now full
blown FREAKS, with coliforms,
necrosis, ulcerated lesions,
staph infections, the works. They
are in hordes outside the diner.*

We find Sheriff being pulled in

from the outside... he's bleeding like a pig.

Chaos everywhere.

INT. JT'S DINER - NIGHT

Chaos everywhere as Sheriff is being pulled in from the outside.

Cherry helps Dakota in with her dead child.

A BLOODY, battle worn Wray patches up Sheriff quickly and impressively.

SHERIFF HAGUE
I figured one of these half cocked deputies would end up shooting me. Didn't think it'd be fucking TOLO.

Tolo looks remorseful...

WRAY
You're gonna be alright. McGraw's here, and a whole bunch of others.

Earl McGraw helps the others re-board up the door.

Dakota is talking to her dead child.

DAKOTA
(hushed tones)
What did I tell you, Tony? Don't point the gun at yourself. Didn't I tell you that?

All the new faces are getting acquainted while in action. We see the twin Babysitters carrying in Skip, owner of the GO GO GO Club. He's got his arms all over the two girls. Pretending to be hurt more than he is. They tear open his shirt and start swabbing him.

Cherry rolls her eyes.

CHERRY
Oh, yeesh.

Hague knows he's dying, the others are wounded, and Wray's the only chance they've got. Wray looks determined to save Sheriff.

SHERIFF HAGUE
Thanks for telling me about...

you know.

WRAY
Don't mention it.
(beat)
And that's an order.

SHERIFF HAGUE
Had I known you were...
(whispered)
El Wray...
(in pain)
I wouldn't have given you such a hard time.

WRAY
Didn't mean to be a prick about it. "Need to know basis," that kinda shit.

Close on Peacemaker coming out of Hague's holster. He hands it to Wray.

SHERIFF HAGUE
You take this Wray. You take this and do what you do best.

WRAY
All the way.

Tolo walks in on this scene and intercepts the gun exchange.

DEPUTY TOLO
No... no, you're not... Don't give HIM the gun. Not to Wray!

SHERIFF HAGUE
Give him that gun, Tolo. You give him that gun. Give him ALL the guns.

Tolo sees the look in Hague's dying eyes. He hands the guns to Wray.

A blood lust rises in Wray. His eyes go wild.

He does some insanely fast gun spins...

We push in on the twin baby-sitters and Skip. Eyes and mouths open wide.

We push in on Tolo who whispers a "holy shit."

We push in on JT. Serious as a heart attack.

JT
That boy's got the devil in him. Wray puts the guns in his pant

belt. More than he can almost carry. Just the way he likes it.

There's something about Wray and guns... information we'll never find out... cause it was all in the missing reel.

One thing is for certain. Wray loves guns and guns love Wray.

WRAY
We've got to fight them off and get to the other vehicles. Everyone behind me.

BOOM! CREATURES suddenly break through the window!

It no longer looks human. The disease has caused total deformation, with bulbous cysts that when hit, pop like giant zits... sending bile and pus goop.

Then BOOM, another splice cut and three are already eating Tolo.

Tolo swings at it with his patented gun fighting Tolo punches of death.

Wray aims his gun at them. So does Sheriff. They can pick them off easily but Tolo is already covered with their pus and blood and is bleeding from unhealable wounds.

Sheriff raises his gun out of a pointing position. Wray does too.

Tolo realizes he's fucked. The creatures PULL HIM IN HALF. Wray then blasts the creatures' heads off.

WRAY (cont'd)
Outside! Now!

They run outside and start firing. Taking out as many creatures as they can.

They wipe out an entire wave of zombies. As their guns click empty, they see a second wave of zombies heading over the hill.

They all look to Wray. Even Sheriff.

SHERIFF HAGUE
What... now... (cough)... Wray?

WRAY
Back inside.

Wray scans all the new weary faces.

They must have made their way here during the missing reel.

WRAY (cont'd)
You. What's your name?

SKIP
Skip.

WRAY
Go out front and start up the Kill Dozer, I'll cover you.

WRAY
Cherry... go. [alt. Cherry, no!]

She runs out.

Wray runs to the window. Starts firing.

Cherry sees what she's up against...plots a course...

CHERRY
Oh dear...

INT/EXT. JT'S DINER – NIGHT

Cherry hobbles/runs for the KillDozer.

through the front door.

Wray leaps out of the way just in time, having shot a zombie off the Killdozer as it was reaching for Cherry...

Now the truck is in the building, having stopped.

They haul the wounded into the back, including Sheriff.

WRAY
JT, you take whoever you can fit in your convertible. I need someone to drive my truck.

SKIP
Are you fucking crazy? I'm not going out there.

Wray loads the rifle.

WRAY
I never miss.

SKIP
I'm not up to it.

Taking the keys from Skip.

CHERRY
It's go go. Not cry cry.

She pushes by Skip.

Thrilling tracking shot as Wray has to FIRE REPEATEDLY, picking off every charging zombie, the last one is SHOT/RATCHETED away from Cherry mid lunge.

Wray is out of bullets, charges to the doorway grabbing fresh guns on the way.

From the door, Wray fires at the GAS PUMPS causing FLAMES to rise to the sky. He has to keep changing out guns as the others reload for him.

Cherry gets in the KILLDOZER and drives it right up and

SHERIFF HAGUE
I'll do it.

WRAY
You're bleeding like a stuck pig. Your vision is blurred, you're on your last leg...

SHERIFF HAGUE
Anything else.

WRAY
(tossing him the keys)
Don't wreck it.

The doors open as JT takes Skip and the twin babysitters with them. Armed to the teeth.

JT
Grab the slaw! Can't pack BBQ
without the slaw.

BABYSITTER
We need guns!

JT hands them shotguns.

BABYSITTER #2
Fucking cool.

*Dakota steels herself as she gets
in the convertible.*

MCGRAW
(with rifle)
You all head out. I'll hold em off
from here.

(to the others)
Who else has a car.

*We pan over to Dakota. She
raises her hand.*

EXT. HIGHWAY - NIGHT

*VROOOM VROOOM - We hear the
start of engines revving up --*

*JT is in the convertible. He has
a rib between his teeth, gnawing
on it.*

*Cherry is on her chopper...
revving it up. Dakota asks the
twins if they can watch over
Tony. They answer with a nod and*

WRAY
Is it fast?

DAKOTA
0-50 in 4 seconds.

WRAY
Ride with her.

*He pulls the pocket bike out of
the trunk. We see it land on the
floor in full size. Looks normal
until he sits on it.*

It's smaller than a tricycle.

*Dakota climbs atop the Chopper
with Cherry.*

Dakota looks back at her father.

MCGRAW (cont'd)
Go on. I can take care of myself.

DAKOTA
Bye. Daddy....

WRAY
You remember how to ride a bike?

CHERRY
Useless talent #32.
He looks at her leg.

WRAY
Use your front brake. If at all.

a cocking of their shotguns.

DAKOTA
Thank you.
(to Tony)
Tony! Listen to your babysitters.
Wray is at Dakota's dead car.

WRAY
The engine is shot. And you have
three blown tires.

DAKOTA
But...I got Tony's pocket bike in
the trunk.

Trunk opens up.

CHERRY
I'm Cherry.

DAKOTA
(eyes on burning building.)
You sure are.

*Cherry finds that to be an odd
comment.*

DAKOTA (cont'd)
(quietly)
Goodbye, Daddy.

*Wray raises up his gun and fires
it to signal.*

WRAY

Head out!

JT looks at his burning diner.
Shakes his head.

JT

A damn shame.

Zombies come up over the hill.

JT levels his gun at them. Skip
ducks as JT fires. Wray also
fires at the zombies then starts
up the pocket bike and peels out.

UP on the overpass, Wray zips
around shooting zombies in the
knee caps. When they drop, he zips
back and shoots them in the head.

Sheriff SPLATTERS the creeps
with the truck.

JT and the ones in the convertible fend off zombies that flood
on top of them.

Cherry runs over as many as she
can.

An accident happens when one of
the zombies attacks JT.

He swerves, sending his poor dog
out into the street.

JT (cont'd)

RUSTY!

The Dog tries to catch up but
gets run over by the Killdozer.
The Babysitters scream as blood
sprays them.

Alt: Tony and Rusty hide in the
seat.

EXT. HIGHWAY BRIDGE - NIGHT

They come to a stop because the
bridge is blocked by a line up of
zombies.

A momentary stand-off. The
zombies raise their arms and
begin their charge.

But machine gun fire erupts.
Mowing down the zombies, and
almost taking out the survivors

as well.

WRAY

Hold your fire, we're not
infected!

The zombies fall over dead and
reveal MILITARY VEHICLES.

JT
(impressed)

Don't mess with Texas...

Soldiers level their guns at our
heroes.

MULDOON steps out up from truck.
Removes his breathing apparatus.

MULDOON

All survivors must come with us.

Two soldiers lower behind Wray
on lines...

MULDOON (cont'd)

Including you... El Wray.

Close on his eyes. They glow that
pale color again.

Cherry makes note of them knowing each other.

WHACK! Wray gets a rifle-butt to the head. He goes down...

Muldoon looks down at Wray impassively.

CUT TO:

INT. QUARANTINE CELL – CELL

Wray on the ground out cold. He comes to. Dakota and Cherry are over him.

Other survivors are in here as well. They are in the army base quarantine cell.

CHERRY
We've been quarantined here with the other survivors.

WRAY
Where's here?

CHERRY
The old Army base.

ABBY
(squints)
El Wray? That you?

CHERRY
He's with them. I saw him earlier tonight with their convoy.

ABBY
I'm a scientist...and a businessman. Not military.

WRAY
It's alright, I know this guy. He's cool. I mean, he's kind of a dick, but... he's 'cool.'

SHERIFF HAGUE
Which is why he's going to tell us what the fuck is going on.

ABBY
They're stealing biochemical weapons.

WRAY
DC2?

ABBY
(nods)
Also known as...PROJECT TERROR. Designed to take out an entire populace in a controlled land locked area.

WRAY
And you were supplying it to them. So why'd they shut you out?

ABBY
They found my supply.
(pointing down)
It's under our feet. 10 stories down.

WRAY
What about countering with atropine and PAM-2?

ABBY
Interferes with the neurotoxin delivery, sets off the cell-blaster and you're gushing blood and pus through every sacred hole in your body.

CHERRY
Appetizing.

ABBY
The only treatment is a regimented exposure to DC2. Delays the negative effects.

WRAY
They need it. Like a drug. Until they run out of it.

ABBY
But we found that a small percentage of people are not affected by the gas itself. And within this small percentage lies the cure.

miss that.

ABBY
The secret to a cure is within our bodies. The uninfected.

SHERIFF HAGUE
Then what do we do? We could still get infected by direct contact with those things.

WRAY
(nodding in agreement)
Mexico. Put our backs against the ocean and defend ourselves from there.

ABBY
No! This infection will spread

to the elevator. Wray tries to intervene and is kicked in the gut for his trouble.

He falls to his knees, watching Cherry go...

He winks at her as the elevator doors close. She sees it.

INT. ELEVATOR - NIGHT

They ride down together. Rapist leans against the opposite wall of Cherry. He pulls off his gas mask to speak.

RAPIST #1
Do you like Ava Gardner?

JT
So how do you find this small percentage?

Abby doesn't answer. Sheriff realizes...

SHERIFF HAGUE
You release the gas into a population.. say, a small Texas town. Land-locked, isolated. Someplace no one's heard of. With no one or nothing around to miss.

JT
Nothing to miss? What about my barbeque? People sure as hell'd

all over the world to every man, woman and child...unless I finish the antidote. We have to get back to my lab.

WRAY
You have an antidote?

Just then two Soldiers appear. Two more are stationed outside. They're wearing breathing masks.

RAPIST #1
You two... come with us.

Cherry and Dakota are escorted

CHERRY
I'm sorry?

RAPIST
Ava Gardner, do you like her?

CHERRY
Uh... Yeah.

RAPIST
Ya kinda look like Ava Gardner a little bit.

Cherry doesn't say anything. She just scowls.

RAPIST (cont'd)
I just paid you a compliment.

Cherry doesn't answer, just looks at the floor.

Rapist reaches over and shuts off the elevator. It stops. Cherry gives Rapist her full attention now.

                    RAPIST (cont'd)
You got something to say to me?

Cherry doesn't answer.

                    RAPIST (cont'd)
I'm not gonna ask you twice.

                    CHERRY
I don't got nothing to say to you.

                    RAPIST
                    (holds up his gun)
It's simplicity itself. You point it at what you want to die.
                    (points at the trigger)
You pull the little trigger.
                    (points at the barrel.)
Little bullet comes out here.
                    (points right at Cherry's face)
Little bullet hits you there. And you know what? You don't look like Ava Gardner no more.

Cherry calms herself. His face is getting really ugly.

An ugly, fucked up hand reaches to pull her hair aside from her face.

goes back to normal.

                    CHERRY
Tool.

Rapist eyes her.

                                        CUT TO:

INT. QUARANTINE CELL – NIGHT

One of the newer soldiers is eyeing the girls... trying to choose from the babysitter twins and Deputy Emmy.

JT eyes the soldiers...and goes up to Wray.

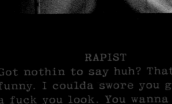

                    RAPIST
Got nothin to say huh? That's funny. I coulda swore you gave me a fuck you look. You wanna say Fuck You?

His face is starting to blister.

                    CHERRY
                    (quietly)
Not at this moment.

                    RAPIST
You know what this is?

                    CHERRY
A gun?

                    RAPIST (cont'd)
Don't taunt me. I'm not one to be taunted. Ya got it?

Cherry shakes her head yes.

                    RAPIST (cont'd)
Let me hear you say, "I got it."

                    CHERRY
I got it.

                    RAPIST
Good.

He puts his mask back on and starts the elevator up again. They ride in silence. His face

                    WRAY
                    (quiet)
What you doing JT.

                    JT
Figured it out. Salt. Blood is salty. My sauce just needed more salt and some thickening agent... I add that, it'll be just like what that blood gave it. I'm telling you. That little bit of blood was the trick.

JT looks a little off. Nervous like.

                    WRAY
Don't do nothing stupid, JT...I got it covered.

JT
Already has my sweat and tears
in it, all it needed was the
blood...

*JT makes a move on one of the
soldiers.*

*Wray quick maneuvers the gun
away from the same soldier, but
JT gets SHOT IN THE GUT by the
second.*

SOLDIER 2
Drop the gun.

*JT doubles over in pain. Wray
stops struggling.*

WRAY
JT?

SOLDIER
Drop it. Now.

*Wray stands and flips the gun
so the barrel is pointing at
himself. The gun is also upside
down.*

WRAY
Don't shoot. You alright JT?

*Wray reaches over to hand the
gun to the Soldier, his eyes never
leaving JT.*

*The soldier reaches for the
outstretched gun, and Wray
suddenly does a DJANGO move
and pulls the trigger, shooting
the soldier in the face without
changing the gun's position.*

*Wray and Abby work the guard
right away and keep moving onto
the next few guards.*

*JT crawls over and falls beside
Sheriff, who's fading.*

SHERIFF HAGUE
JT... you alright, bro?

JT
Well.. I'm shot. My diner's burned
to the ground...I'm not alright,
brother. Not alright at all.

WRAY
Wait here.

*Wray and Abby head down the
elevator. Abby knows his way
around.*

JT
Yeah... we sure will.

SHERIFF HAGUE
Wray!

Wray looks up at Sheriff.

SHERIFF HAGUE (cont'd)
Go clean em up...

*Wray nods as the elevator door
closes.*

INT. CHERRY AND DAKOTA'S CELL
– NIGHT

*The guards and Rapist watch the
girls, who are huddled in the
corner of this smaller cell. They
zero in on Cherry.*

RAPIST
Wait here. I'm gonna go get my
dick wet.

OTHER SOLDIER
She's got one leg, man.

RAPIST
(shrugs)
Easier access.

OTHER SOLDIER
You got a point there.

Cherry looks over at Dakota holding her child in this other cell they are in.

CHERRY
You're a doctor?

DAKOTA
I was earlier today.

learned. It's like... connecting the dots.

CHERRY
I don't know if I can be that optimistic right now. I'm spinning down that drain. No way out.

DAKOTA
She'd tell me, when you're caught in that downward spiral... reach up.

CHERRY
What if there's nothing up there.

DAKOTA
Just reach up.

Rapist comes forward to Cherry.

RAPIST (cont'd)
You're on stage, baby... Dance.

He chuckles and steps back. Gun aimed at her.

RAPIST (cont'd)
Dance!

She starts to dance. The first time since losing her leg.

Her lack of coordination kills her. She keeps falling and he keeps pulling her back up to go at it again.

She looks down at Dakota, who is pleading with her eyes for her to

CHERRY
I wanted to be a doctor. Instead, I can do this.

She does a backbend on the floor.

CHERRY (cont'd)
Useless talent #66.

Dakota smiles. Goes back to petting her dead son's hair.

DAKOTA
A girlfriend of mine had a theory... that at some point in your life, you find a use for every useless thing you've ever

RAPIST
You're a dancer.

CHERRY
I was earlier tonight.

Rapist GRABS her by the hair and LIFTS her to a standing position.

RAPIST
Well, I'm pulling you out of retirement.

The other soldier turns on a radio, and we hear Jungle Julia introduce a new old classic... and TOO DRUNK TO FUCK begins to play.

not give up.

RAPIST (cont'd)
Come on, now... "BREAK A LEG!!"

The Rapist laughs and howls.

Cherry gathers her strength and grits her teeth and leaps in the air, spinning her peg leg in a roundhouse, breaking the peg in half across his face.

He falls back to the ground.

Cherry screams a slo mo feral scream and like a banshee leaps in the air, twisting her body

she flies so that the POINTED
STUB of her peg leg JAMS down
into RAPIST'S EYE.
Blood JUTS out from the wound
and he shrieks.

                CHERRY
Dance for me, motherfucker!

INT. TANK DEPOT - NIGHT

Muldoon and his men enter the
room where the biggest stash of
gasses are kept.

                MULDOON
Get the rest of the shit upstairs
and then we'll detonate the
entire floor.

The room is lined with devices.
But something is wrong.

Muldoon's gas supply runs dry. So
do the two other men.

            MULDOON (cont'd)
Refill.

The two soldiers go to open one

of the tanks. Then the other.
Nothing happens.

                SOLDIER
They've been emptied.

                MULDOON
Get Lewis the fuck down here.

                SOLDIER
He's getting his dick wet, sir.

                MULDOON
Get him the fuck down here.

INT. ARMY BASE/HALLWAY - NIGHT

The two soldiers run off. They
get about halfway down the hall
before they are taken out by
SHAPES IN THE SHADOWS.

INT. TANK DEPOT - NIGHT

Muldoon hears this. He's alone
in the chamber. He gets on his
walkie and tries to call in more
men. There's no answer from
anyone he calls that should be in
the immediate area.

Abby and Wray walk in. Abby
carries something slung over his
shoulder.

                MULDOON
Where are my men?

                ABBY
Got several of them right here.

Abby tosses Muldoon the bag. It's
full and plump and squishy.

                MULDOON
What the fuck is this?

                ABBY
Their balls, sweetheart.

Abby sheaths his ball chopper
knife.

                MULDOON
I'm walking out of here with this
shit, Wray. Let us go.

                WRAY
Tell me why we should.

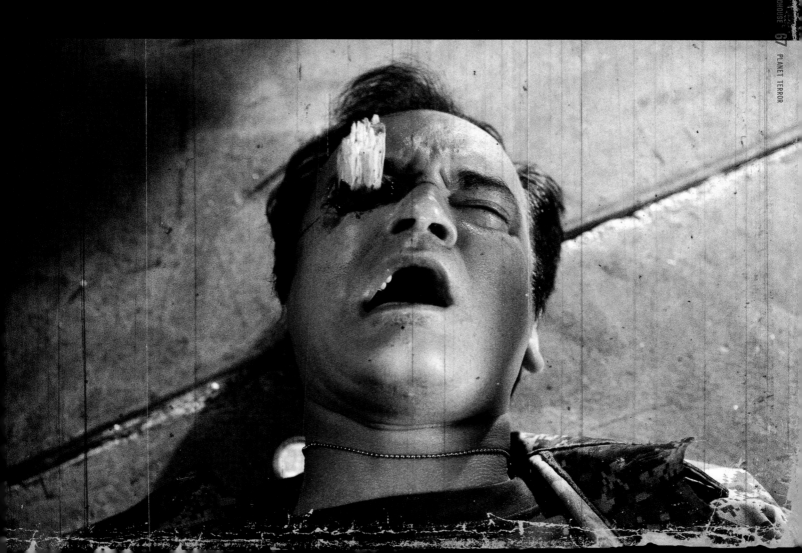

MULDOON
I earned it.

WRAY
How you figure that?

MULDOON
You want the story? I can spin it for you real quick. A termite's nest of caves on the Afghan border. My men and I are walking around with our dicks in our hands and our nads in our throats looking for America's Most Wanted-

WRAY
Bin Laden.

MULDOON
For once our intelligence was right on the money. We turned a corner and BAM!-- There he was.

ABBY
You KILLED Bin Laden??

MULDOON
I put a bullet in his face and two more in his chest.

WRAY
So that was you.
Muldoon removes a severed finger necklace from under his shirt, sitting beside his dogtags.

[ALT DIALOGUE]

ABBY
Then who was that they caught?

MULDOON
Who do you think? An imposter.

MULDOON
Class A Clusterfuck. He wasn't supposed to be there, we weren't supposed to find him and I sure as fuck wasn't supposed to cash in his dialysis ticket. So instead of medals of honor, we got a face full of DC2, fuckyouverymuch. No cure. Not until we found someone on the other side who sold us batches of this shit...

Muldoon is looking at Abby. Wray gives him a look.

ABBY
Science comes first... but business comes a close fucking second.

WRAY
(to Muldoon)
Then you realized if you could infect a large enough populace... and experiment on it's survivors...you'd find a cure.

Muldoon pours the balls out from the bag and onto the floor.

Muldoon looks worse and worse.

MULDOON
I swore to keep my men alive, Wray... and that's exactly what I'll do. Understand...
(he gets to his final stage makeup effect)
...that I had no other choice.

Wray nods. Raises his gun.

WRAY
Neither do I, sir. God Bless you and your service to this country.

In full creature mode, Muldoon/ Thing just stands there. Then lunges forward.

Abby and Wray empty their guns into Muldoon's head.
INT. CHERRY AND DAKOTA'S CELL – NIGHT

The other soldier drags Cherry to the floor.

Rapist stands, blood pouring from his eye.

He opens his pants up.

                    RAPIST
Hold that bitch down!

see what she's looking at.

His dick is MELTING. He reacts with a deep bellow.

                OTHER SOLDIER
The gas! You need your gas!

Rapist doesn't listen, he's so pissed he keeps after Cherry... reaching out to her. Walking faster now...

Cherry starts struggling to get away. The other Soldier tries to keep her pinned, but he too is freaked out by what he's seeing...

at them with a "what the fuck?" look on his face.

He looks up and sees that Dakota is holding the silver needle gun contraption from earlier. She fumbles for another needle reload from the band stretched around her thigh that was hidden under her skirt.

                    CHERRY
Where'd you get that?

                    DAKOTA
Useless talent #37.

Dakota says that as she reloads and shoots Rapist in the eye. Her

The other soldier puts his foot on her hair. Pinning her down, aiming the gun barrel at her face.

Rapist's face begins to blister and warp.

Rapist pulls his pants down around his thighs and stumbles slowly toward her. He's in agonizing pain and pissed as hell.

Cherry reacts to what's between his legs with horror.

Rapist stops and looks down to

He lets go of Cherry and runs for the discarded gas tank.

Cherry kicks and squirms.

We see the fully melted dick and then tilt up to Rapist whose face is melting off as well. He looks horrifying.

The soldier brings the gas tank over to Rapist but before he can reach him...

THUNK THUNK

Soldier gets two needles launched into his legs. He looks

hands are much better.

Unable to see, Rapist's arms are flailing, looking for Cherry.

Dakota goes up to the other soldier with the deadened legs. He's so pissed he's cursing her and reaching for his gun.

                DAKOTA (cont'd)
Don't worry. This's just to take the sting off!

He looks up at her as she fires another needle into his forehead. He falls over dead.

She spins her needle gun like a gunfighter. Flexes her hand. They work again.

Cherry and Dakota get out of there.
The door opens. Cherry runs into Wray.

She kisses him madly.

Abby storms in checks out the place. He shoots the flailing other soldier.

                    CHERRY
I broke my leg.

                    WRAY (cont'd)
So right now I need you to become who you really are.

She now has a sexy bad ass MACHINE GUN peg leg that also has a GRENADE LAUNCHER.

                    WRAY (cont'd)
Stand.

She stands in her iconic pose from the POSTER.

Abby watches as Rapist fumbles for his gas mask. Abby kicks it over to him. Rapist grabs it and breathes into it deeply. Trying to control his deformation.

She launches a rocket, blasting him backwards. It opens the back door that they needed to get into.

INT. BAD GUYS CELL - NIGHT

They walk in on the bad guys that are in an adjacent cell... surprising them.

BOOM!

She blasts the first soldier, does the double kick, first front, then back.

She then does a round house. Spraying the room with bullets.

                    WRAY
                    (smiles)
I made you something.

He sits her down and rips off her BROKEN WOOD LEG.

                    WRAY (cont'd)
I do believe in you. Always have. I believed you could be better. That you deserved better. You even deserved better than me.

Kisses her as he clicks a GUN CONTRAPTION into place on her leg stump. He strokes it.

Gun Fetish close-ups as he arms it.

The gas gags him. He throws up a strange appendage that comes out of his mouth, and still attached somewhere down his throat, falls onto the ground in a grotesque THUD. He looks like something out of THE THING.

He turns towards Cherry, looking very pathetic, but still angry. He growls a horrid sound.

                    WRAY (cont'd)
                    (to Cherry)
Open that door, will ya baby?

Cherry kicks Rapist in the crotch. Her gun leg sticks there.

                    WRAY
That will take you back upstairs with the others. We'll destroy the rest of the tanks and meet you up top.

INT. UNDERGROUND LOBBY - NIGHT

Wray follows Abby who leads the way. Cherry hits the elevator button with Dakota.

She hears voices as the elevator approaches.

They run and hide as quickly and as quietly as they can without making gun barrel noise on the

metal grated flooring.

The elevator opens. Four big soldiers emerge.

Cherry quickly but quietly hides alongside an old fashioned coke machine.

Right across from her is a cigarette machine. On the other end of the hall is the elevator.

One of the soldiers, LEWIS, heads Cherry's way.

                    LEWIS
The girls are in holding cell 6. Primed and ready. Dibs on the one with no leg. You boys can share the one with the broken hands.

They laugh heartily.

Lewis is now directly in front of Cherry. Her gun leg is now trained on him. She fires into his gut, sending him crashing into the wall. She takes his gun and aims both guns at the other two soldiers.

Her back is now to the first guy she shot. She shoves her foot (barrel) against that guy's neck, pinning him.

She is now pointing three guns. Two in her hands and her leg.

The other leg keeps her in perfect balance.

She asks the two she's facing a question.

                    CHERRY
Which one of you has no problem showing me the way out of here?

The smaller, wimpier one raises his meek hand and nods.

She shoots the other soldier, and then machine gun blasts the one behind her before roundhouse kicking him away, spraying bullets as she does so.

                CHERRY (cont'd)
                (to the survivor)
Move.

He leads her.

EXT. ARMY BASE TARMAC- NIGHT

We see soldiers carrying tanks to carts with wheels for loading onto the choppers.

The camera dollies past vehicles to a grate being lifted. Wray's head pokes out. He looks over to reveal the POCKET BIKE in foreground...

He puts on some military infrared goggles.

Looking out at the road in front of them. Sees nothing.

He then activates the infrared.

We see all the shapes of people out in the night. There's at least 40. All moving towards them.

Close on soldiers as they hear the familiar whir of the tiny engine. They turn in time to see a wheelie riding Wray, firing into their tanks as he goes past and even under them.

Abby is picking off tanks from a sniper position up on a catwalk structure.

Gas emitted everywhere.

Wray zips around crazily, firing at everything. He destroys all visible tanks.

And heads back to the quarantine cell.

Abby joins him, firing at any other soldiers headed their way.

INT. QUARANTINE CELL – NIGHT

Cherry's elevator door opens and she leads the guide soldier out.

                    SKIP
Who's this?

                    CHERRY
Our tour guide. HEY!

The soldier tries to make a move,

but Cherry handles him just fine. A gun leg KICK to the face, and then she shoves him into the elevator and sprays it with machine gun fire.

The door closes as we get a glimpse of his bloody body.

The front door opens and Wray and Abby slip back inside, shutting the door.

Their prison is now their fortress.

                    WRAY
We've destroyed most of their supply tanks. Any that are left we'll get on our way to the helicopters. They have two. Big enough to take all of us to freedom.. Who can fly?

Wray is holding up his own hand. No other answer.

                    CHERRY
              (looking at Skip)
Can anyone else fly a helicopter?

                    SKIP
I...can fly...But no way in hell I'm gonna-

She lifts her machine gun leg up to his face.

                    SKIP (cont'd)
Okay. Cool. I'll fly.

He sits back down. A nervous wreck.

Wray goes over to JT. He's got Sheriff beside him.

                    JT
We're gonna stay here, Wray.

He shows Wray his gut wound. Wray hands something to Sheriff.

                    WRAY
You'll take care of this for me then, Sheriff?

                    SHERIFF HAGUE
Yeah...

Sheriff nods...

WRAY
3 minutes. Your brother's a good
man, JT.

JT
Best in Texas.

The two men lay dying there.
Sheriff is coughing.

ABBY
Right now the soldiers are
turning. Once that happens
they'll tear us apart whether
they want to or not.

Wray climbs aboard the chopper
bike and starts the engine.

WRAY
Hop on.

Cherry leaps atop the bike,
hugging him from behind.

WRAY (cont'd)
No, the other way.

She thinks a beat, then smoothly
maneuvers herself onto his lap.

Facing him. Legs wrapped around
his waist.

WRAY (cont'd)
No... the other way.

CUT TO:

EXT. ARMY BASE TARMAC – NIGHT

The motorcycle tears out of
the quarantine cell and onto
the tarmac. All we see is Wray
riding... then he spins and
faces the rear tire towards the
oncoming Soldiers.

As he skids, we see that Cherry's
sitting on the seat behind him,
but she's facing away from
him, aiming the gun leg at the
baddies and letting it rip.

They go flying, chopped to pieces
by her ruthless firepower.
Cherry blows the smoke off her
gun barrel.

Battle ensues...

The others exit the cell, firing
their way out and following
Wray's lead.

They see a wall beyond them they
can't get to as easily.

The others all take cover as
the soldiers all seem to close
themselves off behind the wall.

ABBY
The helicopters are on the other
side.

WRAY
(racking a shotgun)
We make a run for it...

ABBY
No! If we all get killed, there's
no stopping this plague. Don't
you get it? We're the antidote.
There's got to be another way.
(feeling heroic)
Wait here.

Abby takes two survivors with
him to the wall sections. Bad
ass ABBY music plays on the

soundtrack as he takes control
of the situation.

Abby peeks around one of the
wall sections.

His head gets SHOT CLEAN OFF.

CHERRY
Don't suppose any of you are
biochemical engineers?

Wray looks at the ragged
survivors. Clearly, none of them
are. Wray looks down at Abby's
body... and any hopes of finding
a cure.

CHERRY (cont'd)
Take that as a no.

WRAY
We have to get over that wall.

Suddenly grenades and mortar
fire erupt around them.

They take cover. Grenades
explode all around them.

We see soldiers deteriorate into
creatures. They are becoming
featureless. Savage. Faces are
melting.

INT. QUARANTINE CELL - NIGHT

The two men still lying in the
quarantine cell. Side by side.
It's quiet in here.

SHERIFF HAGUE
I was thinking...We could build
a new place....Right there where
the old one was. You cook...I run
the back.

JT
Just don't make the rent so high.

SHERIFF HAGUE
Share the recipe, we'll share the
rent.

JT
Start at 250 degrees.

Sheriff can't believe his ears. He
pulls out a pad and pen.

SHERIFF HAGUE
(scribbling it in his note pad)
I knew it. For how long.

JT
12 lbs?

SHERIFF HAGUE
Sure.

JT
12 pounds... twelve hours.

SHERIFF HAGUE
I'll be damned. Wrapped in tin
foil, right?

JT
No... (cough...) no fucking foil.

SHERIFF HAGUE
Damn, okay. Tomatoes, fresh?

JT
From a can.

SHERIFF HAGUE
No shit? Well, then From Italy,
right? Best tomatoes come from
Italy?

JT
Nope. They get half their shit
from china.

SHERIFF HAGUE
What?

JT
Shhh. Didn't hear it from me.
I get mine from right here in
Texas. Canned. The best shit.

SHERIFF HAGUE
Score me some?
JT
Sure. Cause we're brothers.

SHERIFF HAGUE
Thank you for this JT..

DETONATOR that Wray gave him.
He PRESSES IT.

GIANT EXPLOSION TAKING OUT 1/4
of the BASE.

EXT. ARMY BASE - TARMAC - NIGHT

Wray watches the explosion light
up the sky.

WRAY
That's our cue. Cherry, darling?

Cherry runs.

She is almost blown up with the
bombs all around her…

caps, and as they fall to the
ground she continues her circle
of gunfire, taking off their
heads as well.

Someone fires a launcher at her.

She does her "useless talent"
back bend... dodging it expertly
as it explodes bad guys behind
her on three air rams.

She's out of ammo.

CHERRY
WRAY!

Wray appears on his pocket bike,
gun scraping the ground making

Thank...you.

JT
Just remember...you gotta take
this to your grave.

Sheriff's pen slows to a stop.

SHERIFF HAGUE
I think I can goddamn guarantee
that.

Sheriff dies, pen and paper still
in his hand.

JT holds Sheriff's hand.

JT reveals that Sheriff has a

She cocks her leg and blasts a
grenade into the ground, which
LAUNCHES her entire body high
into the air, catapulting her
OVER the wall.

While in mid air, she assesses
the area beyond the wall,
spotting the main grenade
tossers.

She re-cocks her leg and fires a
grenade into them. Blowing them
to shit.

She lands face down and as the
others run towards her she spins
around, taking out all their knee

sparks. He tosses her a new clip.

He then fires at several of the
soldiers, taking them out.

As a truck with a Gatlin gun on
it rips towards her…

She flips her body over, firing
the grenade launcher into the
truck. Blowing it up and sending
it flying over her.

The truck SMASHES into the
remaining tanks. Big explosion.
Shrapnel flying everywhere. We
see Wray wreck his bike when the
shrapnel hits. Gas pours out onto

the tarmac.

Cherry grabs sunglasses from a dead nearby soldier and puts them on her face to shield her eyes… The shards go past her.

She doesn't flinch. We see the explosion in her glasses reflected…

She stands, her Go Go Girl sunglasses…

Her leg lowering to the ground. The poster image again...iconic.

One of the dying soldiers takes dead aim at Cherry. Wray goes to fire but is out of ammo.

He has no chance but to stand up and take the bullets for her.

He goes down.

The babysitter twins run up and drill the dying soldier with bullets.

Cherry limps out to the open area where Wray made his last stand.

Wray's laying on the ground with huge chunks of shrapnel and bullet holes in him. It's over for him.

CHERRY (cont'd)
Goddammit Wray.

She goes to him.

EXT. ARMY BASE - CHOPPER - NIGHT

The survivors shoot their way to the choppers.

Dakota packs inside with her son. She turns and sees Block, waiting inside...

BLOCK
They told me I'd find you here... I was beginning to lose hope.

He tries to touch her face with his hand.

DAKOTA
Hope of what? Reuniting? That shit's done.

BLOCK
No. I want to eat your brains... and gain your knowledge.

She backs up and falls.

DAKOTA
I'm sorry I lied...

His face is deforming with every step.

DAKOTA (cont'd)
I did want to hurt you.

His face bubbles and distorts inhumanly.

Tight on a shiny pistol as quick hands pull the trigger and hammer back in succession.

BLAM BLAM BLAM BLAM.

Block falls to the ground in a heap.

DAKOTA (cont'd)
No more dead bodies for Daddy
tonight.

*Earl McGraw steps up from the
shadows. Spits tobacco.*

MCGRAW
Never liked that son of a bitch.

DAKOTA
(smiles)
Quick Draw McGraw...

*McGraw holsters his gun with a
fancy flourish.*

*The others climb inside. Skip
makes his way to the pilot's
seat.*

*The Twin babysitters are
hassling him in their panic
to hurry up and figure out the
controls. One is even trying to
fly the chopper herself.*

SKIP
Shut up! Sit down and don't
fucking touch anything!

He starts up the copter.

*We see Zombie Soldiers running
towards them.*

SKIP (cont'd)
Is everybody in?

The last survivor climbs aboard.

*The copter hovers and then Skip
dips it so that it's angled in
a way that the blade chops up
anyone that runs towards them.*

Very effective.

*He gives it gas and flies TOWARDS
the retreating Zombie Soldiers
with the copter at that same
angle.*

*Side view SHOT as the copter
runs over the Zombie Soldiers,
the blade chopping them into
bloody pulps as it overtakes
them all...*

*The blood and guts splat against
the windshield of the chopper.*

*One of the baby-sitter's turns on
the windshield wipers.*

EXT. ARMY BASE - TARMAC - NIGHT

*Cherry tries to pull out the
shrapnel.*

CHERRY
Hold still.

He knows this is the end.

WRAY
No... leave me.

CHERRY
I'm NOT leaving you like this.
Motherfuckers around here EAT
roadkill...

Wray laughs. Coughs blood.

CHERRY (cont'd)
I finally made you laugh. See, I'm
funny.

Now hold still the fires are
getting close.

He stops her.

> WRAY
> It's the only thing keeping me
> warm.

> CHERRY
> Wray...

> WRAY
> Take the copters and go to
> the sea. Put your backs to it.
> Protect yourselves there.

> CHERRY
> Two against the world, Wray...
> remember? Two against the...

He covers her mouth.

> WRAY
> It will be. I promise.

His hand slides down to her
belly.

> WRAY (cont'd)
> I never miss.

The flames from the destroyed
vehicles are crawling towards
them.

> WRAY (cont'd)
> Don't worry, baby. You'll find
> your way.

He dies in her arms.

> DAKOTA (O.S.)
> Reach up! Reach up!

The Copter hovers above her...

A line is lowered over her head.

She leans over and kisses him.

Flames getting closer...

Cherry's eyes never leave Wray.

She simply reaches up.

Close on her hand reaching and
grabbing the line.

Dakota signals for Skip to take
her up.

The copter lifts, taking Cherry
up with it.

Her eyes stay on Wray as she
floats up into the night sky.

We see her POV of Wray laying
amongst the ruin...
The fire overtakes him.

EXT. SANDY DUNES - SUNSET

Close on Cherry riding a horse.

Camera cranes up a sandy
dune to reveal a caravan of
survivors, mostly on foot,
following behind Cherry, who is
riding the only horse.

She rides in this barren desert
of new Earth...a turban on her
head...

She's leading this new batch of
survivors somewhere.

> CHERRY (V.O.)
> It's like you said it would be,
> Wray. I'm like you said I'd be. I
> find the lost... the weary...Those
> who have no hope... I find them..
> and I lead them... To the land we
> have made for ourselves. The
> land by the sea...

We see the coast in the
distance... beautiful...epic.

Kids are playing...off to the side
of her horse. She watches them.

Then a ZOMBIE rises from the
ground with a SHRIEK.

It was waiting for them.

She kicks her leg out and fires.
FREEZE FRAME on her as she
blows off it's head. Hold for a
beat...Then the movie continues.

They cross over a sandy hill
revealing a PRISTINE MEXICAN
COASTLINE.

A BREATHTAKING SIGHT. All the
survivors, the gutted chopper
used as the basis of a small
fortress, live peacefully at the
waters edge.

The group with Cherry runs to
join the other survivors.

> CHERRY (cont'd)
> It's beautiful Wray. She's
> beautiful. I wish you could see
> us. Us two. It's just like we said
> it would be.

Two against the world, baby.

Cherry is wearing a papoose on
her back. A baby is in it, facing
out. Hood over her head.

> CHERRY (cont'd)
> Two against the world.

Cherry turns her head and we
freeze on this image of the two
of them.

Slight post push in as the image
fades.

END CREDITS

ROBERT RODRIGUEZ'S

PLANET TERROR

THE MAKING OF THE MOVIE

Robert Rodriguez and Producer Elizabeth Avellán rely on Troublemaker Digital Studios, their core group of in-house visual effects artists, to research, develop and execute the look of each of their films long before principal photography begins. This process is known as "previsualization" and can involve anything from pencil sketches to high-tech "animatics" (or moving storyboards) created with 3D animation software. This core group primarily consists of artists Rodney Brunet, Chris Olivia and Alex Toader and includes a rotating group of 2D compositing artists and assistants. Although Troublemaker Digital is primarily known for their work in previsualization, they also create many of the final visual effects shots for the films they work on.

ALEX TOADER, Troublemaker Digital Artist: Troublemaker Digital fulfills many roles in Robert's filmmaking process, from creating concept art, previsualization and animatics to finishing complex final shots and compositing. Troublemaker Digital is Robert's creative right arm, if you will, we come up with concepts and do a lot of research and development based on his ideas or comments and he relies on our expertise and talents to bring his ideas to light. From our drawings to our animatics, the art and concepts that we create are used in almost all departments of the production. Robert plays animatics to the camera team and most of the time our rough animations are used not just for the camera moves but for shot composition. We

THE ART OF EXPLOITATION

PREVISUALIZATION WITH TROUBLEMAKER DIGITAL

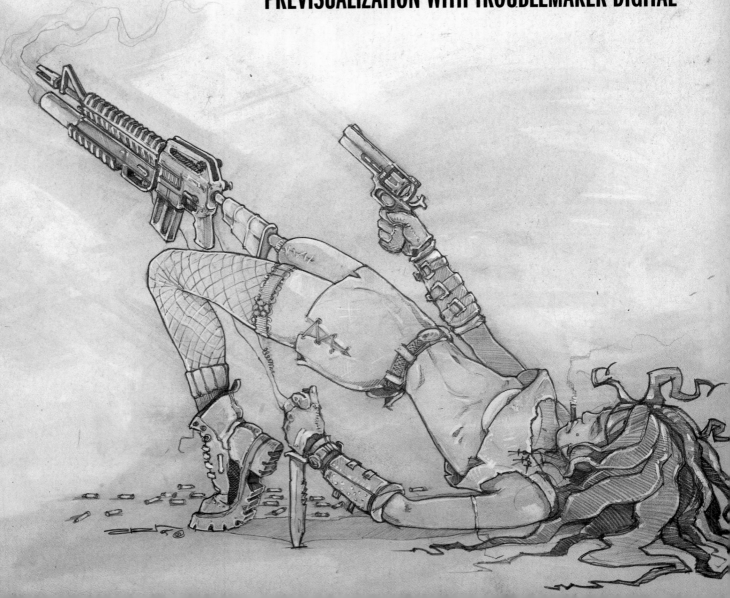

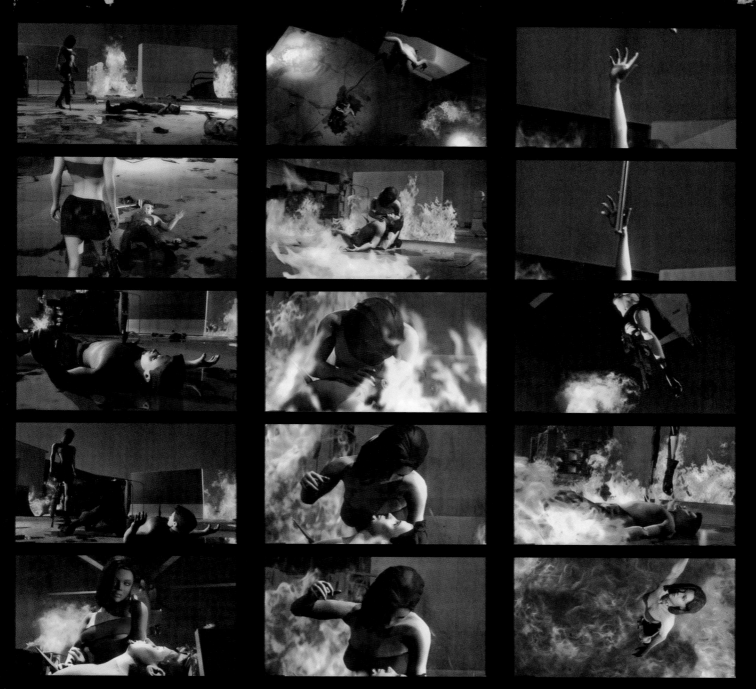

OPPOSITE: Concept illustration by Alex Toader; **ABOVE:** Cherry says goodbye and is lifted away to safety as Wray is engulfed in flames (scene 77). Animatic by Chris Olivia.

are also attempting to solve issues that we anticipate having trouble with later on, during filming or in post. We're basically involved in almost every aspect of the production. Working with Robert is different each time because he always searches for new avenues to create and bring his ideas to life. He always pushes you creatively because he pushes himself. Robert is an excellent artist himself, not just an accomplished filmmaker, but a musician and painter so I have to trust and have faith in his artistic decisions.

RODNEY BRUNET, Troublemaker Digital Artist: As in Robert's earlier films, Troublemaker helped him work through early drafts of his script ideas. We spent a considerable amount of time researching

possible looks and techniques through conceptual art, animatics for camera and environment layout along with tons of rough composites in look and feel by using footage from previous films. During this phase we help create the style Robert has in mind, while giving us a huge head start in developing and establishing techniques for our pipeline. Our first assignments started with research on film damage and we later tested several techniques for object tracking—appendage replacement as well as digital makeup enhancements.

CHRIS OLIVIA, Troublemaker Digital Artist: The way Robert works is that we are always there right from the beginning—the three main artists—and he'll give

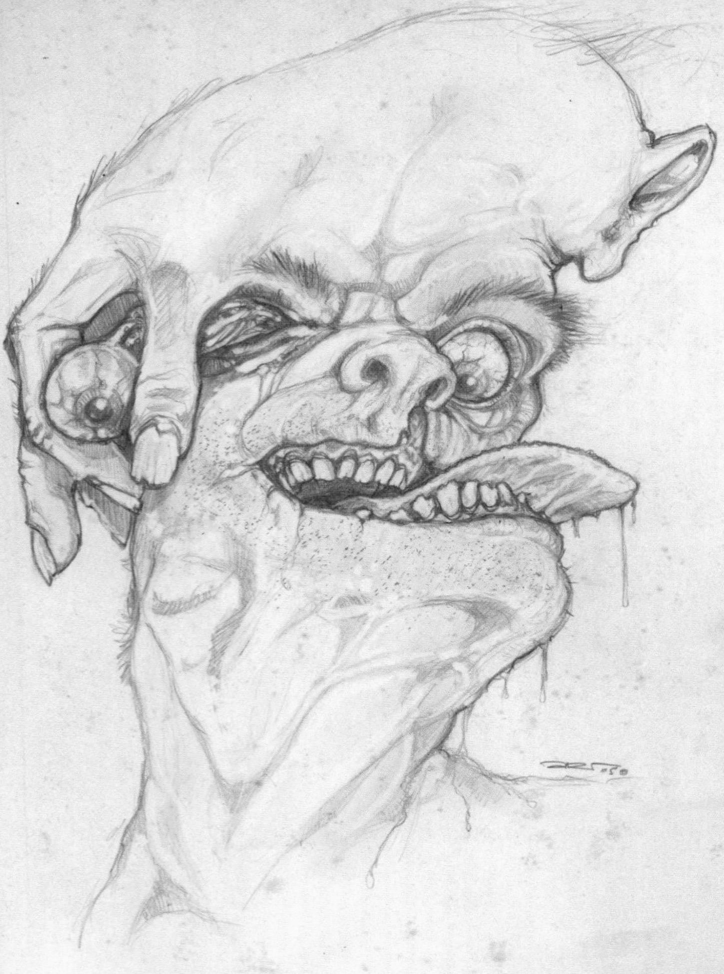

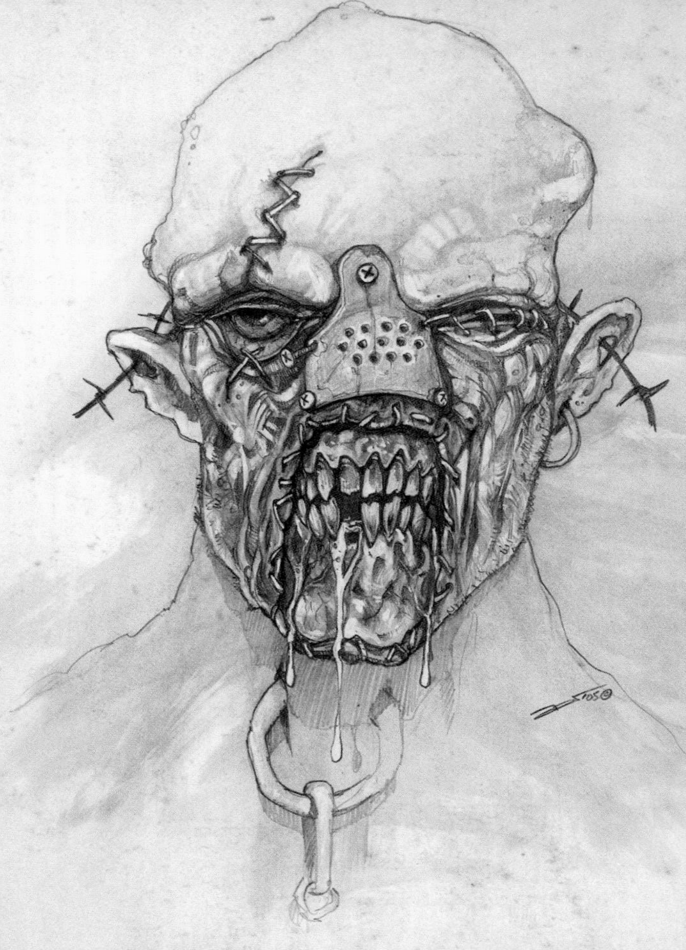

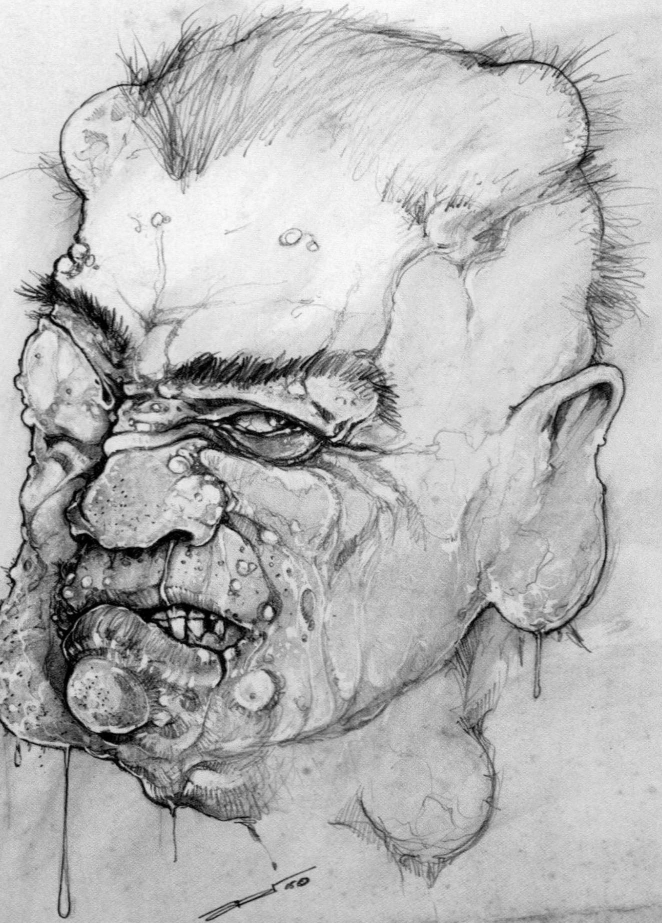

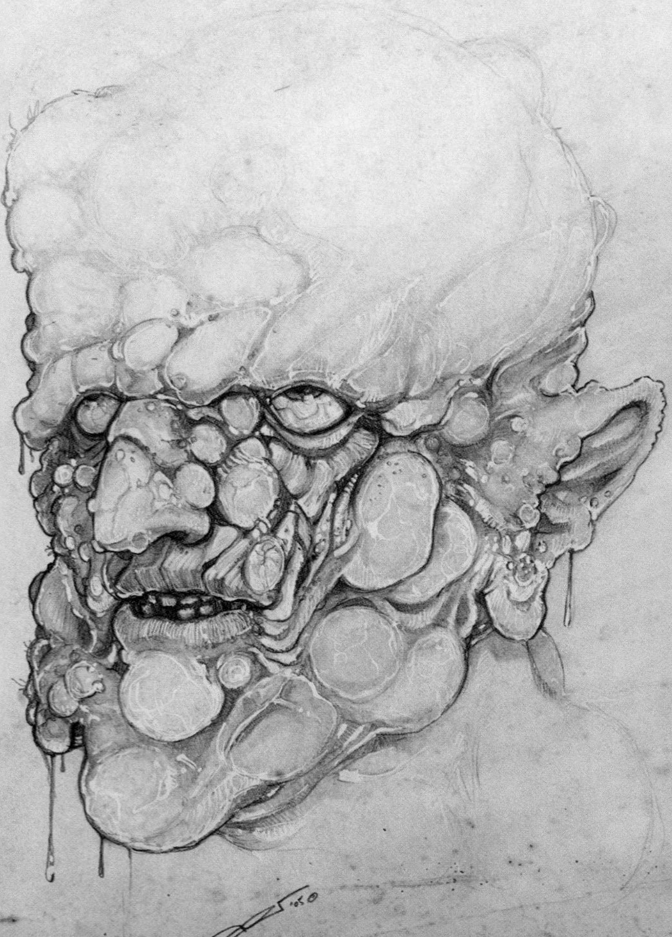

us bits and pieces of ideas and we'll start coming up with looks and playing around with concept designs. Whether it's a drawing, a painting or an actual render from software, we'll come up with these looks and at a certain point he'll use that as a springboard to take to [Special Make-Up Effects Artist] Greg Nicotero or over to the prop department. So a lot of the ideas evolve in different directions, but it's a good starting place for people to come up with stuff. *Planet Terror* was different from *Sin City* in that we weren't designing sets. What's cool about our jobs is that we get to play a lot of different parts. In *Sin City* we got to be set designers and architects by building the world around the characters, whereas with *Planet Terror* we're acting as sort of medical technicians, studying diseases and figure out what's happening with human flesh and the human body. It's all sort of creative design and creative brainstorming.

ALEX TOADER: We are always the group to do the first design pass on Robert's ideas, so in that sense our role was not different on *Planet Terror*. But what happened in this production which did not happen

before was the fact that we were very involved on the set in almost all shots that required post visual effects. One or two artists from the digital team were on the set supervising and making suggestions or bringing forth concerns with particular shots. We had to work very closely with the camera teams, [1st Assistant Director] Brian Bettwy and Robert on the set and locations, which we did not have the chance to do before. We had to get involved in that aspect because we are doing a very large portion of the visual effects. I don't want to speak for the rest of the team, but for me it was a more complete experience of the movie-making process. The fact that we were involved more and had the opportunity to work with a lot of talented guys and gals on the set—not only to learn from their practical work, or them to learn from our digital work, but to cooperate in preempting potential problems, right there on the set during filming.

CHRIS OLIVIA: The most fun I have is actually designing the line of action or sequence of shots. Visual effects shots or not. Just basically coming up with the

OPPOSITE: Zombie concept designs by Alex Toader; **BELOW:** An early concept illustration of Cherry by Alex Toader.

choreography of what's happening during the action of a sequence. And figuring out various coverage for the shots that sell the best emotional impact a sequence can have. Robert gives me a lot of freedom to kind of design a whole sequence and I'll try to give him enough coverage to where he can play with various angles. So the first thing I did on *Planet Terror* was the Cherry leaping over the wall sequence. Those were the first few pages from the script I received, even though it wasn't finalized or finished yet. So I would ask him what he was thinking, and he would either give me an idea or a scene description or I would go off the script a bit and come up with stuff, which was the case in this sequence. So at that stage, it was a matter of coming up with cool shots and angles and action to show off the fact that this character has a gun for a leg. What's going to make it interesting? How is she going to use that as a weapon or how would her walk be affected? So all of these things I was able to explore in a CG environment. There were no constraints. Just seeing visually what would be interesting, seeing what she can do with this device that she has on her leg.

RODNEY BRUNET: *Planet Terror* was different in that we did not shoot on the green screen stages. However, this post production ended up being predominately 2D with most shots requiring object and camera tracking which, in the end, will feel very much like a green screen project.

ALEX TOADER: The fact that *Planet Terror* has very few green screen shots does affect how the artist works on the shot. You have to pay a lot of attention to the integration of the CG elements with the real elements of the plate; set extensions have to be seamless. The integration of CG elements into a plate is far more challenging than creating a whole computer generated shot. In the *Spy Kids* series you accepted the exaggerated architecture and designs because they were part of an overall stylized design. In *Sin City* nearly all the backgrounds and sets were CG. They were stylized, but they were realistic and since all the

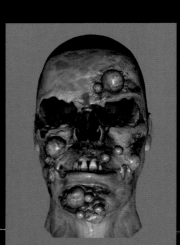

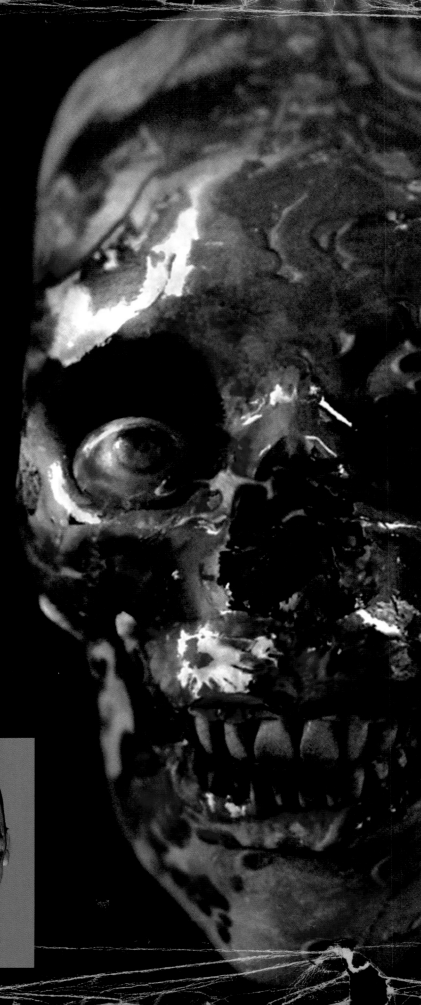

sets were computer generated—with the exception of the occasional door frame—it was much easier to art direct and create it. If you match to a partial set, you have to do a lot of reverse engineering on the lighting set up. You have to have precise notes from the camera department for tracking, removal of cables, lights or unwanted set decoration. Also if there's fog or dust or caustics generated by the lights or reflections, they have to seamlessly match. So there's far less room for artistic license.

use a lot of textures from public domain medical photographs. We would use those for textures or as displacement maps.

I remember one of the tests we started doing was oozing flesh. So other than looking online at tons of medical reference and tons of actual photographs of everything that could go wrong with the human body, inside and out, we started doing animations to see what would end up being CG and what would

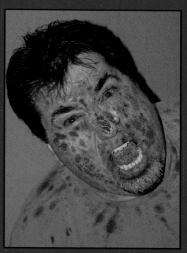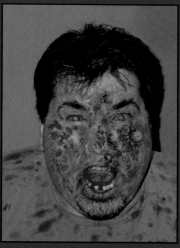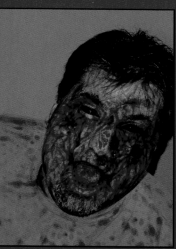

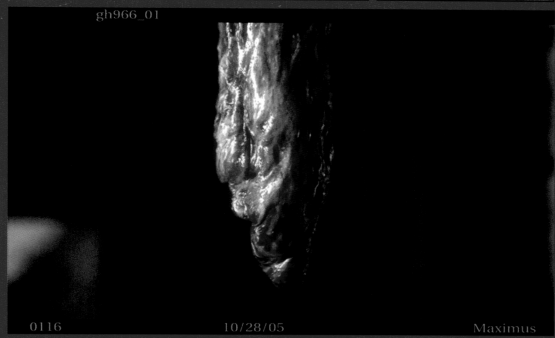

gh966_01

0116   10/28/05   Maximus

OPPOSITE (FROM LEFT): CG melting skin test (stage 1) by Chris Olivia • CG bubbling pustule test by Alex Toader • CG melting skin test (stage 3) by Chris Olivia; **ABOVE (CLOCKWISE FROM UPPER LEFT):** Early concept design of the three stages of infection by (and starring) Alex Toader • Chris Olivia's infamous "Melting Dick" shot.

CHRIS OLIVIA: Early in pre-production, we took existing footage from *Sin City* and did some tracking tests and CG make-up effects, added some boils and stuff and 100% CG effects to see how far we could push the realness of CG flesh. Basically, how could we transform and distort into this diseased state and back and forth. So we looked at a lot of different things from fluid dynamics to cloth dynamics to really simple animated textures. Seeing what the current renderer that we have could do. We were able to

end up being a practical make-up effect. So I came up with some dripping flesh tests. One of the tests I did came out a little phallic. It was just kind of a non-descript oozing flesh thing that dripped down the middle of the screen. I think that's where Robert came up with the idea of Quentin's melting dick.

MARC BAIRD, Storyboard Artist: I cut my teeth on horror films. I started in this business working on movies that literally required buckets of blood, or methylcellulose.

You'd hear people on set say, "We need more blood! More bones!" And horrible things like that. With *Planet Terror*, it's like going back to those types of films.

Robert's really allowed me to go farther than I've gone before on this film, by allowing me to draw actual 2D animatics with 3D elements, sound effects and dialogue. Traditionally, storyboards are drawn on paper, and pinned up on poster board while a scene is shot. As they shoot the scene, they'll check them off. Everyone will take a look at the storyboards to see what the shot will be and once that's accomplished they'll just take a marker and check off the completed shot. I draw my boards on a Wacom tablet, which is a digitized pen and tablet. I draw directly on a flat screen so I no longer use paper, inks, pens or pencils. There's no scanning involved because once I've drawn on the tablet, the image is already digitized. So I preview the storyboards in Thumbs Plus, then I take that into a program called Adobe After Effects. I'm now drawing in layers because I'm thinking ahead of the animation. I take the various layers and pieces of artwork, animate them in After Effects and, once I'm happy with the animation, I take those into Adobe Premiere Pro where I can edit. That's where I add the cuts, the sound effects and the dialogue. Then I output it as a QuickTime and send it to Robert. On the day the scene is shot, they will play the animatic on a video monitor [or as we call it, Video Village] alongside the actual HD image.

Robert is fast, and I have to be fast because everything is happening at that moment. That's the beauty of Troublemaker—that we're all digitized. There are times where I've drawn a storyboard on my tablet, emailed my storyboards to Robert, and the next thing I know they're referring to the storyboards on the set. I think the shortest time I've had for a storyboard to actually became a shot was thirty seconds. I drew the storyboard, emailed it to Robert, and when I went down to the set,

immediately after emailing it, Robert was in a meeting with the stunt guys, his camera operator and his first AD, and they were all standing around the monitor looking at the storyboard. So I think that's a record—thirty seconds.

When I read a script, it's like I'm sitting in the theater eating popcorn and I'm watching the movie. When I'm drawing it, I'm like "I can't wait to see what happens next." And so I'm actually drawing *Planet Terror* from that viewpoint. In the script it said there was a band of people and a fortress by the sea and I was thinking, 'My back is to the sea and if I were these people, I'd want a fortification from something coming from the land.' It was mentioned that the helicopter had been cannibalized and was now part of the fortress. So I imagined what I would do to fortify a structure and made sure to include all those elements. What would they be able to salvage? What sort of things would they be able to carry? What sort of things would keep them safe at night? What keeps a zombie out of your bedroom at night? I tried my best to include that in the sketch. I try to make it as realistic for this world that they occupy, for this world that they are in, within this movie.

It's my job to interpret what is written, what the director gives me. Everything comes from the script. But when I'm feeling very comfortable with the scene, I will add other things; they can always be removed easily. You know I can't completely change the scene, I can't say "Hey let's do it like this!" That's not my job. That's not what I'm here for. But I can embellish. There's always something that sparks another idea that comes from the original material, and I feel confident enough to add that. If Robert doesn't like it, he can just take it out. If he does like it, it stays in. It goes on. And I always try to give a little bit more. I try to give more to make the scene entertaining. What is it that I, as a theatergoer, want to see? What would make me jump or laugh? When I'm right there, it's kind of like I'm not drawing them. Because it's happening on a separate plane in my mind. Even though I'm drawing it, I will see it later, and I'll be like "Did I do that?" I know what's going to happen, but I'm thinking to myself, "What's going to happen next?"

OPPOSITE: Storyboards of the "Sandy Dunes" sequence (Scene 78) by Marc Baird; **ABOVE (FROM LEFT):** Storyboards of Scene 76 by Marc Baird. • Storyboards of Scene 66 by Marc Baird.

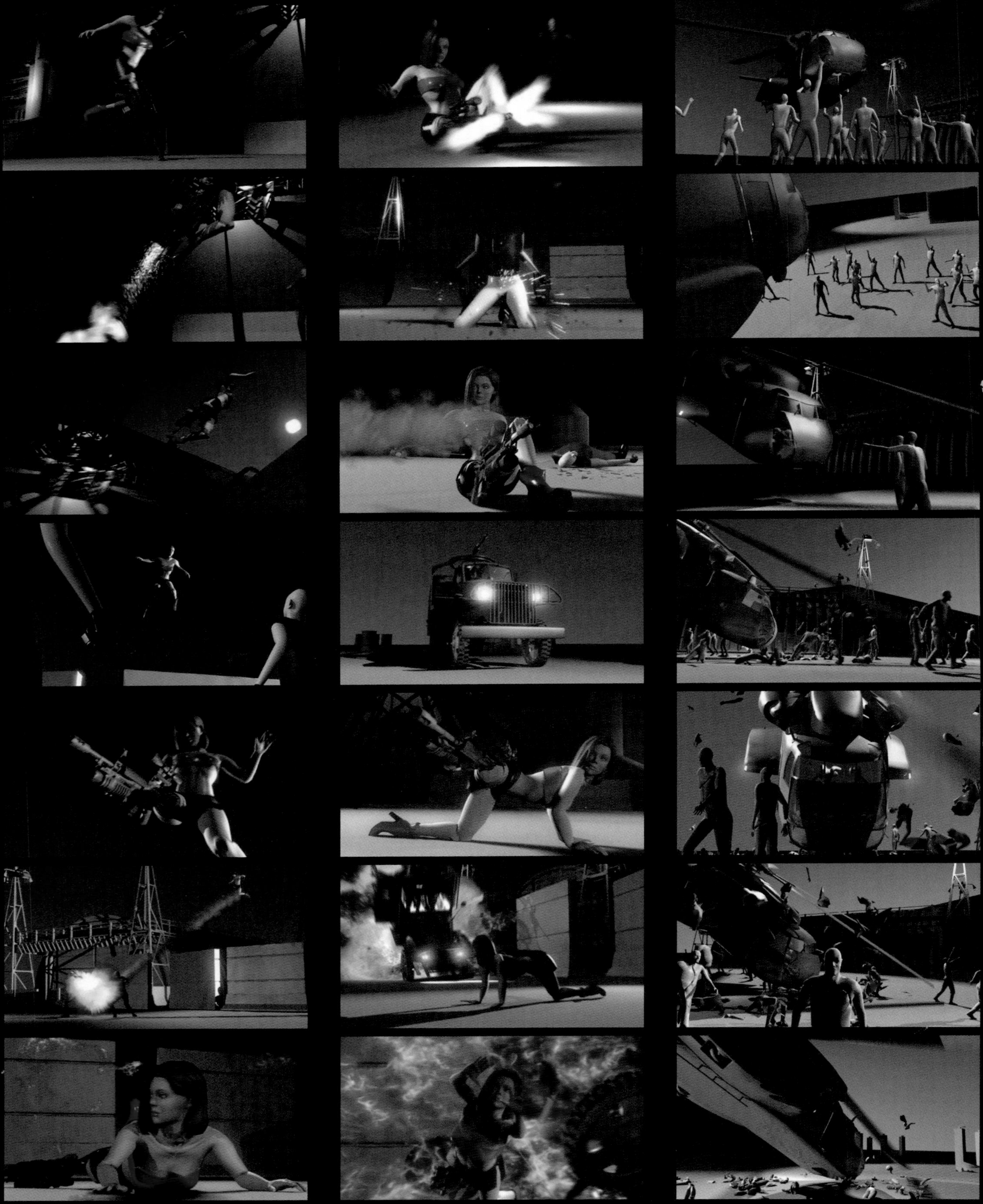

OPPOSITE (FROM LEFT): Animatics from scene 75 and scene 76 by Chris Olivia. • **ABOVE:** Animatic of scene 75 by Chris Olivia. • The Troublemaker Digital team (from left) Chris Olivia, Aaron Burns, Rodney Brunet, Alex Toader, Travis Smith, Amber Kirsch, Andrew Dela Cruz, Emily Davis, Tom Proper, Jud Estes and Carlos Rincones.

THE PRODUCTION DESIGN OF PLANET TERROR
THROWING OFF THE TIMELINE

STEVE JOYNER, Production Designer: One thing about Robert and Quentin is that they both like to create timeless pieces of work. When we worked on *Jackie Brown* back in 1997, one of the small details was that all of the cars in it had 1995 validators on the license plates, per Quentin, to throw the timeline off. Quentin and Robert's movies exist in a parallel world to the world we live in; one that is very similar but slightly off. That's one of the elements that makes them such interesting filmmakers.

CAYLAH EDDLEBLUTE, Production Designer: When I saw *Thelma and Louise*, that was a movie that could have happened at any time. It didn't structure itself to a singular time. Was it in the 50s? Was it in the 60s? Was it in the 90s? It had an ethereal quality to it. When I watch *The Thing*, when I watch *Near Dark*, those movies don't seem like they have a time to me.

That's really the tone that *Grindhouse* had and one that we strive to create. Whatever tools we use need to allow the film to rise above dating itself or limiting itself. Because you want to create a universal story that's timeless. And a great horror movie is timeless.

The production design for *Grindhouse* really began over Thanksgiving weekend 2005. Steve and I spent three days solid just taking photographs of the area around Troublemaker Studios. Our production facility is in the middle of this perfect playground. We're based in an old airport, so all these wonderful found objects exist. Great buildings that have this abandoned feeling. You can feel the wind whistle through old airplane hangars. There are these great objects, reference for our guard towers, all these strong vertical elements. So we went into the back roads around the old airport and saw that

THIS PAGE: CG renderings of the old Army Base by Troublemaker Digital artist Alex Toader; **OPPOSITE (CLOCKWISE FROM UPPER LEFT):** Chipped paint detail. • Lead Prop Fabricator Jeff Poss at work on a detailed miniature of the Army Base. • Troublemaker Studios/ Army Base from above. • Photograph of Troublemaker Studios as "Outpost 31" from John Carpenter's *The Thing*. • Overgrown road. • An old building at the airport.

they really provided a perfect setting for the feel of an abandoned military base. All the paint on the roads had been chipped away, the vines had grown over the fences, rows of lampposts along parking lots, cargo containers everywhere. There was one picture that we took, in particular, that really made an impact.

STEVE JOYNER: It was a cloudy, stormy day. The sky was very gray and when we stood in the corner of our facility and took this picture, we realized that we basically had Outpost 31 from John Carpenter's *The Thing. The Thing* is definitely a movie that we refer to frequently, and Robert does too. It's a movie that is just brilliantly lit and designed by Production Designer John Lloyd.

CAYLAH EDDLEBLUTE: So we showed the stills to Robert and he said "That's really cool. I've got [Alex] Toader working on some renderings." So I think it was a week later that we received these great illustrations and

renderings. Toader's stuff is really a lot of fun. He's a child of Romania and the Cold War, so we really enjoyed his take on everything.

ALEX TOADER, Troublemaker Digital Artist: Robert asked me to do some sketches and a layout of the existing buildings in our facility, to see what kind of action could take place. Basically, block it out to see if we could turn around big army trucks or land a helicopter in the space available. And also to just make it look bigger and to see if we could block out the city in the background. I did a quick illustration in Photoshop using photos I took of the building [which was bright white] and turned it into an old army base with insignia and broken stuff all around. After seeing it, Robert suggested that I deck it out with more massive stuff. Using the notes I got from Robert, I built a set in 3D fairly quick and started to add girders, cranes, guard towers, pylons and all the stuff you usually see around a base.

Within a couple of days, I had fully rendered images from different camera angles of what the base could look like in darkness, lit only by army base lamps. Since this was a night shoot, it was very important to design with that color in mind. Robert didn't want everything to get lost by having the color of the set be too dark. After Robert approved the look, I passed it on to our Production Designer Steve Joyner. The additional designs and details added by Steve and his crew made the outside set outstanding.

CAYLAH EDDLEBLUTE: Both Steve and I are definitely children of the Cold War. We love the idea of having a formidable foe, of an enemy that's tactile and real and not some nebulous element. We pulled a lot of reference—definitely bunkers, blockish, solid structures, solid foundation, elements that have strong footing, nothing feeling spindly, and we knew that we really had to work out some things because the warehouses that we had to work with naturally do have kind of a thin feel.

STEVE JOYNER: We definitely needed to take the warehouses that existed and anchor them solidly. That's a lot of the design that we put into the exterior of the building.

One thing about working with [Producer] Elizabeth Avellán, is that she's very conscientious of the crew and works hard to find, recruit and retain the very best people at every level of the show. One of those people is certainly our great set designer, Jeff Adams, as well as our outstanding construction coordinator, Joe McCusker.

CAYLAH EDDLEBLUTE: Who I really consider a fellow art director.

STEVE JOYNER: Joe contributed to every level here and had some great structural ideas that we incorporated—the fence posts between the chain link fence to increase the mass of the columns were Joe's idea. We had to ring the base and fence in concertina wire. At a large scale, that stuff doesn't photograph well. So to create the drama of actually being trapped behind the wire, Joe's idea was to create these massive concrete pillars between the sections of fence, and they worked as advertised. They really beefed it up.

CAYLAH EDDLEBLUTE: Obviously, you can imagine how much surface area had to be painted in just a few weeks. [Lead Scenic] Tommy Karl and his crew worked overtime to paint everything, from the aging of miles of square footage to the weathered graphics on the runways.

It comes down to the thousands of mind-numbing decisions that you have to make about every element. What color is each door? What is the font of the stencil text? How much aging do you have? How do you separate your warms and cools? How do you have pieces stand out? How do you have them not disappear during a night shoot?

OPPOSITE (FROM TOP): Juliet Guimont at work on a "crow's nest." • Fence posts and chain-link fence. • The bunker exterior (also known as "Level One"); **THIS PAGE (FROM TOP):** A shack made in the style of MacReady's from John Carpenter's *The Thing*. • Abby (played by Naveen Andrews) in front of the hangar doors. The "31" painted on the doors is a reference to Outpost 31 from John Carpenter's *The Thing*.

LEVEL 1

CAYLAH EDDLEBLUTE: One of the first things we did in designing the different levels inside the bunker was to do a really rough floor plan of each level and show it to Robert. We realized we had three levels and that we had to work out the transitions between those levels, figure out how we could segue from one to the next.

Level One is the above ground bunker. Originally, that bunker was going to be a throwaway piece; we weren't going to use it much. But Robert liked Steve's design so much that he placed a lot of the action there. Inside is the Quarantine Cell where all the survivors are based. Seeing as how Level One was above ground, I wanted it to have greens, like grasses—very natural. As if there was still vegetation, still some life and breath in it. We wanted it to be the room where all the life support was for the rest of the levels; that's where the ventilation system is, where the arteries are. We painted all the piping red and blue to represent the lifeblood.

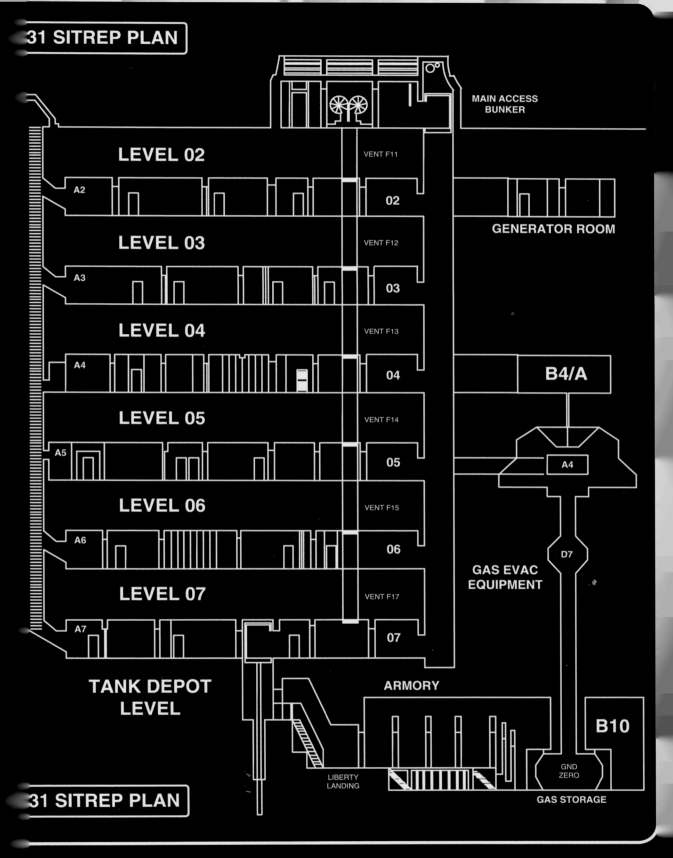

MAIN ACCESS
BUNKER

LEVEL 02

VENT F11

A2

02

GENERATOR ROOM

LEVEL 03

VENT F12

A3

03

LEVEL 04

VENT F13

A4

04

B4/A

LEVEL 05

VENT F14

A5

05

A4

LEVEL 06

VENT F15

A6

06

D7

GAS EVAC
EQUIPMENT

LEVEL 07

VENT F17

A7

07

**TANK DEPOT
LEVEL**

ARMORY

B10

LIBERTY
LANDING

GND
ZERO

GAS STORAGE

P): Abby and Wray prepare to descend in the Level One elevator. • Miniature model of the Level One interior highlighting the ventilation system. • The full-scale Level One

LEVEL 4

CAYLAH EDDLEBLUTE: Level Four was just underground, so we wanted it to be brown, the color of earth. Browns, bits of yellows starting to go into reds. We referenced a lot of fortresses and bunkers from World War II. There's always a feeling in these bunkers like you're being watched. They're oppressive. There are lots of slits everywhere for guns to go through and it always feels like eyes are watching you. These elements also allow for letting light through—cool back light. And Robert is all about cool back light. Signage is also something that's key here. Signage can really bring something to life. When it's lacking, something feels flat. You want your environment to feel real, and the set dressers did a phenomenal job here. There are a huge number of angles in Level Four—it was really tough to get all the piping in—but those guys just got in there and made all the bends, giving the hallways a strong horizontal path to follow.

STEVE JOYNER: Every department worked really hard to bring the different levels to life, but Level Four really shows the work of every individual department that came together as a team: paint, construction, set decorating, special effects. Bart Brown, Dave Hack and Chris Clayton did a brilliant job down there, getting so much material. It looks very real, very simple. But it wasn't. Those guys worked really hard to get that looking right and we really want to thank them.

CAYLAH EDDLEBLUTE: John McLeod and his team also did a phenomenal job building out the soft, lead doors for the stuntmen to crash through.

STEVE JOYNER: John McLeod is one of the top ten guys in the world that does mechanical effects, and he's probably near the top of that list.

CAYLAH EDDLEBLUTE: These are people you truly know you've been in the war with for years. Our ability to communicate with one another, the language we have together is just phenomenal. I feel really lucky to have those people here and we have definitely learned a lot from them. They're a bunch that just does exceptional work.

BELOW (FROM TOP): A photograph by Joe McCusker of a stairwell in the old Austin State School provided the inspiration for the corrugated hallways of Level Four (turn your head sideways to the left). • The Level Four hallway begins to take shape. • Abby and Wray run through the completed Level Four; **OPPOSITE (FROM TOP):** Abby and Wray enter the Armory in Level Eight. • The Level Eight set under construction.

LEVEL 8

CAYLAH EDDLEBLUTE: Next we have Level Eight, the Armory, where we descend into hell. We had just recently seen George Romero's *Land of the Dead*—a movie with great production value for not a lot of money. There's a really cool scene in it where John Leguizamo walks down a trench. I really keyed on that. It seemed really scary as shit to me. We talked to Robert, and we said, "Trench?" And he said, "Cool."

Troy Engel, who does a huge amount of graphics and 3D work for us, rendered out some images and some really key elements came to mind. If you were going through this trench, where would zombies come out from? Are they in the walls? Are they underneath you, coming from nowhere? Are they above you? What are they hiding behind? One of the key things that we worked out was the idea of having a really theatrical set with no walls. I had an image in my head of light passing through weapons and those shadows being on characters as they pass through this passageway and onto the Doom Devices. Ultimately, everything comes down to light. That's why you have elements like this through which light can shine. [Gaffer] John Sandau was superb. He really helped us to be excited about it, and I think we got to learn some cool stuff from him. It all comes down to light and shadow, really. Something

that's scary as hell. We wanted this to be scary. So we created a set that had no walls, and a lot of design went into building the racks so that all you see is the shadows of the weapons.

Early on, we were talking to [Storyboard Artist] Marc Baird and I remember he said the word "catacombs." Obviously, we were thinking a lot about vapor, breathing, the gas in the gas packs. So we made racks of these masks that Jeff Poss sculpted for us. And it really had that feeling of suffocation, like remnants of humanity were buried deep within the levels of this Armory facility.

STEVE JOYNER: One thing about designing and working with both Robert and Quentin is that the design is initially there from them. They are very descriptive writers. You are able to paint a picture of what the environment should look like. So I think Robert and Quentin really deserve as much of the credit for designing the look of the film as the entire team. We could not have done anything without their words.

CAYLAH EDDLEBLUTE: Definitely, those guys create the picture and you feel yourself walking down the road to the end.

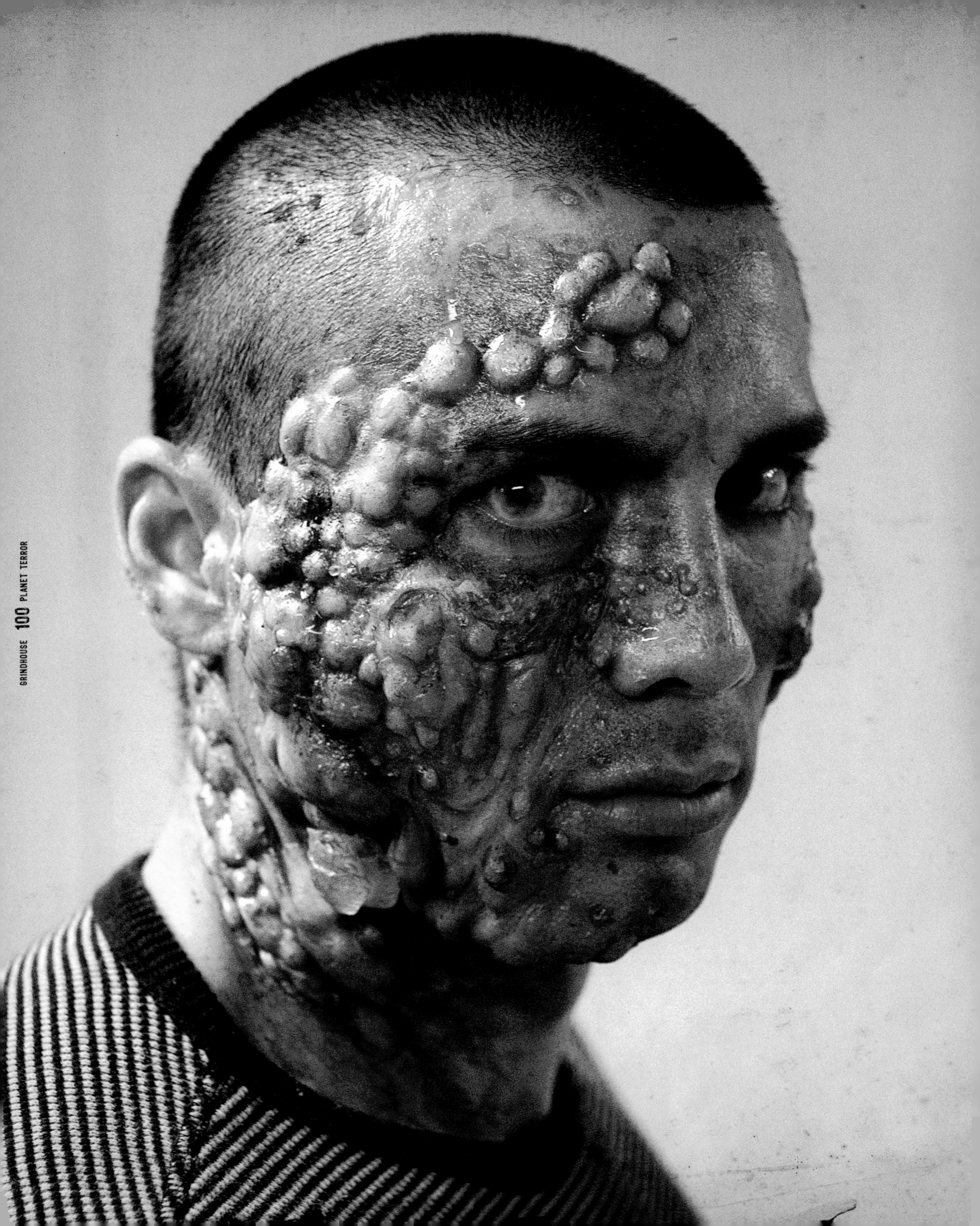

SPREADING THE INFECTION

THE CREATURES OF PLANET TERROR

OPPOSITE: Stuntman Troy Robinson in make-up by Andy Schoenberg; **ABOVE:** Tammy (played by Stacy Ferguson) runs from the approaching creatures.

Special Effects make-up guru Greg Nicotero started KNB EFX Group in 1988 with frequent collaborators Howard Berger and Robert Kurtzman. Since that time, KNB has earned a reputation as one of the leading special make-up effects companies in the industry, culminating in an Academy Award for their work on The Chronicles of Narnia: The Lion, The Witch and the Wardrobe in 2006. Nicotero first collaborated with Rodriguez on Four Rooms (1995) and has worked on every subsequent release, including From Dusk Till Dawn (1996), Spy Kids (2001) and Frank Miller's Sin City (2005).

GREG NICOTERO, KNB Effects: It's interesting, Robert and I share many things—a love of *Jaws*, John Carpenter movies and zombies. So we've always sort of talked about the ultimate 70s horror movie. I remember during the first *Spy Kids*, even back as early as *The Faculty*, Robert said, "Man, I've got this cool idea for a zombie movie. I don't know exactly what's going to happen yet, but there's going to be a doctor and his wife and they're going to be working in a hospital, and then there's going to be this really great scene where we see a girl on the road, and every time a car passes, we reveal silhouettes of zombies getting close and closer to her, and she doesn't see them but the car headlights reveal them to the audience." And he gave me the first twenty pages. This was years ago. And I remember reading it and wondering where he would go from there. So, lo and behold *Grindhouse*

begins, and I get this script and I start reading it. I realize there's a doctor and his wife, and then I get to the scene with Tammy on the road, and I'm thinking that I've read this before. These were ideas that he had a long time ago that he incorporated into the script.

After *Sin City*, I went off and worked on *Land of the Dead*, so I was really excited to come back and show Robert all the zombies that we did and all the gags that we've done in the movie. In *Planet Terror* there's a big misconception that they're all zombies. They don't die and then come back and they don't necessarily all eat flesh. We have a couple guys that eat brains, and people get torn apart and get disemboweled, but generally they don't really die, they just become infected and become mindless killers. The first task was to start designing what these creatures looked like, and Robert had given me a couple tidbits of information—maybe they'll have some translucent skin, we'll see veins and muscle underneath and maybe they'll be infected. So he was sort of throwing these ideas around, and we did a bunch of test stuff, but we stayed away from the traditional zombie look. They don't all have shriveled skin and a grayish pallor with the sunken cheeks and the rotted teeth. We wanted to come up with something fresh and new. Our research took us to skin disease reference as our basis. The idea is that these people get infected with nerve gas. It starts with minor lacerations—little

lumps, and discoloration—and then it just grows from there. It's much more like leprosy where this stuff just spreads. As it takes over the body, you develop these growing, liquid-filled bags of pus. Then you get into stage two which has much larger pustules, bigger wounds, and it starts spreading more. Then in stage three, the heads are misshapen, bodies are built out and there's all sorts of twisted flesh that's melded and grown together. We definitely had an interesting free rein to explore the departure from a standard zombie look.

Q: *Robert told you about this seven years ago or longer. Do you know a lot of directors who come back to ideas like this, many years later?*

GREG NICOTERO: Well, ironically, I happen to be sort of privy to these interesting ideas that some directors have when they have them. We were shooting *Pulp Fiction* and had just done the scene where Uma gets stabbed in the chest with the adrenaline needle. The whole crew went out for drinks at a place in Silverlake. Quentin, Uma, John Travolta and myself were sitting at a table, and they started to talk about *Kill Bill*. "Oh I've got this idea for this bride picture." Quentin even remembered recently. He said "Oh my God, you were there the day the idea for that movie came about." And I feel the same way with *Grindhouse*.

I also remember the *Resident Evil 2* videogame came out while we were shooting *The Faculty*. It had this real elaborate opening with all the zombies attacking the city. I said to Robert, "You've got to see the opening. This is so cool." And then one day I walked past his trailer and Clea Duvall is there and he's going, "Clea, you've got to see the opening of this. It's so cool" and he's showing her all the zombies. He was always talking about wanting to do this sort of apocalyptic/infected people/end of the world kind of movie. He's been talking about it since then, so the

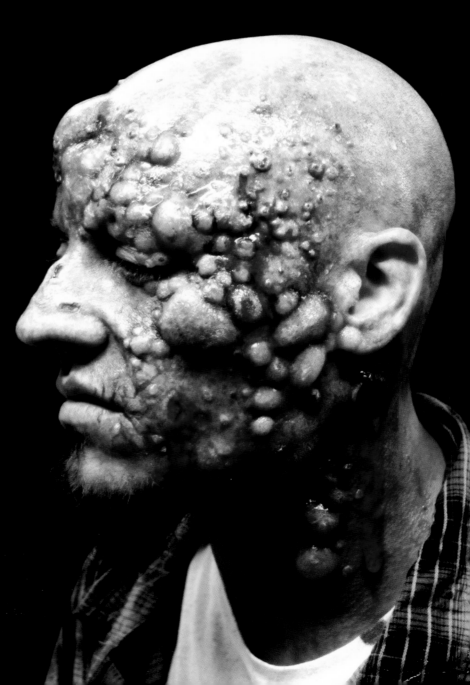

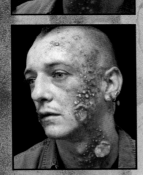

OPPOSITE (FROM TOP): The KNB crew discusses design ideas at their facility in Van Nuys. • Close up make-up test by Scott Patton on KNB's Caleb Schneider; **ABOVE (FROM TOP):** Kevin Wasner sculpts one of the full size advanced stage mutation make-ups. • Dirk Rogers in three stages of "infection." This make-up was created with gelatin and 3D transfers.

irony of this film is he'll set up a shot, or he'll set up a certain angle, and I'll look at it, and it will remind me of a shot from *The Fog*. I think he's subconsciously recreating the look of a John Carpenter movie. John's movies have such a distinctive look and feel—everything's back lit, all the characters are silhouetted. You never really see what they look like. You'll just see a couple wounds, and they'll be shiny and pulsating, but you're never right on it. It's like in a fog bank or something—all real moody and creepy. There were a couple times that I said, "Oh yeah, this is like that shot in *Halloween*. And he'd be like, "You're right." It's interesting because we always talked about sort of paying homage to those kinds of movies.

Q: So is Planet Terror pretty bloody?

GREG NICOTERO: *Planet Terror* is really gory and really graphic. We shot a scene the other night where we had to basically rip the top of Carlos Gallardo's head off and eat his brains. Gino Crognale, one of my key KNB artists, played the creature. The gag was really specific. I told him not to peel the skin back too easily, there has to be a little tension there, you've got to struggle to peel it. Then, once you reveal the skull, you need to crack through it and pick out the brains—made of gelatin filled with strawberry preserves—making sure to squeeze them, so all the goo comes out when you eat them. When they yelled cut, Quentin was the first one going, "That was amazing, that was like the Glenn Strange of

2006—you were so perfect." Gino played the gag perfectly. He had the contact lenses in, he's covered with make-up, and he goes right up to the camera and just chomps on the brains.

For the very first kill of the production, I asked Robert how much blood he wanted to see. He told me that he wanted it be like the Kitner boy from *Jaws*, "I want to see a blood fountain in the air." So [Special Effects Coordinator] John McLeod helped us put all these blood tubes in, and we were spraying blood everywhere. We ended up getting jugs of water that we filled up with fake blood, along with rubber gloves and condoms, so when the zombie grabs someone's stomach and pulls, they're actually just tearing apart blood bags. So as I'm pulling, blood is spraying in the air. The scene where we killed Tammy on the street, it was me and two other stunt guys, and we were literally tearing blood bags apart, and there's blood spraying in the air everywhere. And all you see is a silhouette. You walk away and look at the monitor and think "Oh my god, how cool is that?" People are going to love it.

Q: What's it been like working with Tom Savini?

GREG NICOTERO: It's really been a delight to have Tom Savini here. I feel a little responsible because I keep in touch with Tom and gave Robert a little push to use him as an actor. Tom and George Romero gave me my start in 1984 on *Day of the Dead*. That was my

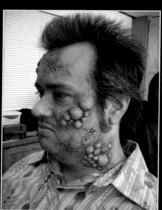

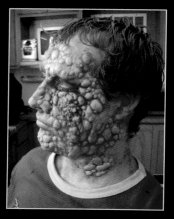

ABOVE (CLOCKWISE FROM TOP): Muldoon in his final stage of infection. • Various zombie face make-up and prosthetic effects; **OPPOSITE (FROM TOP):** Master animator Ray Harryhausen makes a surprise visit to the *Planet Terror* set. (from left) Robert Rodriguez, Tom Savini, Ray Harryhausen, Greg Nicotero and Quentin Tarantino. • A mangled corpse rests on the hospital floor.

first job—a zombie movie, of course. Tom and I keep in touch all the time. I always say to him that he should talk to Robert about this or that, but Tom doesn't really like to promote himself a lot, so I'll sort of throw the bug in the ear. I told Robert that I thought Tom would be great for *Planet Terror* and about a week later he wrote me asking if Tom would be willing to dye his hair white.

I wrote Tom and his response was "I'd do anything. I'd love to work with Robert again." So it was nice because I was able to sort of bring Tom into the forefront of Robert's mind. And I've done the same thing on *Dusk Till Dawn* and on *Land of the Dead*. There have been a bunch of movies where I've just gently said, "Hey you guys should talk to Savini." I think that because so many people associate him with make-up effects and doing his own stunts, people don't really think about Tom Savini as an actor. When we did *Dusk Till Dawn*, everybody stood back and said "Wow." He held his own. Harvey Keitel and George Clooney—and Tom held his own. It makes me proud that he's the guy that opened the door

for me and started my career, and that I can, in a little way, repay the favor.

Q: So has this production been in keeping with the grindhouse/exploitation vibe?

GREG NICOTERO: Well, when we originally started this movie, Robert said it'll be "grindhouse," down and dirty, two takes and we're off. We didn't have a lot of time to prep, and he kept saying stuff like "Listen, anything you have laying around the shop—you got a body bring it and we'll use it." But once we began shooting, this certainly didn't have a grindhouse feel. We wanted everything to look perfect and as we got deeper into the shoot, we realized we were making an all-out horror flick: blood and guts, all thrown in. The grindhouse concept aside, you could cut this movie together and release it and it would be just as equally satisfying as a mainstream horror film. I think originally we were all kind of thinking it'd be one, two takes, and we're out. But it turned out definitely being shot with a lot more love and attention than what they probably did in the 70s, when they had $200,000 and ten days to go shoot it.

Q: How have the actors been handling all the make-up, blood and pus?

GREG NICOTERO: Everybody's been great. It's a really fun cast. We had to do a couple of gags on Rose McGowan, we did a fake head of Fergie, we had to do some stuff on Michael Biehn, and we did some stuff on Freddy. We've actually done a little bit on each actor, and they've all been terrific. I think all of the actors wanted to be monsters at some point. Josh Brolin and I had worked together a few times, so it made his transformation that much more fun. And then, of course, there's Quentin. I've known Quentin so long that it almost works against me [laughs]. Quentin plays the rapist, and after delivering some great Tarantino dialog—and fucking with the wrong person—he literally begins dissolving on camera…starting with his penis. Robert had shown us some skin disorder photos as

reference. He also sent us a CG test that Troublemaker Digital had created of a melting penis. From there we devised a multi-stage disintegration. We created a penis that was made to swell, distend and ooze bloody pus, several prosthetics that incorporated melting flesh as well as a silicone mask that simulated hanging flesh with a muscle stage revealed underneath. Once in the final stage, the rapist then vomits up his insides before being shot by Cherry. For this, Robert had the idea to build a half suit/half puppet that would be operated by a KNB tech in a green suit and removed from the shot, utilizing both state of the art and practical effects techniques to accomplish the sequence.

For the penis melting shot, it needed to swell up and have blood pour out of it. So I'm sitting there prepping the prosthetic with slime and blood, and Quentin's sitting there laughing. We're talking, and I'm laughing. And I look at the corner of my eye and I see Robert flip the camera and start filming, panning up and down as I'm putting slime on Quentin's dripping "prosthetic member," and I knew I was dead meat. I know it's going to be on the DVD somewhere, just a shot of me minding my own business.

THIS PAGE (FROM TOP): Prosthetic version of the Rapist's melting appendage. • Garrett Immel and Greg Nicotero work on the Rapist double. • Garrett Immel and Kevin Wasner sliming the Rapist double. • Gino Crognale and Eric Fielder (in greenscreen suits) perform the Rapist vomit gag as Greg Nicotero applies more slime.

And Quentin's like, "Oh yeah, oh yeah, baby, do it there, I love it!" And I'm laughing because I'm not even thinking about it, and then I see Robert out of the corner of my eye...they got me.

Q: *Can you tell me about the make-up effects crew you worked with?*

GREG NICOTERO: Most of the KNB people actually get cameos in the movie. I play the creature that bites off Carlos Gallardo's arm. If you have a specific gag, sometimes it's easier to have one of your guys in there doing it, so it's executed the way it was built. It's similar to the stunt world; when they have a difficult stunt, [Stunt Coordinator] Jeff Dashnaw brings in a specific guy, and he does this because he's good at that one thing. So for us it's always good to have a make-up effects guy in there to actually execute a certain gag because then you know that he knows exactly how to do it and exactly how to break it and how to play everything to the camera because that's what makes the gag work.

I have to say that this set crew from KNB was absolutely one of the best crews I've ever worked with. Howard Berger and I have brought this company further than I think either of us ever dreamed. It has been an amazing turn of events over the last couple of years. During the prep for *Sin City* we were awarded work on *Chronicles of Narnia*, and Howard—along with a dozen others—went off to New Zealand while KNB built all the effects for that film. Low and behold, six months later we find ourselves with the British Academy

Award for Best Make-up for *Narnia*, a Saturn award and an Oscar! Given our low budget days on *Day of the Dead*, *Evil Dead 2* and *Bride of Re-Animator*, who would have ever imagined this company would receive the highest honor in film bestowed on us for Best Make-up?

For *Planet Terror*, we started with a key design crew in Los Angeles: Scott Patton, Jaremy Aiello and Andy Schoneberg and began working out concepts for the disease progression. Robert had given me a rough idea early in preproduction, so we took what information we had and began working out test stuff for

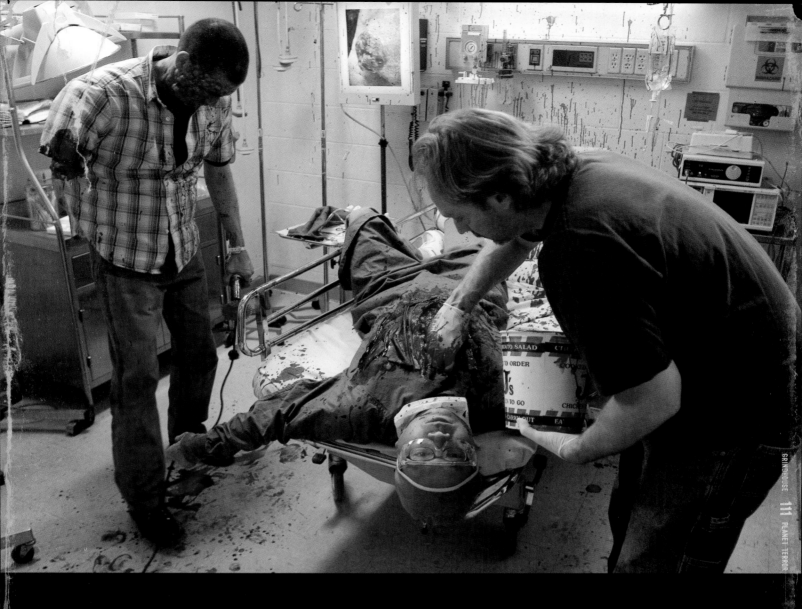

PREVIOUS SPREAD (FROM LEFT):
Robert Rodriguez directs Rose McGowan.
• A very infected Ramona McGraw. •
Eric Fielder threads tentacles into an
insert floor piece (to be shot in reverse)
as the Rapist stunt double holds the
intestine sac; **OPPOSITE (FROM TOP):**
Jaremy Aiello and Kevin Wasner load an
articulated tongue into the dummy head
of an infected creature. • Garrett Immel
and Jake Garber create one of the blood-
filled bodies that will explode upon impact
with the Killdozer; **ABOVE:** Greg Nicotero
dresses blood on the dead surgeon's chest
as Joe (played by Nicky Katt) looks on.
Nicky Katt's make-up by Scott Patton.

approvals. Given that we have done a great number
of zombie films, we wanted to give these creatures
a very different look. We went for more erupting
lesions, blisters and pus-filled sacs that would develop
and grow and, once they burst, would infect anyone
that came in contact with it. The more infected they
were, the more mutated they became.

We went from stage one—two make-ups with gelatin,
foam latex and transfers—to full body foam latex
creature suits, heads and hands, complete with
gallons of pus and blood. Beth Hathaway, Claire
Mulroy, Katherine Sulley and Bruce Mitchell created
all the suits while other lab techs like Kevin Wasner,
Jim Leonard and Rob Frietas built all the other
characters. Once on set, I had Jake Garber, Scott,
Jaremy, Andy, Beth Claire, Kevin, Ron Pipes, Eric
Fiedler, Garrett Immel and Gino Crognale executing
the make-ups and handling gags on a nightly basis.
The shoot was similar to *Land of the Dead* where you

are always dealing with mass numbers of infected
people/zombies, and anytime they show up, people
die. So you spend hours in make-up, then on to set to
prep the effects and execute them.

Everybody here at KNB put a hundred and fifty
percent effort into it. When you do shows like this
you sculpt a bunch of make-ups for specific actors,
and then a lot of stuff you'll create generically, and
someone will sit in your chair, and you literally create
the look as you go—this forehead and this cheek. So I
had an amazing team with me, and they just stepped
up to the challenge and really were enthusiastic
about coming up with cool stuff, "Let's do this when
the guy's face is melting!" and "Let's try putting this
piece on and put some muscle underneath it and add
some dripping skin!" So I'm really proud of the crew
that Howard and I had assembled on this movie, all
the way from the design and build in Los Angeles to
the shoot. Everybody did an amazing job.

SHOOTING FROM THE HIP

REPLACING CHERRY'S LEG...WITH A MACHINE GUN!

CHRIS OLIVIA, Troublemaker Digital Artist: Robert started talking about this character with a gun for a leg, and we were trying to figure out how the hell we were going to achieve this. To find the best way to shoot this on set so it would be easy to get rid of the leg and to digitally track it in post. The actor's leg was supposed to be totally stiff, but you can't completely immobilize the leg without putting the actor in a certain amount of danger. [Troublemaker Digital Artist] Alex Toader came up with a few designs and Robert had me start experimenting with tracking some leg footage that we shot of him. I was trying to come up with a design for a boot that the actor could wear safely, what it would look like and what sort of motion tracking we would use for it.

STEVE JOYNER, Production Designer: The developmental concept from Troublemaker Digital was to provide something green that could be motion-tracked. But what we discovered was that, on a real person, we needed to make her leg completely stiff from the thigh down to the toe and take all the flexibility out of it, putting her center of gravity on her heel as if it was a straight peg. It all came down to acting, getting Rose to feel like she had her leg replaced by a peg. We probably went through five or six generations of experimental legs before we finally got it right.

ALEX TOADER, Troublemaker Digital Artist: We did some early tests actually filming Robert using a green leg sock. After considering the initial leg test a success, we quickly realized that we didn't take into consideration night shoots [the whole *Planet Terror* part takes place at night], particles or debris, heavy motion blur, sequences filmed at different speeds, different lighting and atmosphere situations at the set. [Troublemaker Digital Artist] Rodney Brunet suggested that we do some tests with LED [Light-Emitting Diode] markers that light her leg. We also had to figure out how we could keep her leg straight and mount all the LEDs on the leg prop for tracking purposes.

Rodney and I decided to go two routes: he would build a prop using LEDs powered by a nine-volt battery and I would build one using end-lit fiber illuminated by a 20 LED super bright light illuminator pack, running on a nine-volt battery. [Information Systems Assistant] Jeff Acord came to our aid with his

BELOW: A final, composited shot of Cherry's gun in action; **OPPOSITE (FROM TOP):** Robert Rodriguez acts as guinea pig in an early visual effects test. • The prop version of Cherry's gun leg.

expertise in electronics. Jeff helped us with the wiring harness and showed us the correct way to solder flat-mount LEDs. He custom-designed the LED mounting boards and figured out the necessary battery packs and other components we needed to use. Neither Rod nor I are electronics buffs, so we were really lucky to have Jeff walk us through this R&D project. We did two night tests: one with the LED leg prop and one with the fiber optics prop. They both worked and both props tracked really well, but in the end we decided to go with the LEDs over cost and battery power consumption.

During the shoot, Robert delivered some sequences to us to start implementing the gag, removing the green leg prop and adding the wooden or gun leg. To our disappointment, we realized that the tests we did were only a partial success. While the leg tracked well, there was too much green spill on the other leg. So we had to paint the prop leg gray and dim the LEDs, which made it nearly impossible to key or track. The task of removing a limb, and then adding a thinner prop on *top* of the missing background is already quite difficult, so the one bit of automation that we thought we could rely on—tracking and keying out the green leg—went away.

RODNEY BRUNET, Troublemaker Digital Artist: We then moved on to testing in dim lighting since *Planet Terror* was going to be a night shoot. Testing was conducted outdoors as well as indoors with dim lighting by employing every technique imaginable. To find solutions for tracking data, we tried glow in the dark paint to LED, fiber-optic battery powered tracking lights to multiple colored stockings and rigid casts. In the end—mostly due to discomfort and safety for the actress and her stunt double—the immobilization of her leg became less and less important.

CAYLAH EDDLEBLUTE, Production Designer: As the process evolved, we began focusing on the sleek factor, minimizing awkwardness in the actual device. You want to present something that you would be willing to put on yourself, possibly for an extended period of time—you don't know if the shoot's going to be five minutes or three hours. We're fortunate to be working with [Lead Prop Fabricator] Jeff Poss who's a phenomenal sculptor, really high end. His attention to detail is really superb. Jeff, along with [Production Designer] Steve Joyner and [Visual Effects Coordinator] Keefe Boerner, took the leg through a number of evolutions, ultimately coming up with something very light and very clean.

JEFF POSS, Lead Prop Fabricator: At the very end, the final version was a combination of everything we experimented with. We realized the most important

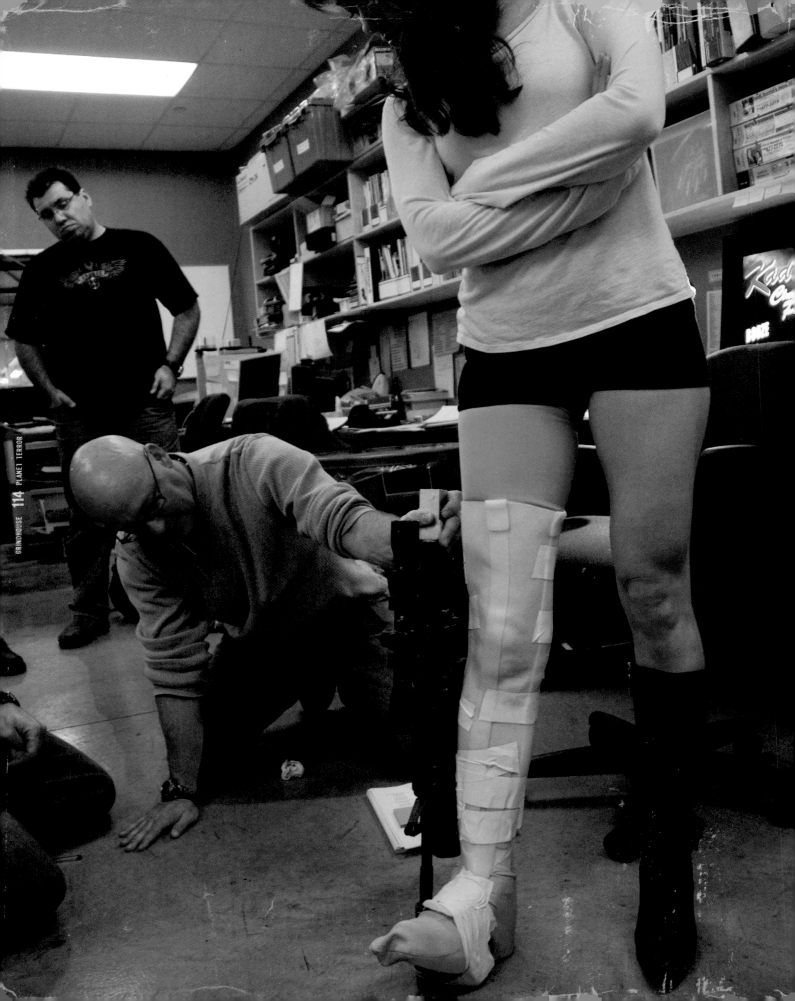

JOHN McLEOD, Special Effects Coordinator: My role on *Planet Terror* was to organize and coordinate the Special Effects. After meeting with Robert Rodriguez and our art department leads, Steve Joyner and Caylah Eddleblute, we met with Producer Elizabeth Avellán and Unit Production Manager Bill Scott to discuss our needs for the startup.

We began the film by shooting a trailer called *Machete* in the fall of 2005. At this time we didn't have the script for *Planet Terror*, but based on Robert's comments, it was going to be a busy project for us. We assembled a base crew of some of the best people I know in the business, sixteen technicians in all. But as filming progressed, our crew size began to swell. Each person had specific talents and experience that covered the wide range of pyrotechnic and mechanical effects required for the shoot. I relied on my shop foreman Richard Woods to lead the fabrication crew and Frank Tarantino dealt with running the set operations.

JEFF DASHNAW, Stunt Coordinator: As the Stunt Coordinator, it's my job to break down the action sequences, find out what the director's ideas are and help to create the best and safest way to give him what he wants. This involves direct collaboration with the special effects department. On *Planet Terror*, the action sequences involved a tremendous amount of pyrotechnics, bullet hits, explosions and mechanical rigs. These sequences involved precise timing between stunts and effects. Having the privilege to work with John McLeod and his veteran effects crew added a confidence level that gave us the freedom to put stunt people in situations that in the past might be deemed unsafe. After multiple rehearsals with John's special effects and pyrotechnics, we were able to put our stunt men and women right in the middle of the explosions. This gave Robert a chance to quench his creative appetite.

I have a group of eight men and women on this show that I've probably killed fifteen or twenty times each. The other night we had somewhere around ninety explosions, with my guys on fire, hitting air rams, flying over cars with debris flying everywhere. I have to say

BELOW: Rose McGowan does her own high-wire stunt to help sell the illusion; **OPPOSITE (FROM TOP):** Tim Trella, in full zombie-garb, is engulfed in flames. • Rose McGowan makes a safe landing after her high-wire stunt. • Stunt coordinator Jeff Dashnaw consults stuntman Josh Kemble.

NEW HIGHS IN HORROR

THE STUNTS AND SPECIAL EFFECTS OF PLANET TERROR

it was one of the most impressive nights that I have been involved with. John's guys in bunkers queuing off the stunt guys, and there weren't any mishaps; it went great. His guys were on the money. The stunt guys hit their marks, John's guys fired their explosions, and everything went of as planned. That's the beauty of working with John—no drama, just a calm sense of confidence.

JOHN McLEOD: Stunts and effects always enjoy working on heavy action films where we're pushing the envelope just a little. We worked very closely with Jeff Dashnaw and his stunt team on *Planet Terror*. Jeff and I have worked together on other films, so there was already a trust between us. This made the changes and last minute decisions easy. We collaborated on a lot of the action scenes that involved mechanical rigs and pyrotechnics. Robert enjoys a good explosion and a bloody hit, so he asked for almost comical amounts of blood from the bullet hits. Because of the large amount of blood, some of the bullet hits packed quite a punch for the stunt players.

JEFF DASHNAW: I have a guy down here named Tim Trella. Tim is widely recognized as the top "burn guy" in the business. Tim is so calm under fire that he literally makes you think it's no big deal to light himself or someone else on fire. In this case it was my 24 year old son JJ and Tim who would be performing the fire stunts. Tim is a veteran of over 100 burns on

film, and JJ is quickly earning a reputation as one of the young all-around talents in the stunt world. The difference this time would be that his mother and I were on hand to witness this burn. We have both seen and performed fire stunts during our careers, but it's a little different when you're watching your kid. Tim and JJ did awesome. They were engulfed by the biggest explosion I have ever seen ignite anyone, and they did exactly what Robert asked them to do after they were lit. This may sound easy, but when you are completely covered in fire and can still have the wherewithal to keep acting, it says a lot about these two. The thing with fire is that there is no little accident. It starts with blisters and just gets worse. But

Tim gives you the wildest burns with all the safety that enables us to push the envelope and make the fire sequences spectacular.

JOHN McLEOD: When it comes to large-scale explosions, working with actors and actresses can be a little nerve-racking. Everyone has a different freak-out tolerance, so we like to start out slow until we get people accustomed to the pyrotechnics. It gets pretty hot sometimes, so it's important for us to remember that our actors and our stunt players have limits. We always need to be aware of the line between being a little uncomfortable and actually being hurt. With some actors, you can't tell how they'll react until you

THIS PAGE (FROM TOP): Special Effects Coordinator John McLeod checks out the mini-bike camera rig with Gaffer John Sandau and Key Grip Ferrell Shinnick. • John Sandau atop the mini-bike tow rig. • John McLeod preparing pyrotechnics; **OPPOSITE (FROM TOP):** John Sandau takes the "rotisserie" rig for a spin. • Stuntman Jamie Ryan and Dana Reed consult with Production Designer Steve Joyner while inside the rotisserie rig.

expose them to it slowly. All the visual input and the heat can really blow your mind if you haven't been exposed to it before. The actors on *Planet Terror* never flinched. We had Rose McGowan and a lot of the talent very close to large-scale fire effects.

JEFF DASHNAW: We flew Rose 100 feet through the air, 30 feet high, and landed her on an eight inch pad on her stomach. I could not even think about trying this without the expertise of my stunt rigger James Ryan. James is tops in his field and brings safety and precision to set every time he shows up. Before we flew Rose, we rehearsed with her stunt double Dana Reed. Dana is one of those special individuals that comes along very rarely. She's great at everything and has a great attitude for this business. She will hit the ground as hard as anybody out there and has no quit in her. I have been blessed in my career to work with some great people, and Dana is definitely on that list. After we were dialed in on the flying stunt where Rose flies over the walls, we were ready to shoot it with Rose herself. She did great. She was able to watch Dana and duplicate what Dana did. The whole stunt crew was impressed by Rose's fortitude performing this and all her action scenes. We also propelled Quentin's character through some metal doors upside down with a ratchet. This was done by Malosi Leonard, son of legendary Stuntman Terry Leonard. Malosi made us all proud. His dad will be smiling when he sees this one.

JOHN McLEOD: The best part for our team was that both Robert and Quentin had decided to do these films the old school way, 1970s-style. A lot of my crew, including myself, had started their careers in that period. These were the days when everything was done in front of the cast and crew on the set— with the exception of miniatures—before the safety net of computer generated visual effects, or CGI, was available. The big difference between special effects and visual effects is that the visual effects can be done after principal photography. They still have a deadline to meet, but they're not dealing with the live action set operations involved with a cast and crew. Production time can be very costly and no one wants to make a cast and crew wait. Visual effects give creative people options that are beyond what live action can offer. The use of miniatures and CGI gives them that option.

For *Planet Terror*, we—along with the hard working transportation team lead by Cecil Evans—fabricated two additional trucks to match the original "Killdozer." We needed to build a lightweight truck that would run fast and stop fast. The original truck had heavy-duty rigging and hardware that was not user-friendly. A third Killdozer was built with a full roll cage and a cannon system for a rollover scene, but that rollover was eventually turned over to visual effects to complete in CG due to schedule issues.

OPPOSITE (FROM TOP): Stunt men Jamie Ryan and Ryan Fitzgerald rehearse a stunt while Director Robert Rodriguez, First Assistant Director Brian Bettwy and Stunt Coordinator Jeff Dashnaw observe. • Stunt woman Tracy Dashnaw stands in for Marley Shelton as she crashes through a second story window; **THIS PAGE (FROM TOP):** Stunt man Chris, "Critter" Antonucci stands in for Freddy Rodriguez as he scales a wall without the help of wires.

The "rotisserie" was designed to simulate the truck during the rollover. Our lead actors, stunt doubles and camera equipment went inside a truck cab that was mounted on a platform. We could then rotate that platform via a hydraulic drive system, spinning at about 45 rotations per minute. We could also crank it manually if we wanted to make the rotation go at a slower speed.

JEFF DASHNAW: Robert always knows what he wants to do. He's so mellow to work with. This was nice to get to do some action with him. We've been on the green screen for a couple of shows, and it was kind of nice to get out and play outdoors for a while. I would have to say my favorite stunt on *Planet Terror* was the other night with the explosions. It was just invigorating. The hair on your arms is standing up all night. It's hard to describe. There was so much action going on, and everybody was really in top form. At the end of the night, you just say, "Wow. That was unbelievable." I got lucky. I put a group of guys together that just gelled, and everybody was helping everybody.

My crew on this has been really amazing. I could not have done this job without the hard work of every single one of them. I would especially like to thank my wife Tracy Dashnaw, whom I call upon to do things as a stunt performer that people ask me "How can you let your wife do that?" My answer is always the same, "Because she's the best." From driving to falling to getting blown up, or just for being there for me, she really is the best.

JOHN McLEOD: Working with Robert and Quentin has been a challenge because they're both so creative, and they both seem to have endless energy while working on their films. Compared to the studio system of making and controlling films, the whole process here is a bit unorthodox. At Troublemaker, we have a lot of departments rolled into one. From a special effects standpoint, we try to approach challenges with a "can do" attitude. They give us the idea and how they want to shoot the gag, and we take it from there. Often the design of an effect will sort of design itself—the old "form follows function" credo. From there we'll show them a test look and they give us a thumbs up or a thumbs down. Sometimes it's a winner, sometimes it's back to the drawing board.

STEVE JOYNER, Production Designer: We have Naveen Andrews from *Lost* playing Abby. One of his character traits is that he collects his enemies balls in a jar—all the enemies that he's vanquished. He has the complete set: ball clippers, ball knife and a jar to keep his specimens in.

JEFF POSS, Lead Prop Fabricator: I kept thinking, 'It's a ball jar. You have to be able to carry it around, so it can't be too big.' And Steve kept kicking me in the head saying, "No. Bigger, bigger, bigger." I actually have a picture of him saying, "See, it needs to be *this* big."

STEVE JOYNER: [Shop Supervisor] Marcia Evers in costumes came through for us by making a beautiful military carrying case for the ball jar and all its accessories.

JEFF POSS: Mark McCord and I worked the ball knife back and forth for a little while. We were really happy with the result—it was figurative, a complete sculpture in terms of balance and form. So we were both really pleased with ourselves when Steve walked in and said that we needed a second weapon. It would be something that served the same purpose, but did so in a completely different way—something with a snipping action. Something really horrible.

CAYLAH EDDLEBLUTE, Production Designer: The guys definitely reacted to this one.

JEFF POSS: The shark knife is so figurative, it was important to make the ball snips in the same way. We based it on the double serrated pincers of a scorpion, while at the same time giving it hip bones and legs. It

THE CHOP SHOP

THE PROPS OF PLANET TERROR

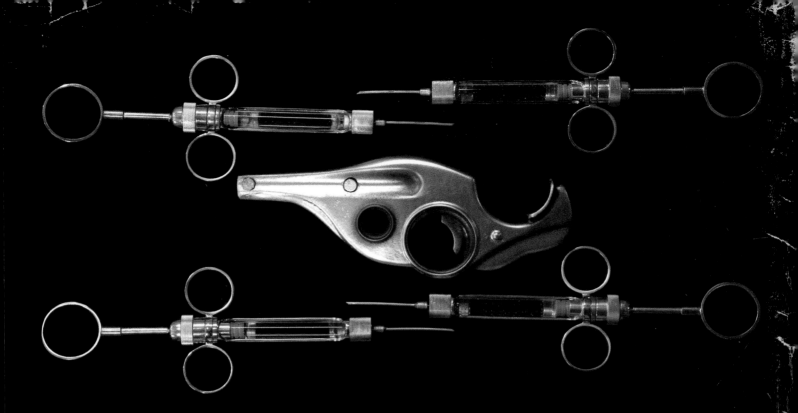

OPPOSITE (FROM LEFT): Abby's "Shark Knife", ball snips and storage jar; **ABOVE:** Dakota's syringes and launcher.

basically creates the area that you're about to snip.

STEVE JOYNER: And you have double cutting action, which is kind of unique. You've got a double cutter because you have two objects that you're trying to sever.

CAYLAH EDDLEBLUTE: There was a lot of statement in the ball clippers.

JEFF POSS: One of my favorite props of all time.

STEVE JOYNER: Because *Planet Terror* was a night shoot, we had to design the ball jar to have very bright LED [Light-Emitting Diode] panels in the top and bottom.

CAYLAH EDDLEBLUTE: The LEDs made it look really cool. If you have a jar full of objects just sitting there in the dark. it just doesn't mean shit. You can't see a thing.

STEVE JOYNER: Because of the night shoot, almost everything we made needed to be light in color or light up from the inside.

STEVE JOYNER: Dakota's syringe is based on a dental aspirating syringe. There are rings on either side that allow the dentist to push and pull the anesthetic in and out of your gums. Even though it looks antique, this tool is still in use today. We were able to locate these from a surgical supply, then we modified them and Kit Casati gold-plated them.

JEFF POSS: They even have a viewing area for the glass vials, so you can see our orange killer juice.

CAYLAH EDDLEBLUTE: For the syringe gun, we were thinking about old surgical tools. The curved quality of them. Stainless. The lines are very specific. When we first started, all the guys were doing renderings of a syringe gun that was very gun-like, and I kept drawing this curved thing. I think Robert actually said "less gun like," which was a benefit to me. The syringe gun went through several revisions. You know we had to really look at the thickness of it. Troy Engel did a great job rendering out the design.

JEFF POSS: In the end, we ended up shortening it quite a bit, so that there wasn't a handle at all. It took a lot of kicking from Caylah to convince us to lose the handle altogether. We finally did, and it worked beautifully.

CAYLAH EDDLEBLUTE: I'm a good kicker.

JEFF POSS: There's a scene where Dakota spins her syringe gun like a revolver, old west style. We kept working on the balance of it to make it easier to spin and Kit came up with the idea of putting ball bearings in the trigger. They ended up being the perfect size. We then made an insert that fit on her finger like a ring and gave it to Marley [Shelton] to practice with. The scene turned out very cool. She was really able to spin it.

CAYLAH EDDLEBLUTE: Anytime you can make something work for an actor in that manner, it definitely makes your day.

JEFF POSS: We wanted the syringes to be as visible

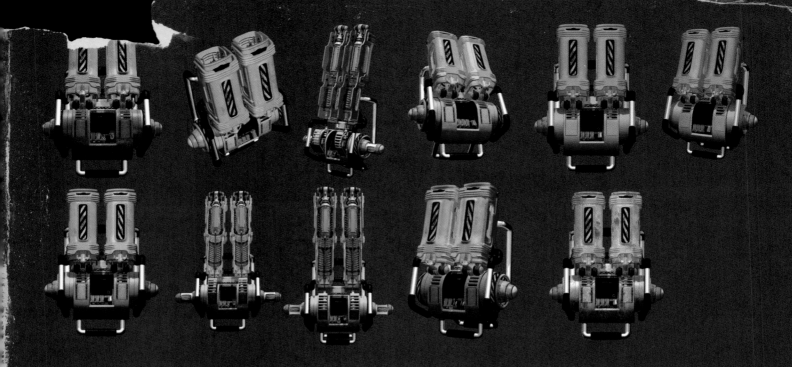

as possible, while being easily removable from the holster. We ended up planting itty-bitty magnets in the syringes and gold-plated the whole thing. It made it very easy to attach. You could just get within an inch of it, and the syringe would click right into place. It even made a nice clicking sound.

CAYLAH EDDLEBLUTE: That's another thing about cool action—you want to create a prop that has a good sound cue. You don't want cumbersome little hooks that the syringe has to seat into. They need to feel cool to the actor when they're using it.

JEFF POSS: I had trouble figuring out how this big, bulky weapon with two big syringes was going to be holstered under Dakota's skirt without looking like an extra thigh. I worked out this elaborate plastic holster—basically a gun holster wrapped in leather.

Caylah looked at it and said, "No, here's a loop attached to a garter belt." It was beautiful. Much better.

STEVE JOYNER: It was more sexy for Marley.

JEFF POSS: Sometimes you keep it simple in design and it works very well.

STEVE JOYNER: One of the first things that Caylah and I saw when we came onto *Planet Terror* was [Troublemaker Digital Artist] Alex Toader's designs for what we call the Doom Device—the device that contains the gas that creates our zombies. When Robert was conceptualizing the story, he had Alex working on pre-visualization for it.

CAYLAH EDDLEBLUTE: Robert keyed in right away on

OPPOSITE (FROM TOP): CG concept designs of the Doom Device by Troublemaker Digital Artist Alex Toader. Notice the "German Gray" coloring at the bottom right. • Prop Fabricator Kit Casati creating a doom device pedestal as Head Prop Fabricator Jeff Poss observes. • Marcus LaPorte airbrushing the final touches to a Doom Device; **ABOVE:** (pictured from left) Construction Coordinator Joe McCusker, Camera Operator Jimmy Lindsey, Production Designer Steve Joyner and Special Effects Tech Mike Reedy check out the final, "hero" Doom Device just prior to shooting.

JEFF POSS: There are three different stages to the Doom Device. First, it had a dormant stage, where it needed a certain ominous presence, a kind of statuesque appearance. It needed to be a little bit higher, a little bit taller than anybody around it. That made it feel a little bit more dangerous. Then it had to be carried. We had to keep in mind that, if need be, two guys could carry this thing. It needed to be portable and to be able to go through all the actions with the stunt people. Then finally it had an open stage. We had to consider the overall height of the set since this thing almost doubles in size when it's open. We angled the top of the Doom Device pack into a leaned-back stance, so that when it opened it created a pretty aggressive action.

STEVE JOYNER: Mike Reedy from the special effects

some of the color schemes. I guess it comes from German military equipment, snow camouflage. Since our entire shoot was at night, it definitely worked to have this lighter color scheme. It allowed the devices to really pop when the soldiers were carrying the tanks around. We also had to work out a good schematic for actors to be able to carry them. To have light-weight versions for actors to carry and have hero versions with working parts. One of the things we also did right out of the gate was to work out our size and scale.

JEFF POSS: There are three different stages to the Doom Device. First, it had a dormant stage, where it needed a certain ominous presence, a kind of statuesque appearance. It needed to be a little bit higher, a little bit taller than anybody around it. That made it feel a little bit more dangerous. Then it had to be carried. We had to keep in mind that, if need be, two guys could carry this thing. It needed to be portable and to be able to go through all the actions with the stunt people. Then finally it had an open stage. We had to consider the overall height of the set since this thing almost doubles in size when it's open. We angled the top of the Doom Device pack into a leaned-back stance, so that when it opened it created a pretty aggressive action.

STEVE JOYNER: Mike Reedy from the special effects

department mechanized the whole apparatus, which was quite a project.

JEFF POSS: Yeah, in the end we went ahead and modeled all the individual pieces, cut them out and made individual molds. We had four "hero" devices that were up front and center and wanted all the relief to be there, all the detail to be there because of the digital world and how detailed it is, how you can catch every single nook and cranny now.

STEVE JOYNER: The script grew from one Doom Device to 25 or 26 Doom Devices, so to manufacture those in time, we had to simplify a lot of the components.

JEFF POSS: I don't think we changed a whole lot on the four hero ones but we did have to take one of those, and we made basically a repeatable vacuform plug for all the background ones. The paint job is the same but there are basically three parts to ones in the background and 30 parts to the hero ones. And only one actual working one. LED components, the actual digital screens on them—there are a lot of little parts to them. But we had to have a lot out on the tarmac for the destruction scene. We really had to crank them out.

STEVE JOYNER: The number grew. Each couple of weeks that went by, it was like "Hey, can we have six more, hey can we have four more?" Fortunately, we had Travis Dean and Ivan Page cranking out parts in the fiberglass shop. It wasn't the first time they saved our bacon.

JEFF POSS: Along the way, we were trying to figure out how to tie the personal gas packs in with the Doom Device. We all worked to make the two props work together as one. When the soldiers run out of gas, they walk up to the Doom Device, push the button and it opens up. Then there are two removable cylinders that pop out that go in your personal pack.

STEVE JOYNER: After the doom device came the soldiers portable gas packs. It became clear that we needed color control in the movie. That's a pretty big hot button for most production designers. I think I was first exposed to it while working with David and Sandy Wasco on *Jackie Brown*. They do a really good job of establishing color and color themes, which really helps tell the story. In our case—because we were shooting at night—we discovered that we really needed to avoid khaki and camouflage. The traditional military green does a really good job of turning black at night. So fortunately, our country went to war in the desert and now there's a lot of great sand-colored camouflaged stuff out there. All of our color choices became about being visible at night.

CAYLAH EDDLEBLUTE: Steve had the idea to make the gas packs operate like weapons, to have a lock and load capability. Your actor can push a button, the tank slips out, they lock in another and it makes a really cool, heroic action. To me that makes a good prop. One of the things I learned from watching Antonio Banderas and Robert work together was that a well choreographed scene is in good musical beats. And Robert is definitely all about good beats.

We really wanted the device to have a single tank. We put it on a sling so it hangs over the shoulder just like a weapon. The handle is based right off an M-16.

OPPOSITE (FROM TOP): Stunt man Troy Robinson models a custom "face hugger" gas mask. • Marcus LaPorte assembles portable gas packs; **ABOVE:** An assembled "hero" gas pack and mask.

JEFF POSS: And some of the venting as well is patterned off of military guns.

CAYLAH EDDLEBLUTE: Again, Troy Engel was so good to work with on this. He sat down and worked it out and just wouldn't quit. He came up with a number of versions, we did a few prototypes and got one that we were really happy with.

Another challenge was the gas mask. Anything that covers your actor's face is a potential problem. You want it to be as unobtrusive as possible.

STEVE JOYNER: We worked for quite awhile to make the masks look military but didn't give them this huge great dane snout.

CAYLAH EDDLEBLUTE: I think I also remember Robert referencing the mask Tom Hanks wore in *Castaway*. I think we tried to get them through France or something, but they were too expensive. So we ended up using

surgical tubing as our anchors.

STEVE JOYNER: Which is a little homage to *Alien* when John Hurt gets the face hugger.

CAYLAH EDDLEBLUTE: Exactly. Steve came up with this cool idea that was in keeping with the color scheme. Instead of having classic green we used orange lights in the masks. It really made them pop.

JEFF POSS: The masks were as involved as the packs themselves really, because they had four five custom elements to them that had to be assembled and then all of those had light packs in them. I think we ended up having more masks than packs since you didn't always see a pack but you always saw if they had a gas mask on.

CAYLAH EDDLEBLUTE: And those little hits of light in the night are just so great.

BLOOD-STAINED SATIN

THE WARDROBE OF PLANET TERROR

Q: *Can you tell me about some of the various over-the-top characters?*

NINA PROCTOR, Costume Designer: Rose McGowan as Cherry. She ends up being something like a super hero. We've played with that idea with her costume, with the black leather skirt, black boots, and the red and black bra top. It really gives you that almost *super woman* look.

We wanted to make sure that we had the right cuts for her top, so we got the best shot of her bust line that we could. It also makes a difference where the bra hits the lower part of her body. So we experimented with different cuts and different fabrics and textures, and narrowed it down to the leathers for the end of the movie, while she starts out in a satin bustier. She looks great in them, and she's been a real sport.

Q: *How did her losing her leg affect her costume?*

NINA PROCTOR: Well, even though we see Cherry with no leg, or a peg leg, she actually has this gray thing

that has lights on it for the CG guys to track. So it's a bit cumbersome. It definitely affected the length of the skirt, where there's a portion of her leg showing above where the bandaging starts. I didn't want her thinking about her costume when she was doing stunts, so we tested different lengths of skirts to see what was going to work best, while still allowing her to do stuntwork.

We wanted Wray to be kind of a normal guy. We didn't want to give away who he was, so we really played it just as a normal guy. Jeans, a thermal shirt and a leather jacket. He could be any guy on the street. But he has these secrets in his past that we don't know about, and we didn't want to give any of that away. So we kept him very simple.

Marley has done some incredible things with her costume. We first see her with a suit and jacket with a blouse that's closed up all the way, and a skirt and heels. Then at the hospital we see her with the lab coat. Then once she leaves the hospital, she just starts becoming more and more sexy. You would think it

ABOVE: A blood-soaked Wray (played by Freddy Rodriguez) sports his "normal guy" attire. **OPPOSITE (FROM LEFT):** Cherry (played by Rose McGowan) in her hero outfit. • Cherry's Go-Go-Go outfit.

would be the other way around, because of all the horrific things going on around her—she falls out a hospital window, then she has to rush home in the pouring rain. She's a wreck. But instead of looking like a wreck she starts to look more and more sexy. By the end, she's in a satin camisole that just looks phenomenal.

For Josh I did the same coloring as I did on Marley because they're both going into this hospital and played with that kind of off-green color. The color is similar to what you would see in hospitals in the 80s. They both have that color on, and all of the nurses have that color on. The hospital is a yellowish color so the off-green worked really well in those scenes.

Q: *Josh Brolin's character keeps getting uglier and uglier.*

NINA PROCTOR: He does definitely get uglier and uglier, but his clothes look good. He becomes infected, so by the last time we see him, you pretty much don't see Josh Brolin anymore, you just see this infected being. Rebel [Rodriguez] was also really fun to dress. He has a tarantula and a scorpion and a turtle—he has different little pets. The Block house was rather big and had lots of animal heads on the walls, so I wanted something that would make Rebel pop. So he

THIS PAGE (FROM TOP): Dr. Block (played by Josh Brolin) sports his off-green hospital attire while entering into the final stage of infection. • Tony (played by Rebel Rodriguez) pops in his red dinosaur shirt; **OPPOSITE (FROM TOP):** Dakota Block's (played by Marley Shelton) conservative coat and blouse outfit. • Dakota in camisole and high-slit skirt.

starts by having a red t-shirt with dinosaurs on it. Of course, being a little boy, he loves dinosaurs. Then as he goes out, we added more layers to him.

Q: *And you've got lots of extras?*

NINA PROCTOR: We had a lot of deputies running around. We also had a full hospital staff. The nurses were all in sterile green scrubs. Then we moved into the hospital with infected patients, visitors, attendants, interns, and doctors etc. We also dressed a number of military men in full uniform. [Special Make-Up Effects Company] KNB did applications on most of the extras, and sometimes it's just these big muscle things that are busting out, sort of like the Hulk, but much messier. So it's a matter of just making the clothes look like they they've been stretched or maybe have some rips in them to accommodate these muscles that are busting loose. There have been so many stunts in this film, and so we end up dressing the extras sometimes three and four times a night. They're getting blown up all the time. So there goes one set of clothes. And we dress them again, and there goes another set of clothes. I gave some of the background characters specific looks, but I wanted to be able to see them without seeing too much about who that person was. So there are lots of muted colors. That

way Robert, in editing, can take different things and edit it however he wants to. Since it's a grindhouse movie, it's not so necessary that everything match. We've been told all along not to bother with continuity. As far as the background characters, I just thought it would make more sense if we went with a muted palette. We did make a few interesting ones that are going to be up front, and there have been a couple of really interesting looks. We had a Rasta man one night, and KNB went in and did all of their make-up, and then he had the dreadlocks, and the hat. It was just wild looking. We did a few character things like that, but for the most part I just wanted the audience to be aware of him without saying so much through his clothing.

Q: *Do you have a favorite costume?*

NINA PROCTOR: Actually, I would have to say Marley Shelton's green skirt. It's got just a touch of glimmer in it, and the skirt, like her top, starts out and as a straight skirt. But then it gets a slit, and then it's slit a little bit more. And then, as I said, she has this teal green satin blouse, so there's a certain amount of shine to it. Button front. The first time we see it, it's completely buttoned up with a tie. Then it just opens up more and more, and Marley just does so many things with it. It's been fun to watch the evolution of that costume. It just did so many unexpected things. That's really the second time I've dressed Marley that way, the first time being on *Sin City*. I think the moment that Robert and Frank Miller first saw her in that red dress was when they decided to put a little color in the movie. She just looked amazing. So we stuck with a little bit of sparkle in the green skirt for this, and she's been able to do so many different things with the costume that it's been fun to watch it evolve.

ABOVE: Zombies close in on our heroes;
OPPOSITE: The Crazy Babysitter Twins (played by Electra and Elise Avellán).

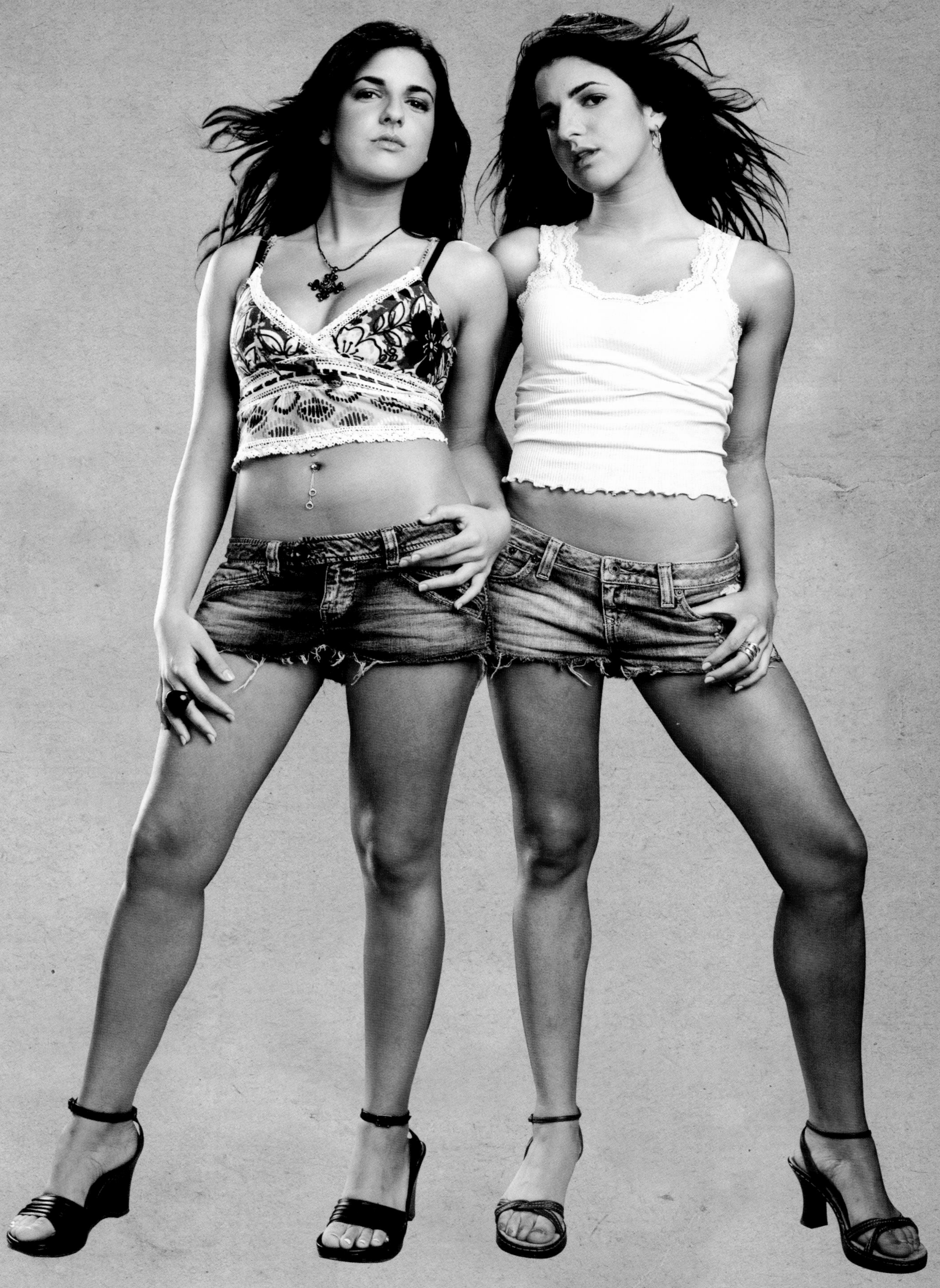

JEFF POSS, Lead Prop Fabricator: Every day on my way to work, for a year and a half, I would drive by a shop called Browning's Auto Repair in Houston. Inside this fenced-in, overgrown yard there was this truck that was rusting away. You'd drive by this truck, and you couldn't help but look at it. It was calling out, like *Christine* or something. One day I saw a for sale sign on the window and I freaked out.

STEVE JOYNER, Production Designer: I was sitting at my desk and Jeff dropped a couple of polaroids in front of me, and I said, "I want to get this truck." We were actually working on another movie called *The Return* that had an evil tow truck driver, so I went ahead and ponied up for the truck out of my own pocket, knowing that there would be a place for it somewhere.

JEFF POSS: We called this guy, Mr. Browning, and told him we'd buy the truck if he could start it. So we showed up ready to take it, he hooked a battery charger up to it and it started right up. We couldn't believe it. We thought for sure it wasn't going to start. This truck, in particular, had such a character to it, right out of that overgrown yard. I think the only thing that we changed was the name on the door and even that is in the same font. We changed it from Browning's to Wray's and I believe the address and phone number are even the same.

STEVE JOYNER: We decided to start calling this thing "Killdozer" because of its massive front grill, and also because of the great grindhouse movie *Killdozer* [based on the Theodore Sturgeon story] about a bulldozer that comes to life and terrorizes a work crew on an island. It's funny, in the original script, the part of Killdozer wasn't a tow truck at all, but a Police van that our heroes take from the Sheriff station.

The original Killdozer is a very heavy, solid-iron truck. In the 50s, it was one of the biggest wreckers available in Houston. They would call on this thing to free stuck cement mixers and semis. We realized very early that we needed a more lightweight truck to do the stunts and road sequences for *Planet Terror*, so special effects and transpo came up with a system where they would get a couple of modern five ton truck chassis and place International L210 bodies onto them. Our production assistant, Erika Jeanne, found one online, and Paul Steel found one 20 miles outside of Shreveport, while on his way to pick up our helicopter. Paul has an eagle eye for hunting out equipment or anything odd. Then Caylah and I found another one on our way down to Luling on a location scout.

CAYLAH EDDLEBLUTE, Production Designer: Looking at how the truck came out, you have to think about all the work from the transportation team, from the paint team, from our fabrication shop, from the effects shop. So many people in this production worked to

JEFFS TRUCK

KILLDOZER

THE VEHICLES OF PLANET TERROR

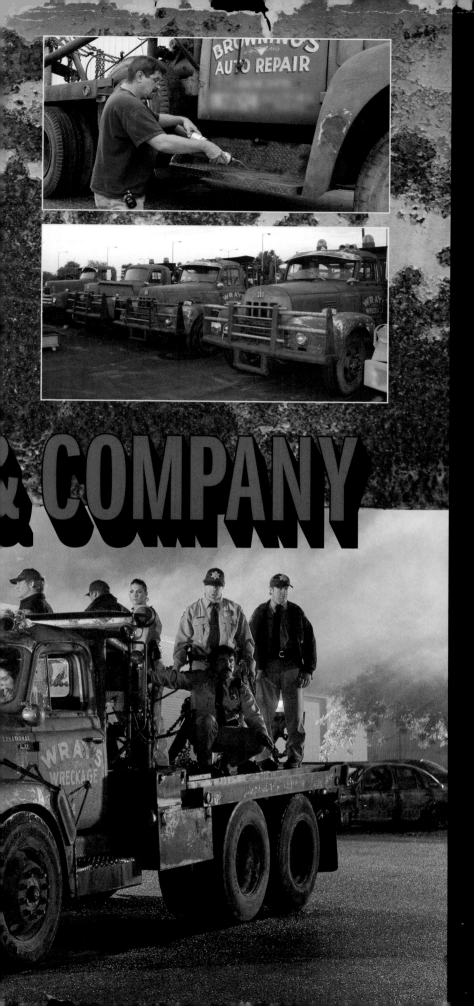

& COMPANY

take our original truck, find the missing parts, make everything sound, so everything could travel and work. These guys really cared, and they definitely made it look cool.

Next, we have JT's convertible, which first appeared in *Roadracers*, a little movie Robert shot for Showtime in thirteen days. David Arquette's character, Dude, ends up driving straight to hell at the end of that movie in his cool Chevy, which we then matched for *Planet Terror*.

STEVE JOYNER: [Transportation Coordinator] Cecil Evans went out and found the matching car, it's a '56, but the original '56 never came as a convertible, and so Cecil, [Mechanic] Bobby Sconci and his fabrication team took the car and chopped the top off and turned it into a permanent convertible '56, which never existed.

On *Roadracers*, Robert had the art department add "teeth" to Dude's car; they found some part somewhere off of some other vintage car. This was before *Monster Garage* and *American Hot Rod*, before the resurgence of things like West Coast Choppers, and all the interest in restoration came about. You could still get all these things and cut them up and get antique parts for them fairly cheaply. They were able to do that, but now when you try to go and find a '57 Chevy it's $50,000.

The one detail that Robert wanted more closely matched to the original car from *Roadracers* was the grill teeth, and we spent a lot of time looking for these teeth that they used and we couldn't find them. I don't think they exist anymore. They've gone back to whatever original cars they were from, so Jeff Poss, our excellent sculptor, actually took wood and carved a replica based on a still from the movie.

JEFF POSS: I use MDF [medium density fiberboard] which is just a nice shaping material that has a specific density all the way through it, so I wouldn't have to deal with grain. And I used an old technique of bolting it to a table and taking a rasp to it and hand shaping it. I worked it back and forth for a day or two until I felt I got the shape right, then through a series of layers and sanding and wet sanding. I thought that was kind of respectful to the car itself because that's how they used to make these cars. So it felt right working on it that way, with layers of lacquer and wet sanding to get a mirror finish. We made a mold of it and we cast them in a fast setting hard plastic, but we used a process that we use a lot here. We pre-paint the surface of the mold with a chrome-type paint. That way, as the plastic sets, the mold bonds to the paint. It creates a much more durable finish and a much more realistic metallic finish, because you get the gloss from the original surface from the mold.

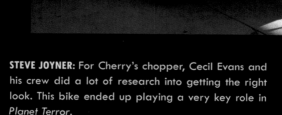

STEVE JOYNER: Dakota's son Tony happened to have this mini bike in the trunk of the car when they escaped. By the end of the movie, it's one of the only running vehicles the characters have left. So Wray rides the mini bike to destroy all the bad guys. It's a very small motorcycle. It almost looks like a toy. I mean, you can pick it up and carry it under your arm, but it still goes 50 or 60 miles an hour with a full size adult on it.

JEFF POSS: Our stunt guys were driving with one hand while they're shooting with the other, riding that little bike around all the explosions and debris and people.

CAYLAH EDDLEBLUTE: It was crazy

STEVE JOYNER: Again, it took a lot of coordination between all the departments to rig up this chase sequence, but it's very exciting.

CAYLAH EDDLEBLUTE: Of course you have to get a feel for what your cast is going to experience. We had the bikes arrive one day for a test show and we got some shots of Robert taking the pocket bike for a test drive.

JEFF POSS: I think he got off the bike and said, "Yeah.

STEVE JOYNER: For Cherry's chopper, Cecil Evans and his crew did a lot of research into getting the right look. This bike ended up playing a very key role in *Planet Terror*.

CECIL EVANS, Transportation Coordinator: Our stunt coordinator, Jeff Dashnaw, had a friend that was working with Jesse James [of West Coast Choppers] in some capacity, and when Jeff came here to start prepping the movie, he mentioned to me that he had talked to this guy and his guy was going to go to Jesse. Robert ended up calling Jesse himself, so he was really the one that got the choppers here. We had pictures of between six to ten other motorcycles that we could've used in lieu of the Jesse James bikes, but of course, when the Jesse James bikes arrived

PREVIOUS SPREAD (CLOCKWISE FROM TOP LEFT): Polaroid of the Killdozer rusting away at Browning's Auto Repair in Houston. • Lead Scenic Tommy Karl ages one of the Killdozers. • The final Killdozers are ready for action. • The Killdozer arrives at the hospital with heroes in tow; **ABOVE (FROM TOP):** Robert Rodriguez takes the pocket bike for a spin while First Assistant Director Brian Bettwy observes. • The "chopped top" 1956 Chevy "with teeth."; **OPPOSITE:** The Jesse James custom chopper.

part to lock off was the back of the leg. We used a combination of really lightweight material and one central rib down the back that was actually velcroed or taped into place. This allowed her leg to breathe a lot. It was really quick to put on and could go right over her boot.

STEVE JOYNER: Because we have such limited time with the actors and such limited time to prepare, a big part of the filmmaking process is experimental. When we actually shoot, it's like war—everybody is really hard on all the props, all the sets, all the equipment. So it's really tested at that point and that is just part of that R&D phase so everything gets better and better, and it will only be perfect on the very last day you shoot it.

CHRIS OLIVIA: It ended up being something that evolved through all the different departments over several months and ultimately changed quite a bit from the original plan. Robert shoots so quickly that we went from trying to be very high-tech with LED tracking markers and a very detailed model to having the brace be really minimal. The thinking was, when we digitally paint the leg out, we're not having to paint out a lot of extra bulky stuff. It just became apparent that the most time-consuming part wasn't tracking the leg, but digitally painting the leg out and replacing the background that wasn't originally there. The thinner the leg apparatus was, the better.

I found that there was enough detail in the bandage itself for me to track it by eye. We have a couple of automatic, 3D tracking softwares, but unless it was a locked-off shot with minimal movement where we

had tracking markers, it was almost impossible t use the tracking software. Because Cherry was doin all these acrobatic twirls and the leg was rotatin completely around, it seemed easier to put a C dummy representation in there, track that by eye an then have a separate CG gun, constrained to th bandage, but with the flexiblitiy to animate the tip it, so you can lock it to the ground.

One of the other challenges was that her thigh an bandage are not solid pieces of material, they'r flexible, they're flesh and blood. That's when we ha to ask ourselves, where do we blend our CG bandag into the live-action bandage, and if we do that, ar you going to notice fluctuations in her actual flesh th you're not going to notice in the hard CG bandag What seemed to be the easiest solution was to do blend half-way between our CG bandage up to he actual leg. That seemed to be easiest, quickest ar most natural solution.

ALEX TOADER: In the end, we had to do the ol fashioned rotoscope process. Sometimes you do ha to use old school skills! In all the shots that you see th wooden or gun leg, they are digital, the actress's le was removed digitally, then the background and th digital prop were added in. We rotoscoped them o using our 2D team: two artists using two Flame statio and three artists using Shake. The 3D models of th props were animated and rendered in Softimag XSI; the cameras were either tracked by hand or wi Boujou and PFtrack. We also used Particle Illusion create smoke and other debris, and all the shots we composited using Shake or Flame.

CAYLAH EDDLEBLUTE: The bikes were sent to us on loan. The thing that was so cool about it was we had no idea what was going to arrive. A bike with a black tank? I don't know. And these phenomenal bikes arrived. Obviously you can see the detail in the work.

STEVE JOYNER: The bikes were just beautiful. The paint job alone would have taken a normal customizer weeks, probably months to do, and Jesse and his crew were able to crank them out and get a pair of matching bikes to us.

Robert had very specific dimensional designs. He knew exactly how he wanted Wray and Cherry to fit on the bike. One thing he was very specific about was the rear tire size and the height of the seat to the ground and the angle of the chop, so I believe that in Robert's conversation with Jesse, he outlined basically the requirements of the shot and left the design up to Jesse. That was the evolution. When Robert writes this stuff, he always has a very specific blocking in mind.

STEVE JOYNER: We hired a guy named Steve Galleon to work on this project, and he has a friend who worked on helicopters in Iraq. He knew we were researching military bases and so he brought in a video his friend had shot of a Sea Stallion helicopter. When Robert saw the tilted way it takes off, he had the idea of using it as a weapon. After all, we're always looking for bigger and badder ways to cut things up around here.

Our lead prop fabricator, Jeff Poss, was prepping the Kevin Costner movie, *The Guardian*, in Louisiana, and they had a deal with the Coast Guard. It was a very positive Coast Guard movie—they were going to provide support and loan them helicopters for the shots and have their people there on set. Right in the middle of pre-production, they got hit with Hurricane Katrina, and the Coast Guard had to divert all its resources to handle it. So it was at that point that they went out and looked for helicopters to build themselves.

JEFF POSS: We were able to buy the one extra shell that the *Guardian* production didn't touch. It was most of the exterior of a Black Hawk, but really rough. It was just a shell. It would've been great as a boneyard helicopter, but shortly before it showed up, we heard it was probably going to be converted into a much larger helicopter, a Sea Stallion. So we started wondering how we were going to do that.

We actually went and bought some little models, we bought models of the Sea Stallion and the Black Hawk in the same scale and ran the Black Hawk through the band saw seven or eight times to figure out what parts we could actually use to scale up to the Sea Stallion.

When you look at the Stallion there are certain things that really make it the Stallion. Primarily, the nose and the engines. Those are really the key elements which set it apart from a Black Hawk, so the nose was crucial. We had a couple of guys focusing on the nose, and then the body was mostly done with panels. We kind of employed a ship building technique of bracing ribs and then skinning that. Then we went in and filled the whole inside of it with fiberglass to turn it into one big body again. At that time, we were still playing with the idea that this thing would end up going on to a truck and being tilted nose down. So we couldn't just screw it together. We had to make sure it was a solid unit, a complete shell that would support its own weight.

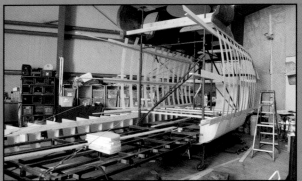

CAYLAH EDDLEBLUTE: One of the advantages of making a set piece like this is that you have access to it at any time. A movie schedule can change at any minute on any day. Something you think is going to shoot in two days may not shoot for two weeks. If you set up a rental for something of this scale—like a military vehicle—and the schedule changes, you find yourself recutting deals and paying fees. Building it yourself allows you to have something available at all times, day or night.

STEVE JOYNER: One of the other factors in building your own vehicle like this is when we work with picture cars, we need

OPPOSITE: A real Sea Stallion in action. • The salvaged Black Hawk helicopter. • The removed windshield before being married to the new body. • The new hull being built "ship style." • The finishing touches are put on the nose before being turned over to the paint department; **BELOW:** The Stallion team from left: Tom Ward, James Cavalucci, Brian McCarty, Tommy Dipple, Bart Bryant and Jeff Poss. • Our heroes escape to the Stallion.

to cut into them in order to place lights or cameras. In this case, we allowed for this flexibility, where we wouldn't have been able to in the real thing. Our vehicles are designed to pay homage to the real thing and look real to the eye, but also allow the camera to get all the shots.

JEFF POSS: Another advantage is being able to move it on a dime. The way we engineered the steering and everything, two guys can move this helicopter. With a real helicopter, or a real Sea Stallion, you put it down, and it's a pretty big deal to move it over a foot.

STEVE JOYNER: There was a giant weight difference, our helicopter probably weighed 8,000 pounds, and a real Sea Stallion is closer to 65,000.

CAYLAH EDDLEBLUTE: I love to break things down to the component parts. When you really see the elegance that everything is hand made. Almost nothing here is a found object. Every piece from the landing gear to the instrument panel to details in the lighting, everything is hand-fabricated.

STEVE JOYNER: Troy Engel drew the "Death From Above" artwork for us. The 31 is a reference to Outpost 31 from John Carpenter's *The Thing*. So we had our Unit 31, which was a clandestine unit, and their motto was "Death from Above" with its hissing black cat delivering a bomb. The classic Ray-O-Vac 9 lives cat was the inspiration for the artwork.

CAYLAH EDDLEBLUTE: Here's the bottom line—we just wanted to make something cool, and in our humble opinion, it's particularly cool.

STEVE JOYNER: We like to get pretty far into a project before we show something to Robert. On this, we pretty much had the floor and the body together with a couple of seats before Robert actually came and looked at it. When he climbed in, his only comment was, "Somebody wake up Hicks."

DRAGGING THE PRINT THROUGH THE PARKING LOT

CREATING THE DAMAGED FILM EFFECT WITH TROUBLEMAKER DIGITAL

RODNEY BRUNET, Troublemaker Digital Artist: The aged look has taken on a life of its own. Robert uses it almost as a character in the story. He described the look as a compilation of lost reels, all spliced together, to recreate this movie. Reels tend to become more damaged at the heads and tails, especially where they're most exposed to editing or the mechanics of the projector. Each of the artists took different approaches. I watched as many old movies as possible and read more than I wanted to know about film damage. Mostly, I waited for Robert to turn over shots and let each frame dictate the effect. Frame flutter, finger print blurs, scratches and flashes were all used sparingly until either Robert or the story dictated they be exaggerated.

CHRIS OLIVIA, Troublemaker Digital Artist: Originally, I think Robert mentioned he wanted to see what we could do with a really grungy, dirty film look. We were trying to find the best way to achieve that, whether it was through plug-ins or stock footage. So we put a lot of research into trying to find things that we could apply to some of the test footage from *Sin City* and the animatics that we were doing. So we just did a ton of different looks. Everything from really grainy, desaturated and scratched looks—basically like the film had been sitting in a warehouse for fifty

years—to going back to something more subtle. So as we were doing these animatics, we would try out these various options. We just knew it was going to be an old 70s look with all the sound problems that those films had. That's kind of how it started.

ALEX TOADER, Troublemaker Digital Artist: The very first tests we did on *Grindhouse* were not the leg replacement tests, but were actually the damaged or aged-look tests. Robert asked us to experiment with different looks. He gave us clips of *From Dusk Till Dawn* and *Roadracers* to work with. We did a lot of research on what exactly happens to film, how scratches can look different by the way they cut through emulsion or if they happened in the negative, for example. We looked at available existing stock of damaged film that was scanned. We looked at actual reels from thirty-year-old prints to see the skips and blurs, the dust and hairs and smears and discoloration and all the sad stuff that can happen to a film reel when it goes through the projector too many times or through too many hands. We also had to keep in mind that Robert wanted the damage to be part of the storytelling process and the overall experience. Plus how the damage would affect sound and so on. So we chose different avenues to achieve three distinct damaged looks, Rod used a library of actual

ABOVE: Troublemaker Digital Artist Rodney Brunet; **OPPOSITE:** The original HD frame grab at left and the final, damaged frame at right.

...scanned film leader that was badly damaged and manipulated it by creating different layers in Shake. I chose a different process by using the CineLook plugin for After Effects. After creating the scratches, dust and flutters, I rendered out a damage pass and brought it into Shake where I created a multitude of distortions and blurs. Then rendered it again, brought it back for a couple more passes in After Effects—putting back in the original crisper scratches on top of the blurred ones done in Shake—then rendered them with an animated vignette created with the Magic Bullet plugin. I added more skips on top of all the created layers and then rendered them again as a final pass. So my process was purely digital, where as Rod and Chris chose to do a more organic pass, using actual film damage. For example, there's a shot I worked on for the *Machete* trailer when he's contemplating on top of a building. In the close up, when he blinks, I chose to blur the whole shot, progressing to a crisper picture as he has a moment of clarity. So depending on the sequence, you will see different looks and the look changes from reel to reel, like the movie was assembled from different reels from different age generations and multiple uses.

CHRIS OLIVIA: I think each one of the artists had a preference for what they liked visually and also what tools they used to create it. I found that using stock footage of organic, realistic footage that you just can't re-create digitally worked best. Like dragging footage across the ground, aging or burning it. I found that overall, that's

different layers to make a realistic look that doesn't just look like a processed layer.

The original test I did involved me trying to figure out what was happening with color. I remember doing some tests where I would take certain channels and bleed them in to one another. I would blow out the reds and stuff like that. It's not as easy as making something more or less saturated. It's really more of a serendipitous process. I know that I was able to achieve some cool looks by getting certain colors, at a certain threshold, to bleed out into the colors around them, giving it more of an aged look. So that objects would have a very subtle halo effect around them. So subtle that it didn't look like a glow, just that the color was bad or not quite right. It's something that all of us who grew up in the 70s were used to seeing when we went to the movies, because of the lower quality of film projection at the time. Even when I would see brand new film, it just didn't look like films today. With HD, everything is so much cleaner. I remember sitting up close in a movie theater, and the first thing I would notice was just tons of tiny scratches.

It's more difficult to create this kind of look with HD because even though you have more options and more opportunities to do what you want, you still find yourself trying to figure out how to re-create things that happen naturally. That's just a part of computer graphics, trying to re-create reality by using something that's based on algorithms and numbers. Say you were to take a

just a cooler look, so I ended up finding as much stock footage online—whether it was ArtBeats or other stuff. Also for reference, we would pull out old DVDs that had really bad film damage. We would usually start with that stuff and blend it into the comp. We really had to understand why that footage looked the way it did. It's not just a matter of superimposing scratches over some footage; it involves finding out if a specific blur is occurring because the film is coming off the reel or whether or not the scratches are on the negative or on the print. Basically what makes a scratch black or what makes it white and how that affects the colors around it. So it's a matter of using various composite techniques, using a lot of

pane of glass and drop it on a rock. Basically, the chaos theory, the breakage. You can always mathematically come up with the way that glass breaks, but there are so many variables going on in there that it's not something you can re-create easily, no matter how much technology you have. So sometimes it's better to go old-fashioned. Even though you have more color space with today's cameras, and you have all these options, it doesn't make it necessarily easier to re-create certain organic looks. Sometimes it's good to just go out to the garage or behind the studio and actually take a piece of film and step on it.

INTO THE CRYPT

A LOOK INSIDE TROUBLEMAKER'S EDITORIAL FACILITY, LOS CRYPTOS

JAY MAHAVIER, 1st Assistant Editor: I'm not sure why the Editing Bay is called Los Cryptos. I think that since the building was going to be for memorabilia storage, it was going to be the crypts. Where, you know, all the past projects were buried.

TIM RAKOCZY, Supervising Sound Editor: My title is Supervising Sound Editor, but probably "Sound Monkey" is more fitting. I work as a middle man between Robert and the sound effects editors and I coordinate the sound that Robert wants for the movie. I also hire the sound editors. Most of the editors live in Los Angeles. They cut the sound, we mix what they cut and what we cut here. Although on more recent shows, we've been hiring some local people to cut here.

BRAD ENGLEKING, Re-Recording Engineer: We also work kind of like filters, Tim gives those guys a list of edits and they bounce stuff to us. We'll bring it over here to the stage and check it out with [Sound Re-Recording Mixer] Sergio Reyes. Sometimes we'll bounce it back to them with notes. They'll recut or maybe we need to mix it a little bit differently. But we're all kind of artistic liaisons between those guys and Robert.

JAY MAHAVIER: I'm the Assistant Editor, but I am also the editorial engineer. As the editorial engineer I'm responsible for the installation and maintenance of the equipment here, all the editing decks, and the infrastructure for connecting the editing decks to the editing systems and routing the signal. Also maintaining the Local Area Network for the computer systems. As the assistant editor I'm responsible for taking Robert's edits and getting all the information to the proper people in the sound department, the visual effects department, and other post production departments including the trailer company.

ETHAN MANIQUIS, Co-Editor: On this movie I'm the co-editor along with Rodriguez, which is tricky because he basically already has the movie cut in his head, and he's an amazing editor. It's definitely a challenge.

TIM RAKOCZY: It also helps, if you're working for Robert, to be good at *Halo*.

BRAD ENGLEKING: Yes, yeah, cause he is good, but not *that* good, make sure that gets in there.

TIM RAKOCZY: Ouch!

ETHAN MANIQUIS: I'm convinced he had the software rigged because he's been winning a lot. I'll still kick his ass on occasion though. *Damnation Alley* is the place I want to be buried when I'm gone.

TIM RAKOCZY: I have to say there is no such thing as a typical Robert Rodriguez movie. They're all different in some way and they all offer different challenges. 3D affects the sound. *Sin City* was all green screen at first, so we weren't sure about everything we were cutting sound for because we couldn't see it yet.

JAY MAHAVIER: There *is* a typical Robert method. In fact, over the years we have worked towards building systems designed around Robert's workflow. You know as the producer, writer, director, editor and composer, he falls into a lot of different categories. While they're shooting, he's on set, not in the editing room. It's our responsibility to take all the material that they shoot on set, all the material from the camera department, all the audio from the sound department and bring it into the editing system. We have to sync it all up and prepare it for him to edit. The system we maintain at the studio lets him start working on edits or looking at stuff in progress when he's ready.

ETHAN MANIQUIS: The editing usually goes through three to four phases. Phase one occurs during shooting. Rough assemblies are made to check if the shots cut well and to check lighting and camera moves. Selects are made and usually after a few weeks a mini trailer will be made to pump up the crew. Phase two occurs directly after shooting. A visual effects cut will be made with all the footage that needs to be turned over to the visual effects artists to start their shots. Then in phase three all the cuts and assemblies are compiled into reels, and the fun stuff—action, stunts, etc.—is cut, because it's fun. By that time the sound department is gearing up and asking for footage which is always an issue. They can't do too much without footage, but the release date doesn't change, so the longer it takes us to turn over picture to sound the shorter they have to work on it, but we've got a great sound team supervised by Tim so they always come through.

TIM RAKOCZY: Typically, we start off by having editors cut things. They get back to Robert and he reviews them, gives notes. We usually edit anywhere between seven to ten weeks and then we usually have about six to eight weeks to final a movie. So over the course of a couple of months, we usually get the entire sound job done.

JAY MAHAVIER: Robert does all his offline editing, all his visual effects reviews, all his music composition, all his sound mixing at his own facilities. The audio editing takes place all across the country, some even in Canada.

TIM RAKOCZY: Foley is one of the few things that we have sent out, that we can't actually do here ourselves.

OPPOSITE: The Los Cryptos exterior;
BELOW: The mixing stage exterior.

We don't have a foley walking stage, so we've had a number of different foley editors on different shows. We try different people out to find somebody that Robert likes and then usually they work with us.

JAY MAHAVIER: Once production's done, he'll come back to the editing room where he begins to refine the edit until he turns over the version one. That will go to all the different departments. Like visual effects will begin working on their visual effects shots based on that, the sound department will begin working on dialogue editing, sound effects editing, music editing, based on that version.

BRAD ENGLEKING: It's a long process.

JAY MAHAVIER: Robert typically delivers about seven versions of the movie that get sent out to the various departments and they refine their work based on those and on feedback from him until we have our online. We do an online since we shoot on HD video.

ETHAN MANIQUIS: Once sound starts predubs and the final VFX start coming in and the music is composed we are in the final edit stage which usually goes on till shortly before release. Along with this, we online the feature as the offline is slowly finished reel by reel, frame by frame. The reels go through multiple versions, even multiple final versions, because of some cut that has to be slipped or trimmed at the last minute.

JAY MAHAVIER: We go into an online suite with all the high definition material and make our final assemble with all the visual effects included. Next comes the color correction. Then we do the film out, and then the picture will get married to the audio at that point. As far as what happens to all the audio in between, I'm sure Tim can fill you in very well on all that.

BRAD ENGLEKING: There are three parts to mixing the audio: there's the pre-dub, the final and then the print master. His guys cut all these effects and then we pre-dub them down which is taking them from a few thousand tracks down to a few hundred tracks. We make artistic decisions in that process and get it into a place to where you can actually mix it all at one time instead of trying to do the whole thing in one big shot. Then in the final, we take those few hundred and mix them down to twenty four. For the printmaster we take those twenty four and mix them down to the six track that goes on the movie.

ETHAN MANIQUIS: To shoot this movie, we used a modern system of HD cameras, decks, computers and technicians and just the right lighting and action so we could create a great looking retro, ragged, raw looking B-movie that you would expect to see playing at one of the sticky grindhouse theaters in Times Square or Downtown LA.

TIM RAKOCZY: Robert wants very specific sound for *Planet Terror*, like a movie that was unearthed from 1972. But not a lot of people would want to sit through three hours of something that sounded awful, where they couldn't hear the sound or where it was poppy and crackly. The first thing that Robert covered with us was that we're going to pick and choose our moments in it.

BRAD ENGLEKING: Most complaints at theaters are about the sound, not the picture

TIM RAKOCZY: Right. People will sit through a movie for 30 minutes and have it be out of focus and not say anything about it, but if the sound is not good or something's wrong with it, people complain. We'll probably let the visual effects, once we see them, dictate how much we do. You could hear a little bit that we've already done in the ComiCon trailer with adding pops and crackles and grime to certain sounds and stuff. It's still going to sound like a Rodriguez movie, though. It's going to be big, the guns will be big, the explosions will be big, the vehicles will be massive. But we'll just pick and choose what moments that we dip in and have a little fun making it sound grindhousey.

ABOVE: Co-Editor Ethan Maniquis edits inside the Sherrif's station location, the Williamson County Jail; **OPPOSITE (FROM TOP):** 1st Assistant Editor Jay Mahavier with an Avid Workstation inside Los Cryptos. • Supervising Sound Editor Tim Rakoczy (L) and Re-Recording Engineer Brad Engleking (R) inside the mixing stage.

BRAD ENGLEKING: Plus it's a good escape net for us because if we make a mistake—hey man, it's supposed to be that way.

TIM RAKOCZY: If it sounds awful, that's the 70s.

BRAD ENGLEKING: Yeah, 70s man. Robert's philosophy sound-wise is: it has to be cool. Every gun is the biggest gun you've ever heard, every explosion is the biggest explosion ever. Everything is huge. We use a lot of surrounds and we use a lot of sub, because that's what Robert likes. He likes to hear it big and fat. Bigger in sound than it is in real life. In Robert's movies, everything is bigger, the cars are bigger, the guys are holding bigger guns. The sound has to reflect all of that.

ETHAN MANIQUIS: We were cutting on the set. So the bay basically consisted of a folding table, chair, hard drive, laptop and a bunch of wires. The explosions were all real, which is always fun. How many times can your edit system get pelted with burning timbers from the explosions going on thirty feet away on set? I think the practical effects, zombies, car crashes, sex and general mayhem of the hectic night shooting schedule combined with all the various crazy personalities on set, both in front of and behind the camera, is going to combine to create a unique movie experience.

BRAD ENGLEKING: Robert's facility is really cool and it's really unique because he has the picture department and the sound department all in the same building. That's cool for him because Robert works so quickly that he needs to have access to all that information at one time.

JAY MAHAVIER: All the editing is done on Avid non-linear editing systems which are all connected to a SAN, a Shared Area Network. All the media for the editing process, all the picture and sound that he's going to use to do his cut is on the SAN. It allows us to share the media between multiple video editing

workstations and to share the actual project files. We're all working on the exact same project at the same time which means a shorter turnaround than we would have without it. From there we do digital outputs of quicktimes for different departments to use.

TIM RAKOCZY: We like to keep it lean and mean here.

BRAD ENGLEKING: We have servers and computers and media that tie the mix stage and the sound department and the picture department together so we can look at whatever they're doing and they can look at whatever we're doing more or less at any time. It's cool because it allows us to work very, very quickly.

ETHAN MANIQUIS: Sometimes, Los Cryptos is controlled remotely. I'll be working at 3am and Jay will call saying "The Unity is at 89 degrees. Lets make sure the AC is working so things don't start exploding." I go down stairs and sure enough the AC had tripped off and it's like an oven in there with all the gear grinding away. Also the computer cursors will start moving by themselves at all hours of the night while I'm there alone. After I figured out it wasn't another acid flashback I realized it was Jay using the Apple remote desktop, in which copying and other tasks can be done from home.

JAY MAHAVIER: The sound department, and the visual effects departments use quicktimes as guides for their work so we don't have to go through the process of making video tapes. We try to keep it all as digital files and we use a high speed network to push all our data around.

BRAD ENGLEKING: On a lot of bigger dub stages, picture department is on the other side of town or in a different city, so if there is a picture change, those guys are waiting a couple of days or a week or maybe they don't even know about it. Whereas Robert is on the stage with us a lot of times while he's editing. So we get picture changes within an hour or two instead of a couple of days. Since we don't use film, the digital picture that we have on the mix stage and the digital picture that our effects editors, Tim, and the picture editors use allows us to just work so much faster.

We deal with so many different types of sound: foley, effects, music, ADR [automated dialogue replacement]. Foley is essentially like the practical stuff: set down a glass, walk across a room.

TIM RAKOCZY: Footsteps.

BRAD ENGLEKING: Yeah, and I guess sound effects would be anything that's not foley. You know, explosions, gunshots, punches—the stuff that Robert is really concerned about. Stuff that's big and percussive and

mean and brutal. That's the stuff he's really into.

And then you have dialogue. The dialogue is obviously recorded on the set, then we bring it here, we cut it, try to clean it up. A lot of times on the set it's real noisy because they have all those machines in there. We bring it out here and we clean it up editorially and then we mix it. When we mix it, we do another clean up process on that. If we can't fix it they'll do what's called looping or ADR. That's when we bring the actors out here and we'll actually have them re-record those lines. If they're not available we'll do what's called an ISDN patch which is where they can re-do those lines in Los Angeles or really anywhere in the world. We can actually run the sessions from here, Robert can give them notes.

TIM RAKOCZY: We've recorded ADR in Los Angeles, New York, Mexico, Florida, I think we did some in Italy.

BRAD ENGLEKING: Yeah, that was in Florence, no Venice, from the film festival.

JAY MAHAVIER: Robert will also compose all his music here. On some shows he's actually rented an orchestra and gone to California to record the orchestra. But on others, he's done the the music straight out of his Pro Tools system downstairs.

BRAD ENGLEKING: We built him a whole new system that incorporates a whole bunch of different computers. I think it's actually eight computers that make up his music scoring system. He pretty much writes most of it all himself.

ETHAN MANIQUIS: Everything at Los Cryptos needs to be as fast and efficient as possible or the process would not be able to keep up with the creative output which drives the movies. We're constantly evolving using new technology to get the movies made more efficiently.

BRAD ENGLEKING: Robert's a cool boss, because in a lot of cases, in the course of any dub, or in the course of any movie, there will be technical problems and mistakes will be made. By definition, what we do is difficult and really complicated. There are so many steps and so many places for mistakes to be made. Mistakes are made, and Robert's cool because instead of ripping somebody's head off or screaming down somebody's throat, his thing is let's just make it right. Let's do whatever we need to do to make it right and we'll fix it and it'll be cool.

JAY MAHAVIER: Mostly, Robert will tell me when he's got stuff that needs to be delivered to the sound department or to visual effects, and he'll tell me what he wants to turn over. It's up to me to clean it up and prepare it and deliver it to the different departments.

GRINDHOUSE **149** PLANET TERROR

ABOVE: Interior view of the mixing stage; **UPCOMING SPREAD:** The cast and crew of *Planet Terror*.

TIM RAKOCZY: Most of my interactions with Robert are based on either playing stuff for him or finding out what he wants something to sound like. I think because we both grew up watching the same movies, we have a shorthand, so that he can say "Hey I want this to sound like *Big Trouble in Little China*" or "I want this to sound like *Shogun Assassin*." I know exactly what he's talking about, because I've seen the movie so I can explain to editors what he wants.

BRAD ENGLEKING: Robert has a good ear. He knows what's good and he'll tell you. It's nice working for somebody like that because a lot of directors don't know what they want and they don't know what's good so they won't be able to give any feedback. They'll just say, "I don't like it, fix it." And you're like, "Well what don't you like?" But Robert knows. He knows sound, and he knows music, and he can tell the difference between what's good and what's bad. It's nice working for somebody who can give real feedback.

TIM RAKOCZY: He's also extremely hands on. In fact, we always say that we sort of bring the ingredients to the table and Robert cooks the meal. We try and get all the stuff together for him and sort of let him pick and choose. Once it comes down to mix time, and even beforehand, in letting us know what he wants things to sound like and giving us notes and

feedback, he's all over it.

JAY MAHAVIER: Being the editor he is very hands on with what goes on. In also being the composer and being on the stage during the final mixes, he's very much around for a lot of the process. Unlike other productions, those responsibilities don't get relegated to various other people.

ETHAN MANIQUIS: Robert has always cut his own footage so he is more hands on than any director I've worked with.

TIM RAKOCZY: I've worked on probably 35 movies, and Robert is the one director that stands out above any of them. He knows exactly what he wants and if he doesn't like the way something sounds he'll recut a sound. And he knows how to work all the equipment and get the work out of it. He has the best ears of any director, and he has a good idea going in exactly what something sounds like. Until we get that sound, he keeps telling us to do it again and fix it because he has a clear idea right from the beginning.

I like to think that Robert doesn't just make movies. He makes rock and roll. It's just huge and loud. That's the way his movies are. They're musical too, they're very melodic, and they just have to be cooler and louder and more fun than whatever's come before.

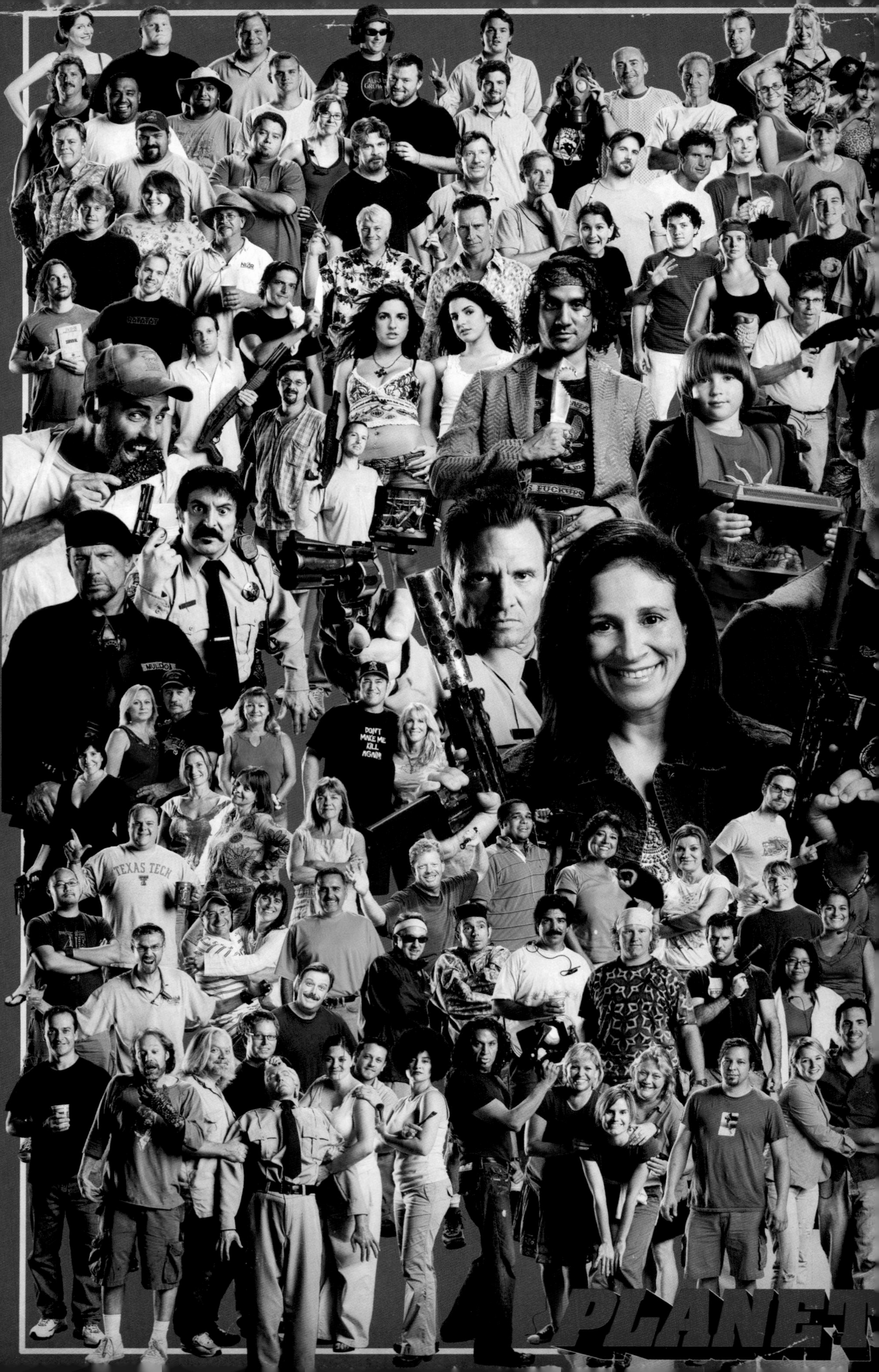
DON'T MAKE ME KILL AGAIN!!
TEXAS TECH
PLANET

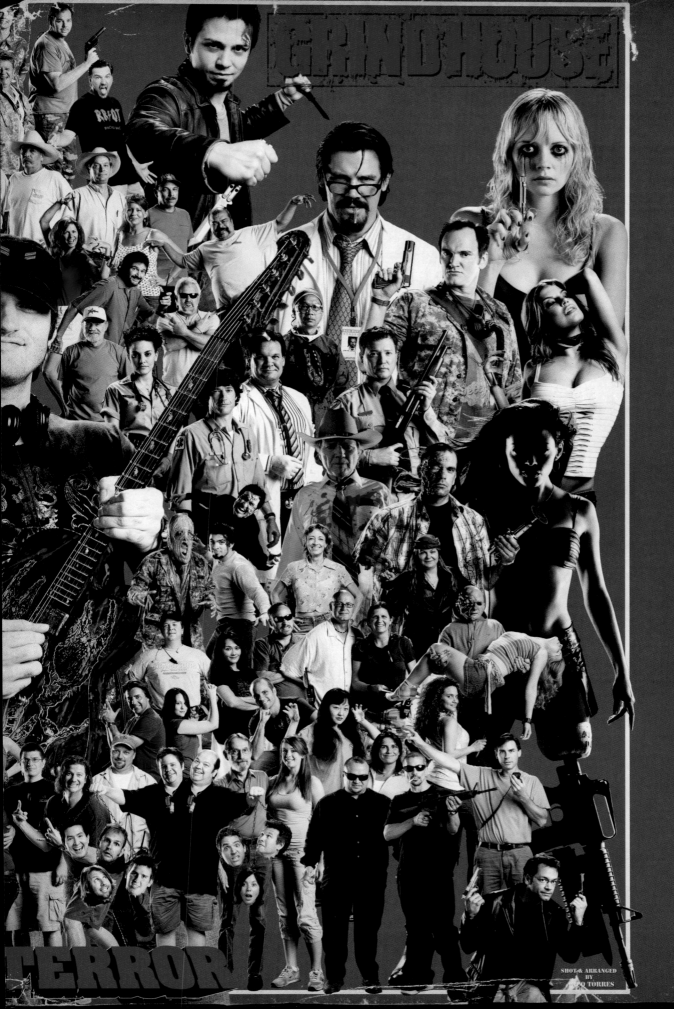

GRINDHOUSE

TERROR

GRINDHOUSE 151 PLANET TERROR

QUENTIN TARANTINO'S

"DEATH PROOF"

THE MAKING OF THE MOVIE

DIRECTING DEATH PROOF

ROBERT RODRIGUEZ AND QUENTIN TARANTINO DISCUSS THE MAKING OF THE MOVIE

ROBERT RODRIGUEZ: I remember when we first talked about doing *Grindhouse*, you said, "Let's do horror movies first." At the time, I had about 30 pages of a zombie script that I wrote a long time ago. If you liked that, I was gonna let you take that and do something with it. I'd always liked it. And you said that you'd always wanted to do a zombie movie. And then the next day, you said "Nevermind, I've got my own movie, a slasher movie with a car." You told me the story and that's when I suggested calling it *Death Proof* because you kept mentioning those words. I think you had the basic idea of it and went right into writing characters. Did you already know where it was going or did you just start off the concept of the killer with the car?

QUENTIN TARANTINO: I don't really remember 100%. It was very piecemeal.

One of the things I do is I examine different genres and sub-genres of B movies periodically. I just watch a whole bunch of them and kind of fall in love with them all over again. I do further research on them, get more entrenched with them and then put them away. At the time we came up with *Grindhouse*, I had just done that with slasher films, so I had just watched a whole bunch of them. I knew I wanted to do a slasher film, because that's what I was in love at the time. It seems like a long time ago now.

ROBERT RODRIGUEZ: I know. That was last year.

QUENTIN TARANTINO: So I sit down and try to think of one. I thought of one idea, before *Death Proof*, and I even wrote one scene for it—a speech in the beginning. I actually read it to Edgar Wright and Simon Pegg while they were in town. They got really

ABOVE: Texas Chili Parlor owner, Warren (played by Quentin Tarantino) pours a drink.

into it, but I realized I had nowhere to go with it. It would be a better trailer than anything else. Let me tell you what that story is.

There's this character in black folklore named Jody the Grinder. He was a slave on a plantation and he had the *biggest* dick. He could fuck anybody. He fucked all the girl slaves, fucked the master's wife, fucked the master's daughter, fucked anybody. One day the master comes home and finds Jody the Grinder in his bed fucking his wife and his daughter in the same bed. So they hang Jody the Grinder.

Jody the Grinder goes to Hell, where he meets the Devil and the Devil's got a big dick too.

The Devil says, "Yeah, Jody the Grinder, I've been hearing about you. I've been hearing about how you can fuck anything in the world. Is that true?"

Jody the Grinder answers, "That's why I'm here. Hey Devil, I'll make you a bet. I'll make you a bet that we can wrestle and I'll fuck you. I'll make you bite the pillow, Devil."

So they get to wrestling and when they finish, Jody the Grinder is fucking the Devil in the ass.

Jody the Grinder says, "Okay, you gonna keep me around in Hell? You can't afford to have my ass around. I fucked you in the ass."

The Devil says, "You're right. You've gotta get the fuck up out of here. Here's my curse on you, Jody the Grinder, for fucking me in hell. I'm gonna put you on Earth, and for all of eternity you will walk the Earth fucking white women. That's your lot in life."

That's the famous story of Jody the Grinder.

ROBERT RODRIGUEZ: So Edgar and Simon were into the story, but it's as far as you could go. Then *Death Proof* is born.

QUENTIN TARANTINO: Yeah, so I came back again to the slasher idea. I've had the idea for a death proof car for a while. Not that I ever knew what I was going to do with it. Basically how *Death Proof* came about was that I used to have a Geo Metro. I bought that car after I got some money for *True Romance*. It looked like a little red Coke can and it was about as safe. And I thought, 'Oh I'm going to be fine. I'm indestructible.' Then after I did *Pulp Fiction*, I thought, 'Well maybe I'm destructible now. Maybe God's plan is that he's not going to take me out before I do what I'm supposed to do. And maybe I just *did it* and I shouldn't be fucking around in a Geo Metro anymore.' So I moved over to a Volvo. But before I moved over to the Volvo—and I'm going to name drop here; it's a guest appearance in my story—I was having

a drunken hotel room night with Sean Penn. And he brought up that any car could be a death proof car. You take the car you want to buy, you give it to a stunt team, you pay them ten, fifteen thousand dollars and *voila*...you've got yourself a death proof car. I've never forgotten him saying that. He said it with a lot of panache and there was just something there in that fucking sentence that I've never forgotten. I always wondered how exactly you would do that? Would it be drivable? What would the role bars be like? All that kind of shit.

The thing that makes the slasher film genre work so well is how similar all the films are to each other. I mean, that's actually one of the comforting things about the genre. That's why you can write about it with a very big picture—because so many movies fit.

It's such a specific thing that if you try to fuck up that balance, you might not be fucking it up to a good effect—you're just kind of fucking it up. I just realized, oh man, this is just going to be too reflective. If I try to do it as a real slasher movie, it's just going to be too early 80s reflective, and that's not what I do—even though people accuse me of doing that. That is not what I do; I reinvent. So I've gotta reinvent it, and I've gotta make it just as good a movie as any Quentin movie. It's gotta be my own thing, I've gotta do to this what I did to heist films with *Reservoir Dogs*. I had to figure out a way in. And then I remembered Sean's death proof car.

ROBERT RODRIGUEZ: What made you want to do a movie about stuntpeople? Was it the people that you worked with on *Kill Bill*? Did the Stuntman Mike character come first or did the Zöe character come first?

QUENTIN TARANTINO: That's a really interesting question. Stuntman Mike actually came first. Since *Kill Bill*, I've been involved more with the stunt community. I was involved with that documentary *Double Dare* about Zöe Bell and Jeannie Epper and I met a lot of them. I went to the stunt awards a couple of times and won an award, so I got to meet a lot of different people. A lot of the stunt men who are like a couple of generations older than me—about Kurt's age.

I've seen that guy in a bar—he might not have been a stuntman; he might have been an old character actor or an old rodeo guy. I've seen him walk up to the young girls and act the old flirtatious fool. I've seen them send him on his way. But I've also seen those girls laugh at a couple of his jokes if they were funny. I've seen that dynamic take place. I've seen the dynamic of credits that used to mean something, but don't mean anything anymore as the girls get younger and younger and younger.

That dynamic was an interesting way inside the story.

It just kind of led one thing in front of the other. I wasn't in any hurry about turning up the thriller stakes. I want people to forget it's a thriller until I remind them again. At one point in the movie, when Vanessa's character notices Stuntman Mike's car outside, I put in some Ennio Morricone music from Dario Argento's *The Cat O' Nine Tails*. That's the first time you hear thriller music in the whole fucking movie! That's the reminder that it's that kind of movie.

ROBERT RODRIGUEZ: Was it always going to be Austin?

QUENTIN TARANTINO: I've always wanted to do an Austin movie and I've been going there for ten years, so I can write about it with a sense of history. You know, the character that I play, Warren, started off as a Cliff Antone character, but the Texas Chili Parlor has a real owner—his name is Zoob and Warren

started becoming Zoob. Originally Warren was the only guy working there, and now I've got some waitresses working there.

I realized, being the director, I didn't want to make drinks in the background, I wanted to be watching fucking scenes. So there's a real good bartender there, Tim, and we cast him as the bartender. Now everywhere in the script where Warren makes a drink, Tim makes the drink. Every time it says Warren gives out the drinks, Tim gives out the drinks. That's kind of what the owner of the bar does. When he's on the schedule, he's there drinking, flirting with the girls and sitting at the tables, while everybody else is doing work. Well that's kind of what I did. They were like, "Man, you're really getting to be like Zoob, man."

ROBERT RODRIGUEZ: What was your approach to the style and the look?

QUENTIN TARANTINO: The aesthetic I was really going for was the aesthetic of watching old prints I own. A lot of these prints are little Frankenstein monsters, as far as how they've been compiled over maybe a couple of different prints. So one reel's washed out, another is red, another one is in technicolor, and then a reel change happens—*boom*—and all of a sudden it looks gorgeous. I really got into that aesthetic. Into the idea that it was not us, the filmmakers doing it, trying to create this artistic palate, but that it's an actual print itself that's this quality. Without really even realizing it, our film just ended up going that way because it seemed natural to me. Because we'd always talked about it that way. I hadn't thought about how weird that would be because it just seemed like the way to do it. From having done my film festival in Austin and having screenings with friends, I know an audience will go with it. That look can be its own cinematic experience, if it's pleasurable and if it doesn't take you out of the film.

ROBERT RODRIGUEZ: What would you say the biggest inspiration for a movie like this is? Movies like [Roger Corman's] *Rock All Night*, the slasher movies of the 80s?

QUENTIN TARANTINO: Well, because it has a bar setting, it can't help but be affected by *Rock All Night*. It really is a weird cross between a slasher film and a 70s car chase movie. There is actually a very specific moment where they switch hands and become different movies, but the audience doesn't know it's happening. It really is interesting, even to people just reading the script.

Oddly enough, it has the slasher film structure, even though I don't really follow it. Once I get to the bar, it starts doing other things. It turns into a Eugene O'Neill play. But before that, it was the slasher structure that I was going on. The girls are talking about sex; the girls are just being the girls. They've got a little better dialogue than they normally would and there's always a guy lurking around. Then they get into the bar, and it plays very much like a Rick Linklater movie. I mean, I put a bunch of the Texas Chili Parlor footage together and it really duplicates a night at a bar.

The second group of girls have some of the most rhythmic dialogue in the whole script. The dialogue in the first half isn't quite as rhythmic as most of my dialogue, because you're supposed to be lounging. You're supposed to be just hanging out in that place for a while. When the second group of girls comes in, it's like a routine. Like straight out of a Howard Hawks movie.

I had the idea that you wouldn't know Stuntman Mike's methods for the whole first half. And that would be part of the thing of the first half, figuring out what his deal is, what he's trying to do. And then you realize

it and you realize it in a big way. Everyone's wiped out. Then we start the movie all over again, in another state with a different posse of girls. Now you know what his plan is. We ignore him for a long time, but we always know he's out there and that he's going to come back.

By the time you're in the third act of the third act, you're not watching a horror movie anymore, you're watching a balls-out action movie. And the girls are completely in charge, they're in control and he's running for his life. Now you're in a whole different movie from a slasher movie, but you didn't notice how you got there. All of a sudden, you're in another genre. It crossed over. If you're going to duplicate the experience of watching our movies together, you couldn't just take a zombie movie and a slasher film and say that duplicates our experience. You can't. You would have to throw in *Dirty Mary, Crazy Larry*. You would have to make it a triple feature to truly get the aesthetic value of what our double feature is.

ROBERT RODRIGUEZ: So when you first conceptualized *Death Proof*, were you already thinking about this big car chase? Did that worry you at all back then?

QUENTIN TARANTINO: Yeah, you know, I did think about it. But I got really caught up in writing the script. I knew I was writing a car chase. I was gonna have to do it and it would be hard, but I wasn't censoring myself in any way. Really, I was just trying to get to the end. I wanted to hurry up and write it so I could see how it ended.

ROBERT RODRIGUEZ: So, how did you conceptualize the chase? Did you draw it out or did you come up with a lot of it there?

QUENTIN TARANTINO: Yeah, well, it's funny because it kept growing.

ROBERT RODRIGUEZ: Was it like The Crazy 88 [from *Kill Bill*] scene in that you conceptualized? How did those two compare?

QUENTIN TARANTINO: How would it compare to The Crazy 88? That's a good question. The chase got to be much more organic because you didn't have to teach Uma the routine. On *Kill Bill*, we changed the routine a lot, especially after we got used to it. Uma wasn't expecting us to change it that much, but she got really good at adapting to our changes. That was her own downfall because we just kept doing it.

ROBERT RODRIGUEZ: So this would be more you having an idea and then just executing it.

QUENTIN TARANTINO: Here's the difference though— we'd have a big routine in The Crazy 88, but once we started doing it, I'd get bored with the routine. So we'd try to figure out how to reduce it down into three or four moves. We'd figure we could teach Uma, and we'd bring it down there and we'd teach her and we'd do it. With this film, we didn't have quite that flexibility to just completely change things the day of the shoot—although even though we did a couple of times. The chase itself just kept evolving. If you read most scripts, they'll say, "They chase" or "They get into an exciting chase." Maybe something a bit little more detailed with plot-oriented shit in it, but still pretty loose. Well my chase wasn't that loose. I wrote a lot of shit.

ROBERT RODRIGUEZ: I didn't see the re-writes. Did you write a lot of the shots in there?

QUENTIN TARANTINO: Not so much shots, but just, 'they do this and they do that and they do this.' It wasn't very laid out, and it was the last 20 pages of the script. But you really can't start putting your chase together until you've picked the location, because that's gonna dictate tons of things too. Is what I wrote more important or is it more important what we've come up with at the location? So, once I found the place, I started doing a little re-writing. We moved all the way to California from Texas. Once I had set up the locations, I did a big re-write with a lot more gags and really opened it up. I made it much bigger. Once we started doing it, I started writing and re-writing just in the way I was shooting. Some things suddenly seemed a lot less important. I'd watch the dailies of this really cool turn across a four lane highway—that I shot with four different cameras—and realize I could turn one turn into three other turns in the movie, depending on the camera angles. I started realizing that's what those fucking guys have done. That's how they were able to do all this shit. They just used a different camera angle for the same gag and made it into a different gag. That's the one thing no one could tell me—the tricks that they used to do. All of sudden I knew why they keep passing by the same fucking VW Bug in *Bullitt* six times! They filmed it six different ways and they used all six of them and the fucking bug is always in the shot no matter where they are!

It was not something you'd ever think to ask. I'd never talked to a director about how to do a chase scene.

I wanted to come fresh. I didn't want anyone to be talking down to me, telling me how to do it. Although, if I could have had dinner with Peter Yates and we could've gotten into a conversation about *Bullitt*, that would have been another thing.

ROBERT RODRIGUEZ: And that was cool that you didn't shy away from it. You knew what you had to do. I don't know if I'd be able to do that, because I know, one, I'm probably gonna get in an accident, somebody's gonna get hurt. You can't really do it like

The Road Warrior anymore. The world's changed. I would opt to do something with a trick, but you do everything for real. I wouldn't have had the stomach for it. I'd want to slow down a little bit, just under-crank the camera. But you're out there doing it for real. That was exciting to me. As long as you didn't get hurt, you've accomplished what I want to see as an audience member. You had the balls to go all the way with it.

QUENTIN TARANTINO: That was my thing. No second unit. No CGI except to erase a wire or cable or two. No under-cranking. It was really interesting to actually watch a bunch of different chases from a lot of action cinema. When I look at a whole bunch of different examples, especially now that I know how to make movies, I know how they did it. Every time I'd have to re-write a scene, I had to shoot it in order the way I was going to edit it. I could never just…

ROBERT RODRIGUEZ: Go back and do that little part…

QUENTIN TARANTINO: Yeah, exactly. I always had to do it cut for cut for cut or I'd get confused.

ROBERT RODRIGUEZ: So did you shoot it that way? Pretty much in order?

QUENTIN TARANTINO: Yeah. We kind of had to. Because the cars kept getting so fucked up. We had to shoot it in order and any time we tried to jump ahead, we had to go back and shoot that shit again because the cars never fucking matched.

ROBERT RODRIGUEZ: Right. Right.

QUENTIN TARANTINO: We only did that once and then we learned the error of our ways.

ROBERT RODRIGUEZ: From now on, in script order.

QUENTIN TARANTINO: That's how I like to do it. In case things happen, it's a legitimate scene. It's not that they're just protruding pieces that will go together when I put them together—it's still a scene. It's still growing; shit can happen. So maybe Buddy Joe overturns the car—maybe that's a mistake and maybe that's a cool re-write!

ROBERT RODRIGUEZ: I didn't realize you had [stuntmen] Buddy Joe Hooker and Terry Leonard. How was that?

QUENTIN TARANTINO: Yeah, Terry Leonard actually did a couple of background car stunts, but he did one *big* stunt. One extremely cool stunt. And he crashed. It was cool though, because the shot had Tracy Dashnaw behind the wheel with Zöe on the hood, Buddy Joe Hooker in the other car, and Terry Leonard in this pick up truck driving right at him. Buddy Joe Hooker is

ABOVE: Quentin Tarantino directs Vanessa Ferlito (L) and Omar Doom (R) inside the Texas Chili Parlor.

parallel with Zöe on the hood and Terry Leonard's car comes in his lane in the other direction and he has to swerve, fall back, as Terry's car goes through. And Terry Leonard rolled the car. He rolled it. It was the pick up truck, and he rolled it three times. You see it in the background, and it's rolling, and you think, 'What the fuck!? That guy crashed.' We didn't know he was gonna crash.

Terry was thinking, 'Well, you shouldn't have given me a crash strap in there or I wouldn't have used it. I figured you wanted me to crash it so I just crashed it. You didn't want to say "Crash it," but I could see it in your eyes. You wanted me to crash it, so I just crashed it.'

ROBERT RODRIGUEZ: What was it like working with Buddy Joe?

QUENTIN TARANTINO: Oh, it was a blast, man. It was so much fun. He's such a funny, fun guy, and I knew all the movies he had worked on. He was just right there, man. And it was just me, him, Dashnaw, and then Tracy driving. It was just us out there, just us out there *doing* it.

It's fun watching these old exploitation movies and seeing some of the stuff that they pulled off. Some

of them weren't exploitation movies but they played in the grindhouses, like the Charles Bronson movies. *Mr. Majestic* has that big truck chase in it that's really cool. All these different chase movies—they just fucking *did* it. They just went out and did it, but no one does it that way anymore.

ROBERT RODRIGUEZ: What way?

QUENTIN TARANTINO: You just go out and shoot the stunts you want to get. You're not going to edit the crap out of it—turn it into little guitar picks in the editing room. No, you're killing yourself to get that shot when the car does it all in that *one* shot.

We never took the fact that people's lives were on the line for granted. But at the same time, that's what they do for a living.

ROBERT RODRIGUEZ: They're stunt people.

QUENTIN TARANTINO: If I open an air circus, somebody's gonna have to fly.

ROBERT RODRIGUEZ: I remember early on you said that you were gonna shoot some of the car chase stuff early, so that if Zöe hurts herself, she has time to heal up. I thought that was strange. That's what she does—

she's a stuntwoman. So you have to think about that.

QUENTIN TARANTINO: Yeah exactly. She's a stuntperson. It's not like they wanted me to come up with pussy stunts for them. They want to come up with big stunts, so they could pull them off.

It really was about pulling it off in my grandiose way. I just kept wondering if I could pull it off. If I could, it would be exciting. I'd have something at the end of it. I wanted it to be one of the best stunts. But the fact that I've got one of the people who is dearest to me on the planet Earth on the hood made it also a really tangible thing at the same time. We were never really worried, but the day we got Zöe off the hood was a really great day.

ROBERT RODRIGUEZ: What also got me excited about *Kill Bill* was the scene in The House of Blue Leaves. That's your take on a kung fu movie, and this is your take on a slasher movie and a car chase. You've seen a lot of that stuff, but you hadn't ever done it before, so you were gonna end up taking a whole different approach to every shot, and when you shot it you didn't have any second unit.

QUENTIN TARANTINO: No, not at all. Not one iota. I really love the idea of getting an opportunity to do these great set pieces of cinema that I grew up watching.

ROBERT RODRIGUEZ: You mean per project?

QUENTIN TARANTINO: Yeah, per project. Whether it was the big martial arts fight scene or the Samurai scene I grew up watching or whatever it is, I'm always throwing my hat in the ring—this time trying to make one of the greatest chases ever. You can be a great piano player, but if you can't play Beethoven, you can't call yourself *the man*. If you can play the piano solo in "Layla" and make everyone in the room cry, you ain't the man. You can play the piano, but you ain't *the man*. You do a great chase and you're the fucking man, alright? Until you've done it, well you ain't the man.

It really hit me how none of the chases I've seen—and I've seen a couple of good chases in the last six years—haven't resonated the way a chase scene used to. Remember when you heard a movie had a great chase scene, and you went to the theatres to see it. You watched it and your heart was in your throat. You'd hear that *Colors* had a great chase scene through Watts and *Basic Instinct* had a really cool chase scene. I went to see it for the chase scene, not to see Sharon Stone's cooch. I actually think the ease of video editing has kind of fucked up chase scenes. Everyone does twelve or fifteen or at least

eight cameras on every fucking crash and tries to milk every last little bitty angle for as much as they can get out of it. That has actually taken the drama, the piss, the fucking blood out of it.

When you're doing an action scene, you write all these inserts you want to get, but you keep on moving them down the list, thinking, "Fuck that." As time went on, I had a couple of inserts that I'd shot, but I decided I just wasn't gonna use fucking inserts in it. I didn't want to cut to the brake, cut to the gas or a cut to the speedometer to get me out of trouble. Even if I have five cameras there, I don't want to use all five angles. If he fucking does the jump and does what I want him to do in one take, that's the take I want. I do that in acting too. I'll cover a scene from all these angles and if the golden moment is the big wide-shot and they're just terrific in there, then you stay in the wide-shot. So the metamorphosis has been interesting. But the weird thing about it was, I have never been more nervous about doing anything in a movie as I was about the chase.

ROBERT RODRIGUEZ: I remember that you thought it would probably take a couple of weeks just to figure out what you were doing, and then after that, you'd be going. And now you're done. It's in the can. You've got a couple war stories, and you've figured it all out, and it's just a great fucking thing. That's putting your life on the line for the fans.

QUENTIN TARANTINO: You know, it's nerve-racking to do a whole movie, knowing that you have this chase waiting for you at the end. This thing that you have this trepidation about. But I also know that there lies my best work. The shit that I'm the most nervous about is the shit that's gonna be the best. There's a reason why I'm nervous about it because I can *fail* at this. My whole thing is, if I don't make one of the best chases, if the chase is just, you know, "It was exciting, it was fun." Then I failed and I'm blaming myself. But if I pull it off, then I've got to come up with something else to test that ceiling.

It's funny because, for some reason, this was really scary going into it. But now the weird thing is that the crew has worked so hard and we've got it, we've got the chase. And every crew member's editing it in their head. Now I've got a new trepidation—now I've got to edit it as good as I know it can be in the short amount of time that I have. Now I know we can do it, we totally have enough time to do it. But now I'm not just editing it for me anymore, I'm editing it for the crew that shot the chase because they're all editing it in their minds and they've got a pretty great chase in their heads. I don't want them sitting in the theater thinking, "Oh man, we killed ourselves for *this*?"

A WHITE-HOT JUGGERNAUT AT 200 MILES PER HOUR!

QUENTIN TARANTINO'S
"DEATH PROOF"

ROSARIO **DAWSON** • ZÖE **BELL** • ROSE **McGOWAN**

A RODRIGUEZ INTERNATIONAL PICTURE • A DIMENSION FILMS RELEASE

GRAPHIC VIOLENCE

THE PRODUCTION DESIGN OF DEATH PROOF

CAYLAH EDDLEBLUTE, Production Designer: Quentin arrived in Austin with a diagram he'd drawn of Jungle Julia's apartment, based on his blocking of the scene. He'd thought about it to the last detail. The scene, as originally written, was far more extensive than what we ended up shooting. Originally, Julia's posse was going to arrive at her apartment and hang out. In the scene, Julia was going to dance on her coffee table, sandwiched between two pieces of art that hung on her living room walls. The first piece of art was to be a huge print of Brigitte Bardot that I believe was taken on the set of Godard's *Contempt*. Quentin handed us a well-worn, rolled up, creased, black and white photo for us to blow up. For the opposite wall, Quentin brought us the cover art to Buffy Saint-Marie's theme song from *Soldier Blue*. It was the paper sleeve for the 45. That, for the uninitiated, is a single on vinyl. A small record with a single song pressed on it. That artwork was about 8" x 8".

Quentin wanted this art to be huge. From these two small, poor quality images we were given the task of wowing Julia's living room with wall-sized art, with source material basically the size of postage stamps.

Erika Jeanne and Steve [Joyner] did extensive Photoshop work. After several attempts, including painting the image, Steve ended up pulling the image of Candice Bergen from a much larger *Soldier Blue* poster that he acquired. *Soldier Blue* became 5' x 5'. The Bardot piece was 7' across. No small feat.

Steve and I have several large Epson printers—a 7600 and a 9800—so we can print poster-size work. We printed our own sample strips for scale and color control, then sent the files to Austin Photo Imaging for the final product to be printed on a single canvas.

Everything in Jungle Julia's apartment was determined

ABOVE: Jungle Julia (played by Sydney Poitier) reclines beneath an over-sized print of Bridgette Bardot; **OPPOSITE (FROM TOP):** Original sketch by Quentin Tarantino outlining the layout of Jungle Julia's apartment. • A sampling of colored rocks and fabric swatches that established the palette of Julia's apartment. • The painted miniature model of Julia's apartment. • The final, interior set of Julia's apartment.

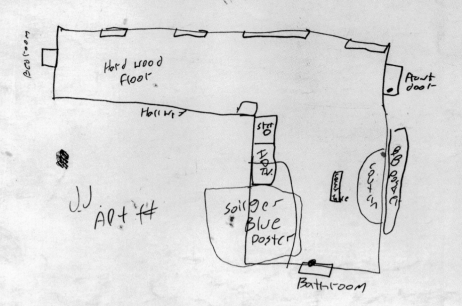

by these two pieces of art—the colors, the length of the living room wall, the size of the couch. So we had to get these two anchor pieces worked out first.

All the sets in *Death Proof* were based on Quentin's love of graphics. He selected art for each set. He'd thought carefully about each choice too. You could tell by the way he talked about the blocking of each scene. As we go through the various sets you'll see this theme as the foundation for the production design.

Quentin's diagram was exact: artwork here, couch there. Widescreen TV here, three albums in frames hanging on the wall there, windows here, a wood floor to get the shot of Julia's bare feet plopping down the long hallway. We carefully considered the floor color and value to accent Julia's feet. Not too light. Not too dark. Just right. Tommy Karl worked with several stain samples to refine the final mix—warm and rich. We didn't want drafty, old-house floors—too cold, walnut, or dark.

On shooting day, the scene was drastically cut. The dance sequence was out, Quentin had wanted Jungle Julia to dance while holding the soundtrack LP jacket from *Candy O*, but he was still able to re-block and move *Soldier Blue* into frame, creating a comical, signature shot. The camera is looking past her feet to the poster in the background.

We had some specific ideas about the interior of Jungle Julia's apartment, based on my old partying and scenester days. I used to write for a music magazine when I lived in Tucson, Arizona, so every night I was out, photographing or interviewing some band, living that scene and the usual partying that followed. Julia was clearly a chick who rocks. Nothing about her was contained. Like her feet, she's all over the place. A splayed out personality. Erika Jeanne, our Production Assistant, who is really so much more, mentioned she knew a few women around Austin not unlike Jungle Julia. She took a camera and went to their houses and apartments. She came back with perfect reference—wood floors, exact light through the windows. I call it "stoner light." Records stacked on the floor just as Quentin had requested.

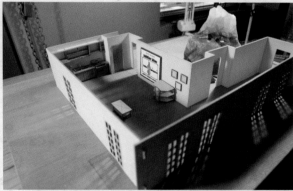

Because of the prominence of the artwork, the interior paint selection was a little tricky. On one wall was the large, graphic, strong black and white image from *Soldier Blue*. On the other side was Bardot, a photograph, with lots of grays and medium values. We intentionally added a blue/green tint to Bardot, so the image isn't pure black, white and grays. It made the image far richer, gave some color to the environment, and provided an anchor to give the room warmth.

Looking at color swatches doesn't always work for me. I have to sleep on color, see it in my mind. After about two weeks, I finally got up the courage to paint the model of Jungle Julia's apartment that Leslie Milligan had beautifully cut out, complete with doors, shelves, stove, artwork, couch and record frames on the walls.

I wanted the room warm and rich, not cold. JJ didn't have a cold personality. Nothing about her was frail or precise. She was hot. I had some Frank Frazetta prints on the reference board, and, of all of those, one in particular, "Primitive Beauty," was Jungle Julia to me. This was long before I ever even saw a photo of Sydney. Frazetta's colors, the greens, tawny browns, purples—you couldn't have better inspiration.

The colors had to compliment her skin, show its richness. The orange-yellow Bardot wall is several shades darker than all the others, an accent. The Bardot is so strong an image, the wall had to act as a frame. It had to be equally rich to balance out the room.

With the model, I placed several found objects and a few fabric swatches to represent the color palate. I referenced colors from a small rock collection that I have to represent accent pieces, window treatments, furniture, tone. Several beads of different colors gave Jeff, Marcus and Kit the jumping off point for the cool lamp they built.

Quentin wanted us to create a time capsule in every scene possible. In JJ's he wanted the Austin Chronicle—

the weekly alternative rag—on the coffee table and that month's calendar from the Alamo Drafthouse on the fridge. The Alamo is a theatre in Austin where you can order dinner while you watch a movie. Quentin wanted a moment preserved in time. So we did this in the details, without dating the movie's overall look.

Jungle Julia's apartment was on a second story. That's how Quentin wanted it blocked. In the shot, the camera comes up from behind Julia and travels past her, through the window and looks with her point of view to the street below.

Since the set was built on stage, we had to come up with a way to shoot the scene where she looks out the

ABOVE: A special rig built for Jungle Julia's apartment allows the camera to exit a second story window; **BELOW:** An "Austin Hot Wax 505" billboard high above Jo's Hot Coffee on South Congress Avenue; **OPPOSITE:** The girls exit the real Guero's Taco Bar on South Congress Avenue.

window and sees her friends below. So we had to find a location with a scenic street, a sidewalk, enough of an expanse to build a platform, with no guy wires, electrical lines or other overhead obstructions so the crane could move and have the forty to sixty feet it needed to travel. There was nothing simple about this shot. It wasn't, "Let's just go down the street and shoot someplace." Not many Austin streets even have sidewalks.

Steve Joyner, John McLeod and Joe McCusker worked out a beautiful set of windows that operated on a pulley system and disappeared as the camera moved—an elegant installation. Our pre-rig grip team of Pete Stockton and Phil Renke and all the grip brothers kicked ass. The crew got the shot quickly and that's always is a sign of success for us. I have to say

for Jungle Julia in her *Kill Bill* costume.

We pulled other cool reference like Wolfman Jack, Rodney on the ROQ from way back, Suicide Girls, photos of the Texas Rollergirls [one of Austin's all-female rollerderby teams], all of whom Quentin knows.

Alex Toader, one of our Troublemaker Digital artists, did a few renderings of billboards for us. One of which was Jungle Julia leaning back, surrounded by stacks of records with her feet up, sticking out beyond the border of the billboard. A cutout. Quentin loved it, since the first part of *Death Proof* is about her feet.

Quentin brought a couple of his friends on board, Dave Evans and Michi Ukawa, for some final concept

I'm glad Stevie J. is an engineer.

Julia works as a DJ at a local radio station. Her spin time is called Austin Hot Wax 505. She's part of the Austin scene, getting her own record label off the ground between slamming shots at all the local hot spots. And she's wired into South by Southwest, the big music festival and party that fires Austin up every spring.

When designing the billboards for her radio show, we pulled reference early on. Some of the first homages that came to mind were the *American Graffiti* poster—I sketched out Julia holding a record player like a platter. Angelyne is another one—anyone who knows Southern California knows this reference. Also, the Black Velvet billboard—Quentin used this pose

art. Michi did some fun stuff for us on *Kill Bill*, making all the graphics for the Japambulances. She rendered out the final billboard art.

Production scheduled a day for a photo shoot of Sydney in all her costume changes for the billboards. With [Costume Designer] Nina Proctor's costumes, including an homage to Raquel Welch in *Rollerball*, the stage was set. Quentin had a lot of fun. Our gaffer, John Sandau got great shots we could work with easily, but Sydney made it all work!

In all, we installed six Jungle Julia billboards around Austin. Bacardi jumped in and helped us out by lending us their billboard space for the time we needed it. Two were on a tri-fold, downtown where the action is, just blocks from the Capital. One was for a Red

Apple Cigarettes—a Tarantino staple—one for 303 Hot Wax and one for Shiner Bock, a beer that's a local favorite. The billboards stayed up around Austin for a month. Quentin wanted the girls to feel like they really lived in the environment we'd created. The rest of us did too. Everywhere you went in town, there was a billboard of Jungle Julia.

We were able to install four billboards for the first day of shooting, a real eyeball bleeder, considering the photos and artwork were approved just a few days earlier. Kevin Jackson at Reagan Outdoor busted his ass, working to get us spaces already being used by clients. Darin Wilson from National Print Group received our artwork, got proofs back pronto, printed the billboards in Tennessee with a great crew there, shipped them back to Austin, and Kevin's crew was installing at 8:00 on Sunday morning. Our first day of filming was on Monday—less than 24 hours away.

Without all these people from across several states who made the production timeline work for this large scale industrial art, we wouldn't have been worth shit. They were up to the task!

A popular Austin hot spot and hangout is Guero's Mexican Restaurant on South Congress. Ground Zero for a margarita or a few dozen, it's a tourist destination as well. QT wanted to use real Austin flavor and all that implies, so we shot our exteriors at the actual location. But we built the interior on stage so we could have control over the environment. Guero's is so popular and it's open all hours, so it would have been tough to shoot at the real place. The owners and staff there were top notch at helping us out, providing food and dishware to the prop department, everything to make the scene real.

Quentin also wanted to change the space for blocking reasons and make the area wide enough to get all the shots he wanted. Set designer Jeff Adams came up with great details for "wild walls" and visual interest. Quentin wanted the chairs a certain size, the table a certain way. He also wanted the interior to pop more. At one point he made a joke about wanting to shame Guero's into redecorating.

Our interior set had an unusual evolution. One of our painters, Tim Dingel, brought one of his art books for reference to work one day. It was Robert Polidori's "Havana." It was a jaw dropper. Page after page of color photos of Havana crumbling. Beautiful buildings, rich with concrete paint textures, beautiful hues. I got to take a look at it for a few minutes back in the scenic shop. Immediately, Steve and I ordered a copy for ourselves and one for Robert as well because he loves to paint and to study different mediums.

It picked a page of especially cool

OPPOSITE (FROM TOP): The painted wall of Quentin Tarantino's office inside Troublemaker Studios provides the inspiration for the interior Guero's set. • Model of the interior Guero's set. • An early stage of the Guero's interior set inside Austin Studios. Note the model of Guero's exterior in the left foreground and the model of the Guero's interior in the right foreground; **ABOVE:** Jungle Julia (played by Sydney Poitier) enjoys some after-dinner margaritas at Guero's.

office to match. Quentin liked his office so much it that it became the inspiration for the interior set of Guero's, with its strong, orange-striped accent wall acting as our "hero" wall behind Julia. Our scenic department with Tommy Karl and his kit of cool techniques hit this one out of the park.

Once again, the set design and blocking were carefully laid out based on Quentin's selection of art. He brought with him to Austin stacks of 70s posters from his personal collection. He especially chose those with two or three strong colors and strong brushstokes, posters with a sketchlike, rugged quality. He brought a few lobby cards too. But he really hit the jackpot when he took a walk down Congress one weekend and stopped by Tesoro's, a shop just blocks from the Capitol. Quentin cleaned them out. They had a treasure trove of old Mexican movie lobby cards. Wow. What a find.

He put posters and lobby cards up in his office and keyed on how the colors melded with the wall paint. He wanted that effect in Guero's.

This presented a challenge for us, however. There was no way we were going to use his original posters as dressing, even though he wanted us to. Many were paper thin, nearly tissue, and when the "worm"—those giant yellow hoses they use for air

conditioning—arrived on set, we knew they'd be ripped to shreds.

Steve rigged up a copy stand system in our office and photographed every single poster and every lobby card from Quentin's collection. It would have cost stupid money to send a job like that out. So he and Ellen Lampl—who does great graphics for us when we need help—finessed all the artwork. Since we have our own large format printers, we printed all the images. Erika Jeanne did a great job aging all the artwork. Quentin is very particular, but the reproductions passed his quality test. We were relieved. And he got all his stuff back safe and sound—also a big part of our job. If I recall correctly, we only ended up using two of Quentin's original posters inside Guero's.

Around this time, Robert had just put on an art show in San Antonio called "Solamente Salma." The show had ended, so these large paintings from the show were waiting for an opportunity to be used. And we had an area, outside Guero's doorway that needed a wild wall. I wanted two of his paintings to be the wall piece. The strong vibrant images, bursting with color and their large scale would suit the set perfectly with its high brick and plaster walls. They would provide a cool, watercolor wash effect out of focus in the background.

I lived in Tucson many years and had the image in my mind of light shining through saguaro ribs, on the sides of the painting. But since we were in Austin, we used cedar tree limbs, which gave it a great rustic effect.

The floor brickwork on set also turned out beautifully thanks to Ron Perkins, a true mason. The traffic pattern of the restaurant had to flow like the real thing. You have to think about all those things. How will the tables fit? How will the traffic work, how will extras pass, how will you get good foreground and background action for a scene that long? Waitresses, bus people, hostesses, diners. You have to make it flow for the action.

We scouted a number of locations—some funky, some skanky and some downright backwater eddies—for the bar sequence. But our first stop was Austin's Texas Chili Parlor. The Chili Parlor is a favorite hangout of Quentin's, and the more we scouted other locations, the more he zeroed in on this rustic, down-home, fun hangout, which is very much in keeping with his sense of a good time. He knew the Texas Rollergirls that worked there as waitresses, and because he has partied there and spent afternoons writing there, he could imagine the growing circle of people around

Jungle Julia's table and the people layering up to party around her. He felt comfortable there. He knew his characters would as well.

We had several meetings at the Chili Parlor, just sitting around a few of the tables, while Quentin worked out the blocking. There was considerable talk of building the set on stage, but Quentin loves the feel of a real environment. The way the bar smells, walking out onto an Austin street—he's very much about every authentic detail.

So our locations crew, Steve White and Jimmy Schwertner, had their work cut out for them. Shooting in a bar is always tough. Local patrons, daily business. Plus we were shooting during football season. Football is big, but it's *giant* in Texas. It was in the shooting schedule—we had to be out by the Ohio State Game. You never know what stipulations you'll run into when sorting out a location.

There were three parts to the Chili Parlor. First, we would shoot the interiors at the actual restaurant. Then we had to pick a location for the exterior shots, where we could build the back porch and park cars in the parking lot as well as put up the Jungle Julia billboard. Quentin chose the parking lot of a popular

ABOVE: Julia and her entourage enjoy a few cold ones at the Texas Chili Parlor; **OPPOSITE (FROM TOP):** The back porch of the Texas Chili Parlor on a soundstage inside Troublemaker Studios. • Exterior of the real Texas Chili Parlor on Lavaca Street in Austin, Texas. • Warren's famous jukebox, a 1962 AMi Continental 2 appropriately named "AMi" (pronounced *Amy*). See the upcoming spread for AMi's complete track listing.

Austin breakfast joint, the Omelettry. So we set about constructing a back porch set for this location.

Quentin decided he also wanted to build the exterior parking lot and Chili Parlor porch on our soundstage to match the Omelettry. This was so he could better control the long dialogue portions of the scene. Then we could shoot at The Omelettry location for just a night or two for the car shots.

It was a good idea. A lot happens on the porch, intimate stuff between the characters, so the crew ended up shooting on stage for several nights.

We built the porch set on stage, complete with a gravel parking lot and fence, dumpsters and a billboard. This set was scaled up for action and blocking and for people, while the Omelettry set was scaled down due to the constraints of the site. We had to fit all the cars in the parking lot and have enough room for Stuntman Mike to peel out in the *Death Proof* Nova with Pam. Joe McCusker and his construction crew were super nimble.

This meant John McLeod had to set up rain towers on stage as well as at the Omelettry exterior and the Texas Chili Parlor. The on-stage rig naturally presented its own set of opportunities for creative thinking. John, Steve Joyner and Joe McCusker worked out a drainage system and cut out two holes in the concrete floor of the warehouse to install pumps. Joe McCusker's crew built a dam around the entire set to control the water flow and channel it outside. Quite a project. This was a labor-intensive set—keeping the greens fresh daily and dehumidfying the stage after the crew finished shooting each night so they wouldn't return to a stinking swamp. We had to keep the air crisp and the set dry. And mosquito free.

Quentin arrived for the first night of shooting on stage. They had been shooting at the Chili Parlor a couple of weeks by then. It was time for a change of scenery. He walked through the door and said, "This is like the snow garden in the House of Blue Leaves" [from *Kill Bill*]. What a shocking compliment. It makes me a little weepy even now. Yohei Taneda's design for that set in *Kill Bill* remains one of our inspiration keystones.

It really did feel like a theatrical set, which we loved. We even hauled out some of the old walls from Club Kadie's in *Sin City* to give the feel of an alley in the background.

The Chili Parlor has great tables, chairs and set dressing, like the old Shiner Beer sign—stuff Quentin loved. Authentic stuff. Nothing pretentious. They lent us their set dressing to use on stage as well. We also hung Kurt Russell's shirt from *Big Trouble in Little China* on one wall. Stevie J. has it in his collection, a gift from a crew member a few years ago. We put our

Red Apples graphic in the cigarette machine and we were set.

Front and center, a character all her own was AMi [pronounced "Amy"], Quentin's own jukebox. AMi *was* the Chili Parlor. She was trucked to Austin in her very own rig. Along with AMi was her original instruction manual as well as the phone number to her tech in LA, Brad Frank, who helped us out of a couple of tight spots over the phone. The list of songs was handwritten by Quentin. She worked beautifully.

Quentin was fired up about the sequence at the Big A convenience store. His plan to pop from black and

Sometimes you're so busy thinking about all the individual elements of a set, that you get a great surprise of actually taking in the whole picture for the five minutes before the hive of the shooting crew descends. The Big A was like that for us.

The original Big A is from Richard Linklater's *Suburbia*. Quentin wanted that store, that artwork, that logo. A scout revealed that the original location used in *Suburbia* had shut down just a couple of months earlier, so we had to find a mini-mart that was willing to let us come in and completely change their store. Obviously, a big chain was out. The American Food Mart graciously opened their doors and let us wreak havoc.

AMI'S COMPLETE PLAYLIST

ISAAC HAYES............Theme from Shaft / Ellie's Love Theme	MICHAEL ZAGER BAND............Let's All Chant / Love Express
BARRY WHITE.....You're the First, the Last, My Everything / Can't Get Enough	SANTA ESMERALDA.......Don't Let Me Be Misunderstood / You're My Everything
BOB DYLAN..........George Jackson (Acoustic) / George Jackson (Big Band)	JIGSAW............Sky High / Brand New Love Affair
STEVIE WONDER............Lately / If it's Magic	GEORGE BAKER SELECTION...........Little Green Bag / Pretty Little Dreamer
THE CHI-LIGHTS............Have You Seen Her / Oh Girl	THE SWEET............Blockbuster / Need a Lot of Lovin
THE T.H.P ORCHESTRA............Theme from S.W.A.T, Pt 1 / Oh Girl	EDDIE FLOYD............Good Love, Bad Love / Things Get Better
STEVIE WONDER............I Ain't Gonna Stand For It / Knocks Me Off My Feet	JOE TEX............The Love You Save / If Sugar Was As Sweet As You
BLOODSTONE............Natural High / This Thing is Heavy	BOB DYLAN.....Gotta Serve Somebody (long version) / Gotta Serve Somebody (short version)
DON MCLEAN............American Pie Pt 1 / American Pie Pt 2	DICK DALE............Miserlou / Eight Till Midnight
THE SWEET............Little Willy / Man From Mecca	LEE WILLIAMS............They Told a Lie / I'm Tore Up
THE ISLEY BROTHERS.......Take Me to the Next Phase Pt 1 / Take Me to the Next Phase Pt 2	WILLIAM BELL............Formula of Love / You Don't Miss Your Water
THE MIRACLES............Love Machine Pt 1 / Love Machine Pt 2	DINAH WASHINGTON............Mad About the Boy / Stormy Weather
BOB DYLAN............Subterranean Homesick Blues / She Belongs to Me	THE BOX TOPS............Cry Like a Baby / The Door You Closed To Me
HONEY CONE............Stick Up / V.I.P.	THE CHECKMATES, LTD............Black Pearl / Lazy Susan
EARTH, WIND & FIRE............Shining Star / Yearning, Learning	THE SWEET............Fox on the Run / Miss Demeanor
AMII STEWART............Knock on Wood / When You Are Beautiful	THE DELFONICS.......Didn't I (Blow Your Mind This Time) / La-La Means I Love You
HONEY CONE............Wan & Ed's / We Belong Together	BROTHERS JOHNSON............Get the Funk Outta Ma Face / Tomorrow
KOOL AND THE GANG............Hollywood Swinging / Jungle Boogie	BOB DYLAN............Hurricane Pt 1 / Hurricane Pt 2
BOB DYLAN............Band of the Hand / Theme From Joe's Death	ABBA............Waterloo / Watch Out
THE SWEET............Wig-Wam-Bam / New York Connection	T. REX............Jeepster / Life's A Gas
THE FRIENDS OF DISTINCTION......Grazing in the Grass / I Really Hope You Do	MELANIE.......What Have They Done To My Song Ma? / Ruby Tuesday
MARVIN GAYE............Trouble Man / Don't Mess with Mr. T	COMMANDER CODY............Hot Rod Lincoln / Beat Me Daddy Eight to the Bar
BOB DYLAN.....Stuck Inside of Mobile with the Memphis Blues Again / Rita May	ROBERT MITCHUM............Thunder Road / The Tip of My Fingers
PACIFIC GAS AND ELECTRIC............Are you Ready? / Staggolee	DEAN MARTIN............Rio Bravo / My Rifle My Pony and Me
DONNA SUMMER............Love to Love You Baby / Need-A-Man Blues	DAVE DEE, DOZY, BEAKY, MICK & TICH.......Hold Tight! / You Know What I Want

white to a profusion of color at this Tennessee minimart was carefully planned early on. He was acutely aware of what he wanted on the shelves. Rows of repeating shapes, bright bottles—Sunny Delight, Go Juice [which also appeared in *Kill Bill*].

Quentin's love of neon colors came into play here. We worked hard to have color, but tried to avoid "over art direction" which Quentin has a keen eye to spot. Keeping that austere quality at the Big A made it a lot of fun to noodle out.

The yellow Mustang parked front and center next to Big Red soda gave the scene a real pop. Big Red was a specific request from Quentin based on a vending machine he spotted at Cartwright's Barbeque in Bastrop during one of our location scouts. His eagle eye saw that thing before the front door had swung shut behind us and we'd taken our first whiff of brisket.

For us, this set was all about graphics, all of which we produced in house. We have two Roland vinyl cutters so we were able to prints sheets of graphics and

OPPOSITE (FROM TOP): Abernathy (played by Rosario Dawson) picks up the latest copy of Allure featuring Lee (played by Mary Elizabeth Winstead). • The yellow Mustang parked outside the Big A. • The Old Chattanooga truck.

labels on adhesive papers of various stocks, and then run them through the vinyl cutters for perfects cutouts. We made all the Chattanooga beer labels this way for the bottles and cases alike.

[Graphic Designer] Michi Ukawa and Steve Joyner worked out a fun logo for the beer truck we had in the parking lot, Chattanooga Lager. I heard that on shooting day one of the crew noticed that the beer truck sure had been sitting in the parking lot a long time. We were glad the logo looked so real.

A scout of this location also revealed a perfect billboard opportunity. The script's reference to filmmaker Jessie Letterman inspired Dave and Michi to create a billboard for *Potheads 2*. They came up with the artwork and I think the crew got a kick out of it.

When we arrived in Buelleton for the second half of the *Death Proof* shoot, we knew we had a few things to build, but the show didn't seem extensive for us. That changed quickly.

Quentin added a drive-in movie marquee. I'm sure glad he did too, because it turned out to be great fun to make at the end of a long shoot. In the midst of grading roads and building car ramps—endeavors that require considerable thought and time—the marquee was creative and lighthearted. After all, no

one ever says, "Hey wow, look at that cool pile of dirt!"

Quentin drew a sketch of what he was thinking. The "Starlight". Steve and I were thrilled because that was the name we wanted as well. He also referenced the Burnet Road Storage sign in Austin, which happens to be the old Burnet Road Drive-In that's referenced on the *Death Proof* poster. So that was a great starting point.

We didn't have a lot of time and the whole installation had to be built as a breakaway. I thought about it for several days. The marquee was two sided to get all the shots. The structure had to accommodate all lettering and design regardless of side. Pretty tricky. We divided the structure into three sections which made it more likely to stay in one piece and easier to construct.

One thing I've learned over the years—it isn't just about how cool something looks. It also has to be well engineered. Thought out through all steps— construction, assembly, transport, support tools, reset time.

It was a daylight shot, but we wanted the marquee

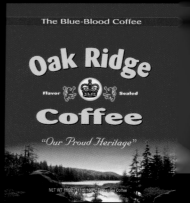

to read with all the magic of night. That included neon, of course. Jeff Poss made a jig, then heated and shaped acrylic tube into cool rope forms per the specs. A little spray paint and the acrylic looked like glowing neon. We were lucky that Laurel and Beth, whom David Wasco had hired as scenics on *Kill Bill*, were available to work with us on this portion of *Death Proof*.

Quentin wanted debris to fly all over place when the car hit it. So we designed the marquee like a sandwich. Between the readerboards, we installed aluminum shelves that Davy Pahoa in effects built. Then we loaded the shelves with shards of colored acrylic, so the guts of the marquee held all this extra material that would fly out on impact.

For the titleboard, we didn't have much time, so hand-

might've thought the marquee was a little small when he first saw it. But in the end it worked out because he was able have the Charger approaching and the marquee in the same shot.

Quentin also picked the movies—*Scary Movie 4* and *Wolf Creek*. Both were movies from the same company, one a first run, one a second run. The first thing he did when he arrived on set was walk up to the marquee, pull off the B and the P for Bill Pullman and reverse the letters. The sign reads Pill Bullman. He had the biggest grin on his face when he did it too. That is the total imp in Quentin, the complete kid.

Buddy Joe flew through the marquee perfectly on the first take. The company moved down the road to shoot a couple of other shots while we re-set. So we got the old sign out, cleaned all debris, got the

OPPOSITE (CLOCKWISE FROM TOP): Lee (played by Mary Elizabeth Winstead) steps into the Big A parking lot. The *Potheads 2* billboard can be seen in the background. • Oak Ridge Coffee can artwork. • Old Chattanooga label artwork. • Red Apple Cigarettes advertisement. **ABOVE (FROM LEFT):** Painters work on the marquee in Buellton. • 2nd Assistant Director David Rimer (L) and 1st Assistant Director Brian Bettwy (R) pose with the marquee, shortly before it's smashed to pieces.

drawn lettering was out. That was tough because both Steve and I are sticklers about font and type design. Fortunately, Steve found fonts that had the right pop.

Gene Kelly, our construction foreman, and his crew were killer fast. Remember, we had to build two marquees, double sided. That turns out to be a hell of a lot of letters all cut, shaped and sanded by hand. This was all happening just before Christmas, so it felt just like Santa's workshop. These guys were flying—making dozens of letters from their patterns. The scenics had their Hudsons filled with oranges, greens and blues. It was a great time and a great energy.

John McLeod helped us scale the marquee so it would be just the right size for the Charger to fly through it and wreak complete havoc. Too big and it would've just left a hole in the center of the sign. Quentin

second marquee up, filled the inner shelves with our colored acrylic shards, installed the reader boards and got the letters up. We got the second take at magic hour. It was a great way to end the day.

The roadside was a mess. But everyone helped us clean up. Cast and crew alike. That's what's great about working on a Quentin crew—everyone jumps in. Quentin has a lot of heart and you see it in the people he brings to his movies.

I guess the biggest compliment that day was seeing several crew members taking their pictures in front of the marquee. That meant more than any words.

NINA PROCTOR, Costume Designer: Quentin was here while we were shooting *Planet Terror*, so I did have the opportunity to meet with him on several occasions before we began prepping *Death Proof*. Quentin had been shopping in San Francisco for t-shirts and I'd been doing the same thing here in Austin. When it came time to put the two groups together, we discovered they were pretty much the same color palette. So that was a good way to start.

Quentin did an incredible job casting *Death Proof*. The girls are all perfect for the roles, and it was a lot of fun coming up with their looks. He wanted it to look like Austin in the summertime, so the girls wore cut-offs and t-shirts. We tried to show a lot of local flavor in the film. I was really excited when he said that we're shooting it for Austin, we're not shooting a film here and trying to make it look like somewhere else. So we went out to some of the local diners, some of the local clubs, just to see how young people dressed around the city. It's also a matter of knowing what the girls are comfortable in and how they were going to feel about the clothing. I think we came up with the right formula for each of the girls.

Basically, I broke the film up into the two different stories. We have the first set of girls: Jungle Julia, Arlene and Shanna. They've been friends for a long time, they went to school together, and they're seeing each other for the first time in a long time. They're doing the Austin party scene, they're going out every night. This particular night, they're going to have some dinner, go to a bar and then go to the lake. So they're dressed very casually: cut-offs and t-shirts.

First we have Jungle Julia. She's a local Austin DJ

JUNGLE LOVE

THE WARDROBE OF DEATH PROOF

OPPOSITE: The "first" set of girls: Jungle Julia (played by Sydney Poitier), Arlene (played by Vanessa Ferlito) and Shanna (played by Jordan Ladd) show off their threads outside Guero's Taco Bar; **ABOVE:** Various Austin Hot Wax 505 Billboards featuring Jungle Julia; **UPCOMING SPREAD:** The Allure magazine spread from the film and featuring Lee (played by Mary Elizabeth Winstead).

and she would be reaching a young audience. So we wanted her to feel very real. We played with the *American Hot Wax* cover art, made a few changes to it and came up with Austin Hot Wax 505. That's the radio station she works for. I ended up screen printing t-shirts with the logo. It's a 45 record—the exact size of a 45 record. That t-shirt, along with her custom-made, little black denim shorts, were kind of a uniform for her. And since Sydney has such long arms and legs, we went very light on her jewelry. Just a little snake band on her arm. It was also a lot of fun doing the costumes for the Hot Wax 505 billboards all over town. We had several different looks. First, for the "Jungle" look we had her in a Tarzan/Jane costume, complete with leopard print and feathers on it and a really wild hairdo. Then we have her roller

derby costume, the yellow jump suit from *Kill Bill* and a couple with the "uniform" I just mentioned.

Next we have little Shanna. She's little, but she's bad. She's managed to get kicked out of all the local bars in Austin, which is a really hard thing to do. She's got a little bit of an edge to her. And Arlene is from New Jersey, so she certainly had an edge too.

Then we have Rose McGowan who was also in *Planet Terror*. A completely different character this time around, a complete turnaround. This time she's a blond, so that opened up a whole new color range. We wanted Pam to be very much a hippie. I looked at lots of books and reference from the 60s and 70s. We used brighter colors and a lighter fabric

that allows for a little bit of movement. Pam is in bell bottoms and a peasant top while the other girls are in t-shirts and shorts, so she's really stands out from the other three girls in the first section of the movie.

The second set of girls are a little bit older, a little bit tougher. So we moved completely away from the shorts and t-shirts. We have Rosario Dawson as Abernathy. She's a hair and make-up person, so that opened some doors for us. We could take that character a little bit further. Her t-shirt had the sleeves cut out of it, it was low-cut, and the back was completely cut out. But Abernathy is also a mother, so she has a unicorn on her shirt and she's got a little necklace with clouds and rainbows. As for her pants, I'm not sure what we're calling these. They were cut like pants, but looked like a skirt. The day Rosario came in for her fitting, I was still playing around with what we would do for her footwear. I had just finished a fitting for Kurt Russell a few minutes earlier, so I had cowboy boots all over the room and Rosario went straight for them. We found a great pair of boots for her and the first time she put them on, she loved them.

Then we had Mary Elizabeth Winstead. She plays the part of Lee, who's an actress playing the part of cheerleader, so it was fun coming up with the right

colors, the flirty little skirt, and the right shoes for her. We also did a photo shoot with Mary Elizabeth for a magazine layout, which was also a lot of fun. It was kind of a concept photo shoot which [*Death Proof* Unit Photographer] Andrew Cooper shot. Andrew would give Mary Elizabeth a little bit of information, like we were shooting these mini movies. I found this orange, chiffon, kind of genie-looking outfit—high fashion from the 70s. And we found the perfect head scarf to go with it. Then we got the idea to have her coming out of a yellow taxi cab. So the transporation department found this vintage cab in perfect condition. Even the little driver that came with the car was perfect. He had his little hat that matched.

Then we have Tracy as Kim. She plays the part of a stuntwoman, so she's very tough. She's in a camouflage t-shirt, tight jeans, and camo tennis shoes. She brought such a great attitude to the film. You totally believe her as her character. When it was time for her to go home one day, she said, "You know what? I'll take a later flight. I want to stay and work." So we were able to get some things with her that we wouldn't have been able to otherwise.

And then we have Zöe Bell. She is such a natural in front of the camera. She's funny, she's pretty, she's

ABOVE: The "second" set of girls: Abernathy (played by Rosario Dawson), Kim (played by Tracie Thoms), Zöe Bell (playing herself) and Lee (played by Mary Elizabeth Winstead) at Jasper's farm; **OPPOSITE:** Pam (played by Rose McGowan) and Stuntman Mike (played by Kurt Russell) examine the "death proof" car behind the Texas Chili Parlor.

tough. The pencil leg jeans are in this year, and Zöe is really tall, so she was able to pull that look off well. Then we did a pink t-shirt on her. It's actually something that Quentin uses a lot in his movies—Jasmine tissue paper. We took the logo and screen printed it on a t-shirt. It's funny because these girls end up kind of taking care of Stuntman Mike, so there's a little play with this being the tissue paper. They wipe Stuntman Mike away.

For Stuntman Mike, Quentin definitely wanted this silver jacket, not a dark gray, not a light gray, but a shiny, silver jacket. I think Kurt's first thought was just like mine, "What are we going to do to make this thing look tough?" So I met with Kurt and Quentin and we tried on a sample jacket, kind of showed them what we could do by adding some detail on the back to make a place for the Icy Hot patch to live.

That was something that was really important to Quentin, that it have this Icy Hot patch on the back

of it. We also broadened and toughened Kurt's shoulder's up a bit, not that he needed any help there. But it did add an element. I also had some patches custom made. Different things that maybe a stunt guy or a race car driver would have. A Pennzoil patch and some old oil companies that aren't around anymore. We covered it with different patches. This really helped give the jacket a stronger presence. Other than that, we dressed him in black jeans and a black t-shirt, which helped give the silver jacket a stronger presence. For the second half of the movie, we just had him in the jeans and t-shirt, but changed him into blue jeans. In the first half of the movie, he knows these girls, he's stalking them and plans this whole attack plan on them. He's planned the car crash and he's dressed for it. The second set of girls, he doesn't know. He happens upon them by pulling into a parking lot at a convenience store. He just happened to pull in for coffee and it's his lucky day. He doesn't know that morning how the day's gonna end, but he finds out.

THE POINT OF IMPACT

CREATING DEATH PROOF'S CAR CRASH SEQUENCE

JOHN McLEOD, Special Effects Coordinator: Quentin definitely wrote a very intricate car crash sequence that had everyone scratching their heads. We had so many questions that it was hard to figure out a starting point to find out how to do it and what we needed to fabricate. We realized that this would have to be done by presenting pictures to the man and having him give the okay. Once we had the pictures, Quentin took off with info and then we had one hell of a sequence on our hands. Along with a huge build list.

[Stunt Coordinator] Jeff Dashnaw and Quentin were trying to figure out how to achieve a very difficult part of the scene when Stuntman Mike first makes contact with the Honda. The Nova was supposed to go up and over the Honda and take off the roof of the vehicle. It needed to tie into the inserts that Quentin had devised for the girls' deaths. They decided to have us build a Honda that we could tow unmanned. It would have a ramp off the front end that we could pull into a head-on collision with a Nova test car that Jeff would be driving. In the Nova,

we put in a full cage for the head-on collision test, along with the full safety systems we always install to make the car as safe as possible for the stunt drivers. We tried to make this car strong enough to maintain its integrity but also absorb some of the shock. The day before the test, we had needed to check that the steering mechanism was running true so I pulled the car from an offset line with my pick up truck at 45 mph. I was a good 25 feet from the line of the Honda. The car pulled down the line like it was on rails but it was strange to see that car in front of me without a driver. It was not a good feeling to imagine pulling that car into head-on crash with my truck. The next day Jeff decided he would pull the cart at 40 mph into a head-on collision. The cars were 1200 feet apart and pulled into an impact point at 600 feet at 40 mph. Since both cars were traveling at 40 mph, it gave the car an upward lift of 80 mph off the ramp. The ramp we had built into the Honda had created a strength that kept any real damage from occurring to the Honda. It was a tough little opponent for the Nova. The Nova, however, flew like 23 feet into the air and traveled 75 feet forward. And during the

ABOVE: Stuntman Mike's "death proof" car takes out the girls' Honda; **OPPOSITE:** John McLeod discusses the pendulum rig prototype with Quentin Tarantino and Robert Rodriguez. • Stunt Coordinator Jeff Dashnaw drives the Nova head-on into an unmanned Honda in a test crash on the Troublemaker Studios backlot.

flight, it rolled driver-side down and contorted on its landing. It was hard to watch Jeff come back down to earth on the driver's side. After that, we abandoned the idea of a manned vehicle for the crash. We went back to the drawing board, and Jeff headed to the doctor. He was a lucky guy.

JEFF DASHNAW, Stunt Coordinator: John McLeod and I put our heads together and talked about the best way to bring the two cars into each other for a head-on collision. We designed a ramp that attached to the front of the Honda that Stuntman Mike's Nova would launch off of. So we built cages, attached the ramps and determined the speed we would go.

I drove the Nova in the original test, pulling the Honda into myself. Both cars were going 40 miles per hour, which made for an extremely violent 80 miles per hour collision. Quentin really liked what he saw, but you could tell that something was missing. Ultimately, we decided that we could be more efficient and more violent and get more speed by towing both cars into each other, unmanned.

So John came up with the two-to-one pull system to create the effect. I've seen a lot of systems where the car wanders when you're towing them into one another, but these cars tracked so straight, it was unbelievable. This new system allowed Stuntman Mike's Nova to go 80 and the Honda to go 40. We also lowered the ramp on the Honda, so we could take more of the car top off and make it look more violent. For the final shot, the car flew unbelievably well, stayed on its wheels when it hit, bounced a couple times, turned sideways and went into a sideways barrel roll, which we were later able to reenact with Buddy Joe Hooker for the overlap. He came in at 70-75 miles per hour and did a cannon roll for us and it just cut together great.

JOHN McLEOD: For the interior car crash sequence—where you actually see the girls get crushed—we had numerous meetings between the departments to develop a list of questions before we presented it to Quentin. It really became quite comical at times. Each girl had a very detailed and choreographed ending to her life that only a guy like Quentin can put into words. We would listen to his descriptions and reasons for each gruesome scene and somehow the majority of us would end up laughing. Maybe because we were so nervous about how to pull all of this off.

The script actually seemed fairly simple—except for the detailed car crashes and chase sequences. Those really caught my eye. And since I had heard through the grapevine that Quentin was intense about the details of some of his action scenes in previous films, I realized we would not be taking the easy way out on any of these scenes.

Quentin was full of endless energy and seems to truly enjoy the process of making films. At certain points, he seemed to slow down and mull over ideas a bit as far as story points related to our mechanical gags. So we

tried to provide visual aids like models and videos of our tests. And then he would spring back with a keen sense of direction and then we were off to the races. If we started to stray from his direction—which, of course, we tried to avoid—he'd give us a quick and decisive verbal redirection.

GREG NICOTERO, KNB Effects: One of the first things Quentin said to me was, "If these dummies don't look real, then I won't be able to shoot them. And if I can't shoot them, I don't have a crash." He didn't want to rely on computer-generated effects. Quentin's a practical guy. It was the same on *Kill Bill*. With the exception of maybe one or two shots, the only CG stuff we had on *Kill Bill* was for wire removal. Quentin's a purist; he wants to be able to see it, to touch it, to be able to figure out where he wants to put his camera.

What made this crash sequence even more difficult was Quentin's desire to shoot it as if it were crash test dummy stock footage. Everything was going to be at super slow motion. We're talking 150 frames per second. Generally, when you're watching a movie, you see a dummy on screen for just a few frames. The gag happens and you cut away. With this, we

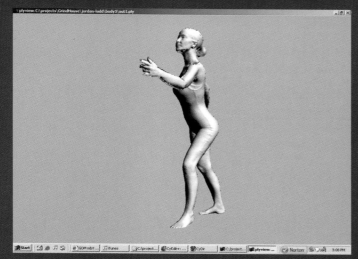

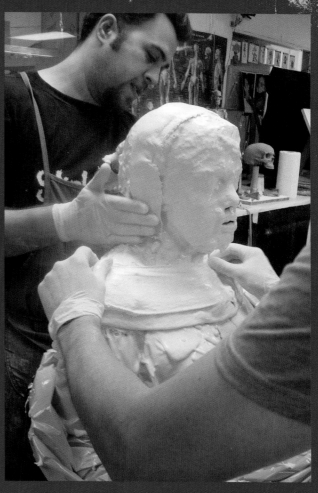

OPPOSITE: The Honda crash rig on the Troublemaker Studios green screen stage; **ABOVE (CLOCKWISE FROM TOP LEFT):** The cyberscan of Jordan Ladd. • KNB Moldmaker AJ Venuto creates a headcast. • The Honda crash rig under construction.

literally had to build dummies that had to act. You had to be able to stay on them for a long enough period of time to sell the shot, but they also had to look completely realistic and move realistically. So we had to do perfect replicas of each actress in the exact position, completely articulated, so once the impact of the car hit, they would move realistically. And we had to do all this in eight weeks.

The rigs that John McLeod came up with were just absolutely amazing. It was probably one of the best experiences in terms of interface with a physical effects department that I've ever had. But we tested the hell out of everything too. We made dummies that I flew down to Austin with, we stuck them in the car and we actually tested all of them. And then showed everything to Quentin.

As soon as I read the script, I knew how I wanted to build the bodies. And it was interesting because when we got down to it and we were on set, he came up to me and he said, "Hey, I looked at all the videotaped test footage you did. And a lot of the angles that you shot tests of, I really like. I want to duplicate those angles." I think it really helped him visualize the scene by being able to look at the tests that we had done so that he could see which angles were successful and which angles were less successful.

Now we had done two films earlier in the year where we had been experimenting with new ways to create bodies. One was a Tony Scott film called *Deja Vu*. We had to create a burned autopsy cadaver of a woman that would move realistically and be heavy. So we actually built an armature where all the joints were machined. The elbow would move in the right place, the wrist would move, the shoulder would move. So we spent a lot of time building these custom armatures that were totally articulated, put those into the mold and then we ran the bodies out of solid silicone. Silicone is a material we utilize for fake heads. You can tint it flesh-colored, put a little paint on it, punch hair into it and it looks completely realistic—more so than foam latex or latex would. Silicone is sort of the standard that we use for making fake bodies.

For us, the first task at hand was determining the position each girl would be in at the moment of impact. I had to get Quentin to commit to who was sitting in which seat and what position they were in well before we started shooting. So Lanna Frank's hands were on the steering wheel, Julia's leg was on the window sill, Arlene was behind the driver and Shanna was reaching between the two front seats, fucking with the radio. So we stood outside of Troublemaker Studios with a camera, put four girls in a car and I got Quentin to sign off on the position of each body.

Then the actresses came to KNB and we individually cast each of their heads, hands and feet. Then we sent them to a facility in Burbank called CyberFX, where each actress was scanned in the exact position that her body would be at the moment of impact. CyberFX then provided us with a one-to-one scale foam replica of the actress' body, and we re-sculpted areas to add muscle detail and to basically clean it up a bit.

At the same time, we were cleaning up sculptures of their heads and hands. So we then grafted the heads, hands and feet onto the foam bodies, to create complete foam bodies of each actress. Then we molded those out of fiberglass. Concurrently we were building the articulated armatures, so we would open the mold, take the foam out, put the armature in, seal it back up and fill it with silicone. That took three days. Then you'd open that, trim all the excess off, paint it and then you're into the hair work. For Sydney, we literally had to make all of the wigs custom because she has that long, black curly hair. So we had to hand tie each of those wigs as well

wheel crushed the chest, it would force all the blood up through the throat and out the nose and mouth. We built it anatomically correct so that we could get the blood shooting out the mouth. That's really what would happen if your chest was crushed by a steering wheel. Quentin also wanted to do something really specific with her legs. He wanted the entire engine block to come in and crush her legs. So John McLeod and I came up with a rig. We built anatomically correct legs that started with resin bone, then we laid layers of silicone muscle, then we put a skin over that. So the idea was that when the engine block comes in, we put pointed shards of metal that would catch the flesh and tear the flesh backwards, revealing all the muscle and all the blood and all the bone underneath. We really wanted it to look like someone was scraping the top layer of skin off. So we had three sets of legs since we had three versions of Lanna Frank. We did three different takes, Quentin picked three different angles, and right before each take, I would make incisions in the silicone and inject blood into the leg with a syringe, so that when the flesh came off, you would see instant blood. And one

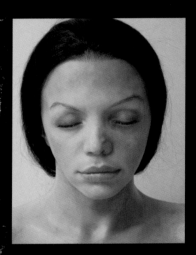   

as the ones for Jordan, Vanessa and Monica. Once the bodies were created, we had to start thinking about how many bodies we needed to make, based on camera position. If you're inside a car, you're not going to be able to just see something happen to Julia without seeing everybody else in the car at the same time. We weren't just making one dummy of each girl; we had to make three dummies of each girl. So we ended up making 12 fully articulated dummies—three dummies of each girl so we could get three individual takes.

Lanna Frank [played by Monico Staggs] was the driver. Her body was created hollow because originally Quentin wanted the steering wheel to crush her chest and we were going to fill the whole thing up with blood. There were tubes. There was basically a reservoir in her chest that we were going to fill through the mouth. So that when the steering

of the most effective aspects of that was that her neck was so well jointed, that there was a camera that was straight overhead looking down and all the rigs that John McLeod built all had "jerk" cables on them and pistons on them. The entire car could move forward and backwards really quick to simulate the action of the car impact. So when you're watching the footage, all of the dummies are reacting to the physical rigs that John McLeod built, so Lanna Frank's body fell forward when the car was jerked backward and then when the car stopped, she fell backwards and her head and her chin tilted back, looking right into the camera. So it looked like the thing was literally acting. It was pretty amazing.

Arlene is sitting in the backseat and is the only one with her seatbelt on. So for a split second you think that she's going to survive. But the idea is that Stuntman Mike's car drives over the top of their car and his wheel tears through the roof and rips her face off. This was one of the first gags that we started building because I wanted to test the whole thing out even before we started working with the actress. So when we were shooting *Planet Terror*, I had one of the guys at KNB sculpt a generic torn-away face, so that we could test it to see exactly how we wanted to do it. So the idea was we got a cast of the actress, got a clay

to build a leg that we could pull off and on top of that, we had to put a scoop underneath the dummy to push the dummy's body upward so that we could clear the window sill when we wanted to pull the leg off. So again, this whole sequence couldn't have been done without John.

The idea was that we had to mount the cameras onto

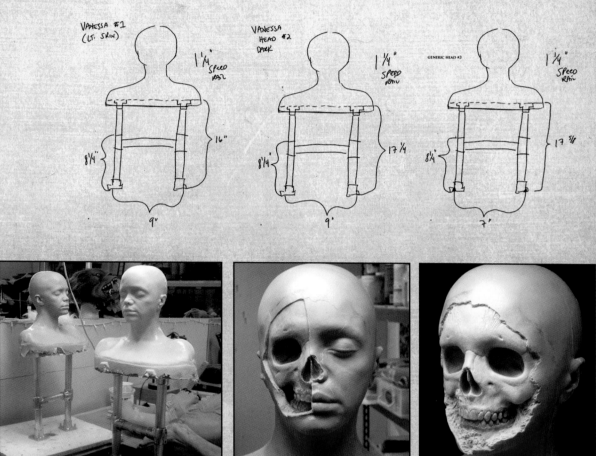

OPPOSITE: KNB's dummy versions of the crash victims; **ABOVE (FROM TOP):** Schematic drawing by John McLeod of Arlene's "face peel" rig. • Various stages of the Arlene dummy.

version of her head and then we sculpted away the face, which revealed the skull and the muscle. Once we molded that, we made a little plug that filled in the areas that still had her face detail on it. We stuck that on there. Then the whole neck was jointed and then the jaw was jointed. So, one of the first tests that we did, when the wheel is coming through and hits the chin, it pushes the head back against the chair. As the face gets crushed and torn off by the wheel, it actually opens up the mouth of the dummy. When Quentin watched that in slow-motion, he couldn't believe how realistic it looked. Again, these dummies all had lives of their own.

With Julia, because Sydney is a really tall woman, Quentin was specific about wanting her leg to get torn off. The way she's sitting in the car, her right leg is dangling out the window. She's sort of lounging in the front seat of the car. So the idea was that we had

the platform that moved the car back and forth. And on action, the car would jerk, there was a piston that John put underneath Julia's body that would push the body upward and there was another cable rig that would tear the leg off. So we filled the joint where the leg attached to the hip with fake blood and condoms and all kinds of viscera, so when the leg flew out, there was this trail of blood and viscera that would follow the leg. And I think we hit the camera on every take with the leg and then of course with the trailing guts and viscera. And it worked out amazingly well.

So at the point of impact, Lanna Frank gets pinned behind the steering wheel, Julia gets crushed in the passenger seat and her leg is torn off and Shanna, who is in between those two front seats reaching for the radio, goes face first through the windshield. John rigged a cable that we attached directly behind the head of the dummy. There was a scaffold that

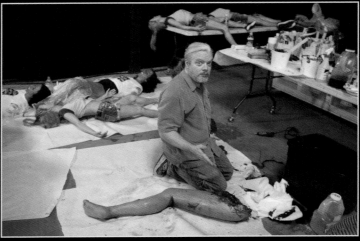

was built around the car rig with pistons that, once activated, would pull the dummies in whatever direction we needed them to go. So for the Julia leg gag and for Shanna going through the windshield, they squibbed the windshield and pulled the dummy out. We're talking about 60 or 70 pound dummies that we were pulling. The amount of force to actually pull those bodies was astounding. But when we did it, they launched like they weighed five pounds.

Myself, Andy Shoenberg, Eric Feedler and Alex Diaz flew down to Austin, got the dummies all dressed and it pretty much went like clockwork. We did three takes of each version. And then at the end of the first night Quentin said, "You know this stuff looks so great, I want to do another couple of takes. Do we have any more dummies?" And I said, "Well, they're a little screwed up because we've been tearing them apart, but we can certainly put something together for tomorrow." So we ended up shooting extra coverage at different angles once we got into it and he realized what he had.

Quentin took a lot of pleasure and glee in bringing each girl over to her dummy to look at it. They were all really mesmerized. I know Sydney and Vanessa were probably the most creeped out looking at their dummies. Especially after we did the first exterior crash, because when we did the first exterior crash, we put all the dummies in the car and I actually put

several well-placed blood bags in the car. Once the impact happens and we all walked over, we were basically looking at four slumped over dummies covered in blood and glass. It really felt like we were walking up to a real accident scene. All the bodies were slumped, their hair was all messed up, there was glass everywhere, there was blood everywhere. It was really disturbing because you could almost imagine if a crash really happened and you were the first person to walk up to it, that's what it would look like.

This is going to be one of those sequences in modern American cinema that people are going to be talking about for years to come. Because there is virtually no CGI, it's all practical, it's all in camera. And it's certainly a tribute to Quentin's initial vision and John McLeod's work and the people here at KNB that did an astounding job building these dummies. When we were finished, Quentin came up to me, put his hand on my shoulder and said, "You've outdone yourself." He said, "I think that this is some of the best work that you've ever done."

I love the challenge, I love the fact that Quentin and Robert challenge us. I feel like our company that's now been in existence for 19 years, we welcome those challenges because they test us. And I love that. I want to keep getting better and better and when you have

ABOVE (CLOCKWISE FROM LEFT): KNB's Alex Diaz holds Jungle Julia's dummy leg. • KNB's Andy Shoenberg with Jungle Julia's dummy leg and various full-body dummies in the background. • The Shanna dummy is ejected from the Honda; **OPPOSITE:** Quentin Tarantino makes last minute adjustments to the Shanna dummy before shooting the car crash aftermath; **UPCOMING SPREAD:** Crew members observe the full-scale pendulum rig as it rotates Stuntman Mike's car.

directors like these two guys, they push you. And I like being pushed because it inspires us to do better.

Quentin told me last week that he was talking to the editors and he asked for an angle of Lanna Frank's dummy in the front seat of the car and the editors, who study this footage over and over again, said, "We don't have a shot of Lanna Frank's dummy, we only have the actress in the car." They had no idea it was a dummy. Quentin said to me, "If that's not knocking it out of the park, I don't know what is."

Andy Shoenberg was basically our key shop supervisor. He really supervised a lot of cosmetic work. Eric Feedler and Wayne Toth, in conjunction with the rest of our mechanical department, built all the armatures. It takes 45 people to make these, you have different departments, you have sculptors like Jaremy Aiello and Kevin Wasner and Alex Diaz. Then you have moldmakers like Jim Leonard and Rob Freitus. Then you have the guys that run the silicone. Steve Hartman was basically the key guy that ran all of the silicone bodies. He and Caleb Schneider really worked out how to make the bodies. And then

fabrication and final cosmetics and then hair work. Mark Boley, Annalise Boies and Jack Bricker did amazing work on the wigs. In all, we had eight or nine people working on hair alone.

JOHN McLEOD: Quentin had a very specific idea for the interior of Stuntman Mike's car during the crash scene. The movement of the car was hard for me to grasp at first, so Quentin simulated the movement with his cell phone.

The idea was that the car would move like a plane flying in a loop. Cameras would shoot Kurt Russell in the car's interior, giving the impression that the background was spinning. I was still a bit unsure of the concept, so the next day, I put together a prototype model to help both of us understand it. Quentin liked what I showed him and we were off to the races.

We had four days to build the unit. After we designed the device, I was a still a bit nervous about the main shaft, so I enlisted the help of Mechanical Engineer Larry Slate to double check our calculations. Most guys will not touch devices like this due to the liability

involved. Lucky for me, Larry is always willing to give me advice when I'm in a jam. I always want to triple check myself when it comes to safety. We based our design around the materials we could gather quickly. Our boys worked hard at it for four days, swinging a lot of big steel.

We installed the rig on the backlot area of Troublemaker Studios on the day before we shot it. Kurt Russell was very brave and trusting. He hopped right in and seemed like he was having a ball.

Over the course of this fifteen month production, there were many crew members that helped make these two films possible. Too many to name, but I'd like to at least mention our core group. Shop Foreman Richard Woods headed the shop that dealt with the gadgets and mechanisms. He's very good with hydraulic systems and fabrication. I leaned on Richard to guide the crew of effects fabricators through the various projects. Set Foreman Frank Tarantino dealt with the day to day operation of the shooting company. It was a handful between the two films. Car Shop Foreman Andy Miller was in charge of cages and general fabrication of the *Death Proof* cars. He played an important role for us. We were prepping cars for *Death Proof* while shooting *Planet Terror*. Setting up a second shop was a huge project and Andy was able to bring in some great help. Gang Boss Mike Reedy was my go-to-guy when I had difficult rigs or gags that were hard to describe in one sitting. He can take intricate projects from design to on-set operation with ease. Mike also

pre-rigged a lot of the large sets for us on *Planet Terror*. This is something that you cannot teach or tell people—it comes only with experience. Gang Boss Rob Clot also was a clutch guy for me. I put him in charge of the pyrotechnic inventory and recording for all the pyro on *Planet Terror*. I also had Rob with me during all of our testing with the unmanned cars for *Death Proof*. Special Effects Buyer Brian Montgomery took a huge load off my shoulders by dealing with purchasing and buying for the set and the shop. Brian also dealt with the crew and the drivers for all the various rigs and jobs. Driver Billy Chambers was critical to our operation. He does so much for us during a shoot and has a great mechanical sense. I trusted Billy with the position of driving the vehicles that pulled all of our mechanical rigs for the car crash in *Death Proof* and the motorcycle rig in *Planet Terror*. Our resident Machinist, Keith Haynes, who is a key player in our group with his knack for gadgetry and machine tool operations. Car Shop Foreman Elia Popov took over when Andy had to leave for a prior commitment. He brought in some great help during a tough time in the schedule. Special Effects Technicians Wes Mattox, James McCormick, Dan Yates, Marc McCord and Bill McGinnley were key guys for me both in the shop and on set. Lead Prop Fabricator Jeff Poss was also a huge help when it came to the interior car crash sequence. He, along with his great crew of techs, made duplicate parts for the interior Honda that interfaced with our mechanical rigs. A great crew, across the board.

CECIL EVANS, Transportation Coordinator: On *Sin City*, we were looking for a specific vehicle that we could rent for a week or two to use in the movie. We actually only bought one car, which was the '55 Chevy police car. For *Death Proof*, we were looking to buy eight 1970 Chargers, six Challengers, and eight Novas—which right now are the premiere muscle cars.

We found these cars for sale anywhere from $80,000 to $160,000 and we just couldn't afford that. So instead we found parts of cars that were of this vintage and essentially built new ones. Also, because the cars in this movie needed to be high performance stunt cars, we had to rebuild the motors, rebuild the transmissions, shocks, steering—everything

in the cars—to make them run good and sound. We didn't want to have the wheels fall off while we were shooting.

We normally find cars by networking, really. We run ads in the paper, we contact car clubs, we do all kinds of things to try and stimulate a response when we're finding particular cars. It boils down to finding a guy with a car who knows a guy with a car who knows a guy with a car.

In the first half of *Death Proof*, Stuntman Mike's car is a 1970 Chevy Nova. We got the car running to where it would perform from a stunt standpoint—motor, transmission, powers, wheels, steering. Then

BELOW: Stuntman Mike (played by Kurt Russell) and his "death proof" car, a 1970 Chevy Nova; **OPPOSITE:** A fleet of Novas are gutted, rebuilt and painted. • Stuntman Mike's hood ornament of choice is identical to the one found in Sam Peckinpah's *Convoy*.

WHITE-HOT JUGGERNAUTS

THE CARS OF DEATH PROOF

we essentially threw out the seats and everything inside the cars, put in our own seats and the effects department built a roll cage in each of them.

CAYLAH EDDLEBLUTE, Production Designer: In our pre production meetings, Quentin was very specific about everyone in the crew watching the great car movies:

Vanishing Point, Smokey and the Bandit, Bullitt, Dirty Mary Crazy Larry, Dixie Dynamite, Ride in a Pink Car, The French Connection, Gone in 60 Seconds [1974 Version] and *White Lightning.* That was basically

our assignment early on and we pulled shots and sequences and stunts from all of those movies.

STEVE JOYNER, Production Designer: Quentin referenced Sam Peckinpah's *Convoy.* In it, Kris Kristofferson drives a semi that's emblazoned with a very iconic hood ornament. It's a duck, actually. And Quentin was very clear about wanting to use that *exact* duck in *Death Proof.*

CAYLAH EDDLEBLUTE: We eventually found a guy by the name of John Billings, Sr. He had the original mold of the *Convoy* duck. In two days time, we could get any number of ducks needed and with that resource, it made everything come to life for us. The duck somehow brought Kurt Russell's character to life and it took on a life of its own. The duck really became a part of Stuntman Mike.

Quentin was also very specific about the battle of cars between the girls and Kurt Russell. He wanted a Challenger vs. Charger battle.

STEVE JOYNER, Classic black vs. white—a cowboy showdown.

CAYLAH EDDLEBLUTE: The homage to *Vanishing Point* is another key thread throughout *Death Proof.* There were a number of references, chief among them, an exact replica of Kowalski's white 1970 Dodge Challenger.

CECIL EVANS: *Vanishing Point* was filmed in 1970 when these Challengers were brand new. For *Death Proof*, we needed to find six of them. In an early version of the script, this car had four doors. I had told Quentin early on that this car didn't come in four doors; it only had two, and putting two other doors in there would be a real stretch. Ultimately, he changed the script a little bit to where we tear off a front door instead of a back door.

Challengers run anywhere from $80,000 to hundreds of thousands of dollars, depending on the condition of the car. Again, for most of these, we found car bodies rusting in a field, bought the body and frame and built the car from that.

CAYLAH EDDLEBLUTE: We spent a great deal of time on all of the very small details in the cars including the Challenger emblems and all the little extra pieces that go into the exterior of the car. Obviously, we had all these pieces continually being fabricated.

STEVE JOYNER: When we got them, none of the cars came equipped the exact same way. We had to make our own Challenger logos and our own 440 logos. Fortunately, Jeff Poss was able to mold them and cast them and make very realistic logos. Darren Patnode on set was able to keep sticking these things on, since they would get knocked off on almost every take. We must have gone through 40 or 50 of the little logo plates.

CAYLAH EDDLEBLUTE: We really worked hard to be absolutely accurate to Kowalski's Challenger from *Vanishing Point*. Right down to the gear shifter, the seats, the seat upholstery, interior and exterior, including the hero shot of the engine when the girls open it up at Jasper's farm.

STEVE JOYNER: We had a crew of five people working on the interior of that engine for that shot.

OPPOSITE (FROM TOP): A pristine engine lies underneath the hood of a 1970 Dodge Challenger, the same car Kowalski drives in *Vanishing Point* (1971). • Custom emblems created by the Prop Department for the Challengers; **ABOVE:** One of the six 1970 Dodge Challengers used in the film.

CAYLAH EDDLEBLUTE: The effects department and our mechanics up in Buellton, Pete Mandel and Sean Ryan, literally worked seven days a week. Often late into the night, after being on set. All these cars would come in wounded with gaping holes and all manner of debris and parts all over the place. Having these cars ready for shooting the next day was quite an endeavor. Pete and Sean, along with John McLeod's team were heroic.

Every night when the Challengers and Chargers came back to the shop, my chest would ache.

STEVE JOYNER: It looked like a demolition derby. They'd come in smoking, with parts dragging.

CAYLAH EDDLEBLUTE: Crippled, wounded.

STEVE JOYNER: There were several times when wheels were broken off. Buddy Joe was still able to drive with one of the front wheels actually wedged under the car. I don't how he did it; he's amazing.

John McLeod and his crew worked really hard with the mechanics to keep the cars tough enough to keep taking the hits and keep running. John and his crew did a lot of work internally—behind the body panels and in the back and the front of the car—to reinforce them so they could actually hit without sustaining any real damage. The sheet metal looks terrible, but underneath those cars are completely fine.

CAYLAH EDDLEBLUTE: One quick element to address is that this really became a movie about Tracy Dashnaw. She spent weeks driving that Challenger with Zöe on

the hood and those two obviously had a huge amount of trust in each other. Day after day, they were able to go out and make it all happen take after take. Tracy was one of our main stunt drivers on this show. She doubled for Tracie Thoms and she really came into her own on this. The work she and Buddy Joe did together was absolutely ballet. They were perfectly choreographed and their sense of timing was spot on. I remember one morning they came out and did a rehearsal and she said, "Well, I didn't even have my contacts in!" They did three rehearsals right in a row. They were just sweet, good spins.

STEVE JOYNER: With the cars in the state they were, they rode with the windows dirty and the mirrors knocked off and all the camera rigs on them. Tracy really drove by sense of smell. Buddy Joe and Tracy had a really good intuition of each other. They could drive without any real visual clues, because they really couldn't see.

CAYLAH EDDLEBLUTE: We had originally been slated to shoot everything in Austin, Texas. But Quentin had early on mentioned that after we shot the first segment of *Death Proof*, that he wanted to take a break and really analyze the chase. It was very complex and he wanted a little time to think about it.

He made the assessment to move the production back to California. We ended up shooting in an area about 2 1/2 hours north of Los Angeles—the Solvang/Santa Ynez Valley. It provided a great range for all these stunts and all this car action. A lot of roads there really had the quality of different elevations, so you could get great shots of cars sweeping down these fantastic hills. We had a particular area called Figueroa Mountain Road, which basically became our backlot. It was available to do almost any kind of stunt. We were able to re-create the road, take fencing in, take fencing out, re-paint fencing, put in a windmill, take it out—just do different things. But in that grindhouse way—a single location, without lots of company moves but still having lots of cool action—keeping the company stationed in one area and really focusing on shots, instead of moving from location to location.

STEVE JOYNER: We also got to take advantage of some of the new rigs that are available—the Escalade, the MTV, the push-pull rig; new equipment that people who do car commercials came up with to create those crazy, dynamic camera moves. Some of it was actually employed for the first time in a movie on *Death Proof*. All these new gadgets allowed Quentin to quickly set up shots and execute them without dealing with

ABOVE (CLOCKWISE FROM TOP): Stunt driver Tracy Dashnaw, slams into Stuntman Mike's 1970 Charger, driven by stunt driver Buddy Joe Hooker. • Smashed-up cars outside the Buellton production office; **OPPOSITE:** Stuntman Mike inside his Charger. • Kurt Russell inside a "push-pull" rig. • The MTV camera vechicle. • Interior detail of Mike's Charger.

process trailers and long set-up times—things that can really cut into the flow of action.

CAYLAH EDDLEBLUTE: Another big part of the shooting style was the use of plain old car mounts. They gave that old style feel that helped balance against the new dynamic rigs. It gave a really nice beat to the scenes and to the takes and was really in keeping with what Quentin likes as far as that old style grindhouse feeling. And boy it was funny because you would see these cars rigged to the hilt with stuff all over the place and Kurt barely able to see over all this gear while he drove but it really, really worked.

Kurt obviously can really drive like all get out. He knew what to do. Totally a pro. Totally in control. It really came together.

In the beginning stages of planning the car chase, we referenced Steven Spielberg's movie, *Duel*. There's a behind-the-scenes feature on the *Duel* DVD that shows Spielberg's entire production wall covered with a map basically from downtown Los Angeles all the way out to Barstow. They were able to map out their sequence. They knew exactly what stunts were going to happen where—all on this huge sheet of butcher paper. Quentin really wired into that idea

and was able to separate out the beats of each part of the sequence and figure them out. Tools like this really help the entire crew map out and visualize how to breakdown a huge sea of data, which is really what a car chase can be until you distill it down and separate out the different components.

STEVE JOYNER: When Quentin wrote *Death Proof*, he envisioned the girls arriving in the second half of the film in a bright yellow 2006 Mustang. Unfortunately, in sitting down and blocking out the scene, we determined that the 2006 model wouldn't work because of the configuration of the windows. So we went back to the drawing board. Cecil Evans and his picture car wrangler, Russell Scott hunted down a Mustang with a different window configuration. The '72 Mustang is what we ended up going with. We found a couple of matching Mustangs, repainted them, striped them and redid the interiors. Basically we created an homage to our *Kill Bill* Pussy Wagon, which was designed by David Wasco. This became the Lil' Pussy Wagon.

Quentin was very happy with the result and the girls were very happy with it. It's also worth mentioning that the Mustang's license plate says "Brand X," which refers to the stunt company that [Stunt Coordinator] Jeff Dashnaw and his crew are all part of.

CAYLAH EDDLEBLUTE: The Lil' Pussy Wagon is also an homage to the Lil' Red Express, which was a Dodge logo from the 70s that was on one of their pick-up trucks. We also referenced it on the original Pussy Wagon.

Having worked with David Wasco on *Kill Bill*, we knew we needed to make our interior really sweet. Quentin, of course, has the original Pussy Wagon in his driveway. He drives it all the time, so he knows what the interior should look like. So I called David Wasco and he gave me the name of the original upholsterer in Los Angeles, Fast Ed's. I talked to Fast Ed, and he gave me the exact upholstery color numbers and materials that they used on the original Pussy Wagon on *Kill Bill*. I was able to reference the exact materials, the exact colors and go to a wonderful upholstery team here in Austin, Ben and Virgie from Ben's Upholstery and Paul from Leather Menders. This team kicked ass.

We went over the top from the original Pussy Wagon, even doing all the door panels, all the consoles, everything. Not just the seats, but the piping, the floor, the carpet. We were really thrilled with the outcome there. It looks simple and elegant but, like all things, requires a lot of thought to get it right.

ABOVE: The girls inside the "Lil' Pussy Wagon", a 1972 Ford Mustang; **OPPOSITE:** Details of the Mustang.

Lil' PussyWagon

BUDDY JOE HOOKER, Stuntperson: I was actually supposed to do another film in Yugoslavia when [Stunt Coordinator] Jeff Dashnaw called me and said that Quentin was interested in having me double the lead in *Death Proof*. He mentioned this car chase and that he was trying to get Terry Leonard involved so I said yeah. It's quite an opportunity to work with Quentin because I've been a fan of his from day one. He comes from the same school as I come from: CGI, computer-generated stuff—throw that stuff out. He likes to work in real time, and that's what we like. He gives us the opportunity to do a lot of stuff that nowadays you don't get to do.

TERRY LEONARD, Stuntperson: As soon as I heard that Quentin Tarantino was directing this, I got excited.

He is the John Ford of this era. He is so enthusiastic and loves stunt guys. You just love working for guys like that. Same goes for John Milius. I worked every picture he made since way back in the late 60s. You really like working for guys like that.

JEFF DASHNAW: Quentin didn't want to use any tricks for the stunt driving. He didn't want to change the camera speed to make the cars look like they were going faster than they actually were. The challenge for us was to go as fast as we could, safely. We're always looking for that, but we really got a chance to do it on this show. There are circumstances where you have an actor in a car and you want to make it look like you're going 100, but you're really going 30. If you run the cameras at regular speed, it looks like 30

ALL OR NOTHIN' DAYS

THE STUNTS OF DEATH PROOF

unt Drivers Tracy Dashnaw
hallenger) and Buddy Joe
black Charger) jump two
eously; **ABOVE (FROM
Santos, Crissy Weathersby,
Quentin Tarantino, Malosi
Dashnaw, Zöe Bell, Terry
ddy Joe Hooker.

miles per hour. So if you're not going to undercrank, your only option is to go *really* fast.

ZÖE BELL, Stuntperson: The day that Buddy Joe and Terry were on set together was fucking beautiful to witness. I'd met Terry a bunch of times and I'd obviously worked with Buddy for a long time at that point. Just to see them on set—everyone on the crew, not just the stuntpeople, were aware that we had a meeting of legends. It was like I'd stepped back in time. Like I was there for a reunion of some sort, and it was way more moving than I was expecting it to be.

TERRY LEONARD: On this show, Buddy Joe Hooker and I are doing what they call a near miss, a head-on configuration where we come at each other at pretty good speed; he ducks off one way, I duck off the other. Buddy Joe pulls out alongside the car that Zöe Bell is strapped on to. She's out on the hood and they're looking at each other and all of a sudden here comes a pickup truck. He's going into oncoming traffic—which is me—and of course I force him off the road, he forces me off the road and I end up turning the pickup over. Then he goes out on the road and keeps on going with the chase.

The near miss is one of the most underrated stunts

there is, because of the outcome—you don't hit the other car. But you can't veer even a little in the wrong direction, because at that speed even a slight impact is devastating. For a good effect on screen you need to get it as close as you can; to be safe you need to be as far away as you can. So it's a judgment call. When you do something with a stunt guy like that, you want to make sure that he doesn't panic and give you a false move or a false reading. You're coming at each other about 50 miles an hour each so if you hit each other head-on that's 100 miles an hour and both guys are going to get killed.

BUDDY JOE HOOKER: It's like when it goes well, it's not difficult at all. But there've been some incidences where these don't go well and you have a 100 mile-an-hour head-on. It's all sweet until it's bad, and if it's bad, it's *really* bad. Working with Terry is great because I know he's steady on that end. It's up to me to dive into him as deep as I can, next to the girls, and know that I can get out and not get out too early or too late. So there's that little fine line in there. Too early looks horrible. Too late looks horrible. So you have to find that little window that makes it exciting and safe at the same time. It's a little stressful. You know—once it's over, it's great but when you're barreling down the highway and you have a car coming at you at

50 and you're going 50. sometimes you wonder, "I hope everything stays together, so I can make that decision." You don't want to blink.

TERRY LEONARD: I've had some pretty serious injuries off and on throughout my career, but the worst I've ever had was a highfall from about 60 feet in a picture I shot up in Pasadena called *Black Samson*. I misjudged the construction of the catcher—that's what we land in. I went through it, hit the street and landed on my spine. I was paralyzed, I couldn't move my legs. I also hit so hard that it blinded me. I could see a little peripherally, but it was like a test pattern on the old TV sets. I couldn't see. So I was in the Pasadena hospital for three days, then I got the feeling back in my legs, then my sight started to come back, and the only explanation they had was that I hit so hard I had nerve paralysis.

On the way to the hospital that day, I was thinking about what I was going to do. I didn't know if my

pay the price. When you're making a living with your body, it's going to catch up with you.

JEFF DASHNAW: I hate to use the word "legend" while someone is still out there working, but Terry's a legend. When you call a guy like that and say, "Hey, you want to drive up to Buellton and stay at the Split Pea Inn and drive an old piece of shit pickup truck, do this *Dixie Dynamite* shot with us?" He was so excited to come up and do it. We had his son Malosi up there on the show and Terry told me that it was the first time in his career that he and his son had worked together as stuntmen. Terry ended up doing a stunt where he turned a truck over the old-style way—with a grab strap, no roll cage. And you just knew he was gonna do it. That's how these guys grew up, doing turnovers. Malosi was his safety guy, so it was pretty cool to see the son pulling his pops out of the truck and walking away with him.

BUDDY JOE HOOKER: This is actually the third time Terry

days as a stuntman were over. I was thinking I could be a sound man, that I could run a sound board on set from a wheel chair. I already had a game plan in mind. I could sell this, this and this, put the money in the bank, maybe make some good investments. Then three days later, I started coming to. I spent the weekend in the whirlpool and went back to work on Monday. The accident was on that previous Tuesday.

But I don't like to talk about injuries. If you're doing stunts for a living, you're going to get hurt. Being a stuntman is like teasing a dog on a chain. You go past the neighbor's yard on the way home from school, and you see this bad dog, so you tease him. But that chain might be a couple of feet too long and you'll get bit. And that's what stunt work is—it's going to get you sooner or later. There's no way out. Guys that say they do movie stunts and haven't been hurt haven't been doing movie stunts. It's part of the game, like playing pro football or anything physical. You

Leonard and I have worked together. We've both been in the business for a few years and it just seems like after we passed our stuntman careers, we both became second unit directors or stunt coordinators. Either he was running a show or I was so we always communicated but we would almost never work together 'cause both of us were running shows. So working together was the fun part—it was great.

JEFF DASHNAW: I've known Buddy Joe Hooker for over 30 years, and he has done every stunt there is to do, and he's probably done each of those stunts ten times more than anyone else in the business. He's probably the most talented physical stuntman that has ever come down the road. And when I called him to ask him to do this movie, the whole company got excited when he said yes. To his credit, he probably turned down five shows while he was on this one. He was unbelievable. Over the years, he hasn't changed a bit. He's married and he has twin boys, yet I always

ABOVE (FROM LEFT): Quentin Tarantino and Stunt Driver Buddy Joe Hooker get ready to take the Charger for a test spin. • A father/son stunt team: Malosi Leonard (L) and Terry Leonard (R) pose with Terry's overturned truck. **OPPOSITE (FROM TOP):** Tracy Dashnaw sends Buddy Joe Hooker's Charger flying into the air as the MTV camera vehicle captures all the action. • Stunt Coordinator Jeff Dashnaw demonstrates Zöe Bell's car hood stunt with Tracy Dashnaw behind the wheel.

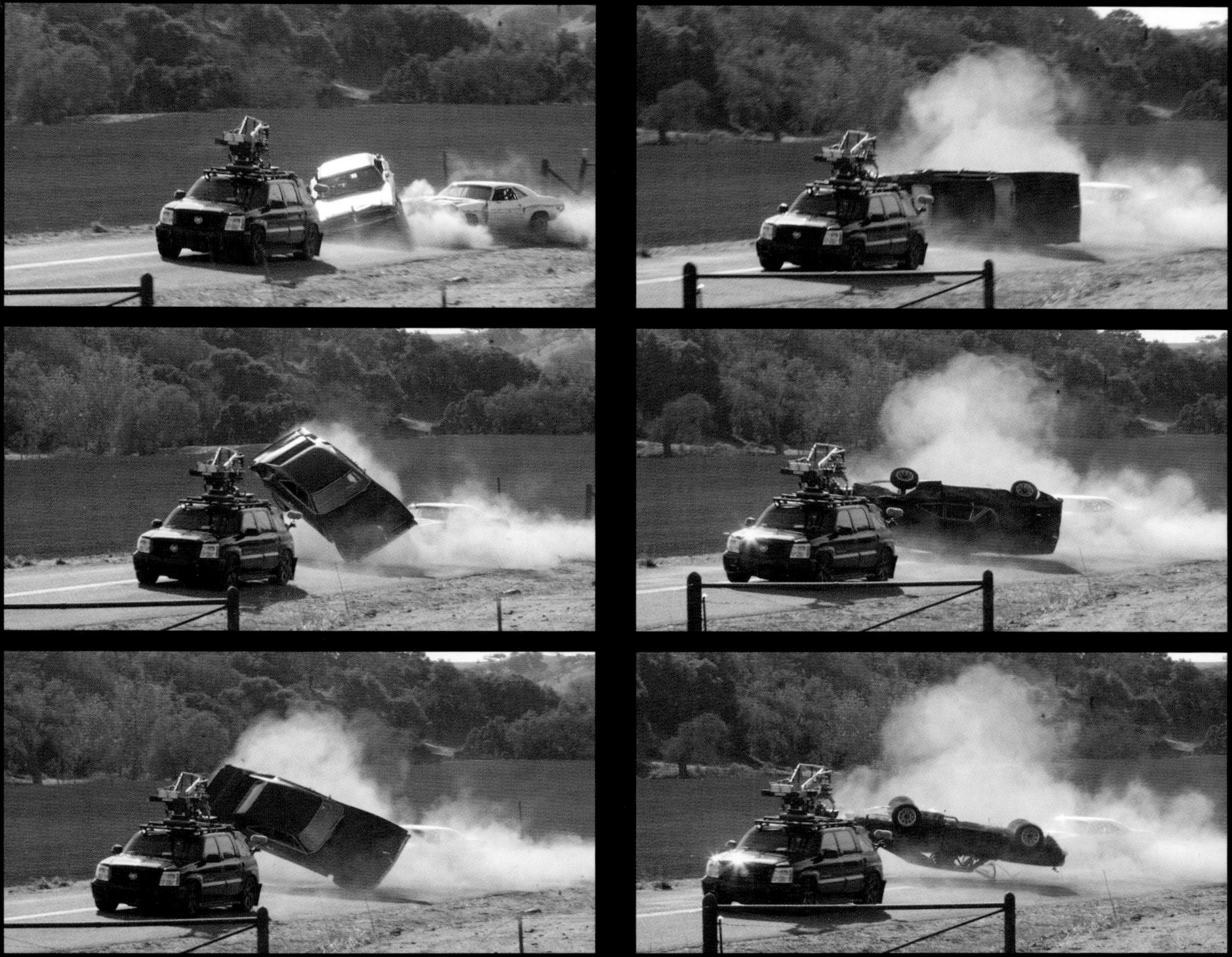

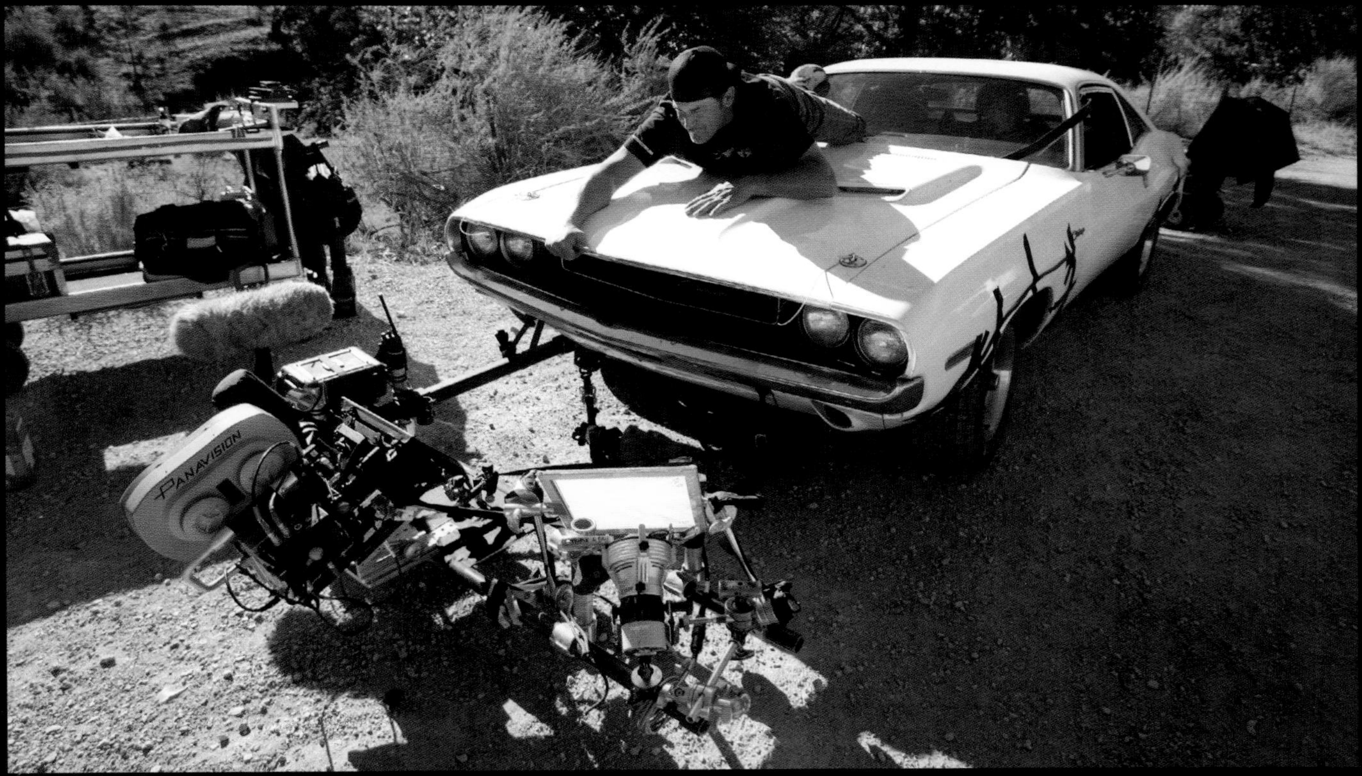
PANAVISION

picture him as a guy in his 30s that will never change. Unbelievable.

TERRY LEONARD: Buddy Joe's reputation is worldwide. Every time I hear the words, the name Buddy Joe Hooker, I get a grin on my face, because I know —there is a stunt man. He's done so much stuff, and he's so cool. When this stuff comes at you at 97 miles an hour and you've got to make a decision like this, you know that he's going to be cool and make the right decision. I know he's not going to get me; I'm just worried I may be hitting him. When you work with guys of this caliber and talent, you're always comfortable, because with these guys nothing is a big deal. They just do it. He gets it done, he's cool. I like those guys because they're cool all the way through. The whole thing about this job is you can lay it out and figure it out but in that instant split second when something goes wrong, you know you're in good hands working with a guy like him. Because he's a pro. He's a legend. Buddy Joe Hooker. Man, I'm grinning already.

TRACY DASHNAW: You hate to say something's never been done before, but to our knowledge, we've never seen a car jump quite like the one Buddy Joe and I did on *Death Proof*. Buddy Joe was in front of me, I was in back and we basically needed to jump our cars bumper to bumper. I think we went almost 80 feet before we landed. Then we were able to drive onto the 101 freeway and pull the whole thing off together, which was absolutely amazing. The cars were built with full cages in them, so if we landed wrong, got hung up in midair or even ended up flipping the cars, we knew we'd be safe.

Ideally, I wanted to be on Buddy Joe's bumper, pushing him off the ramp. Our biggest challenge was that my car wasn't running as well as Buddy Joe's. With my car in back, it would have been better for my car to be faster than his. We wanted as much speed as we could. So the hardest part was just trying to keep my speed up and Buddy Joe trying not to pull too far away, so that we could stay as close together as possible. We ended up hitting in the air. It was really cool.

It sounds weird, but that was actually one of the easiest days I had. Our rehearsal basically consisted of determining the distance we had before we hit and then figuring out how we could hit 50 miles per hour by the time we were airborne—in my case with a car that just really didn't want to run.

As far as the actual jump, it was a blast. There was nobody on the hood to worry about and I didn't have any passengers in the car with me either. I only had myself to worry about. Buddy Joe and I were caged in, we had our helmets on, we were okay. So it wasn't nearly as stressful as having a woman on your hood while you're crashing into another car and

OPPOSITE: Buddy Joe Hooker takes out a movie marquee; **THIS PAGE (FROM TOP):** Buddy Joe Hooker, Quentin Tarantino and Tracy Dashnaw celebrate their two-car jump. • Zöe Bell simulates flying off the hood of the Challenger as Stunt Coordinator Jeff Dashnaw observes.

into guard rails while there's a camera car a foot off your bumper and her feet or her head are between you and the other vehicle. That puts a bit of a strain on you. You don't want anyone to get hurt, you want to keep everybody safe. In that particular job, that was my main concern—making sure Zöe Bell was safe on the hood.

ZÖE BELL: *Planet Terror* was my first experience working with Jeff Dashnaw. I was a stunt zombie and I died like

three or four times. I love working with Jeff. This team of people, including Jeff, Tracy and Buddy Joe is sort of like the closest thing to feeling like I was at home with my team, with my boys that I grew up with since I was 18. Jeff and Tracy kind of became surrogate parents to me during the movie. Being away from my family was hard and they just slipped into those shoes really comfortably and willingly. It was lovely.

Jeff made me feel so comfortable and so safe and I felt like I was given the respect that I earned. Like I didn't have to keep proving myself over and over. But at the same time, if I wasn't up to par, he told me. Then it was my job to come up to par. He gives you trust where you deserve it. He gives you respect where you deserve it. The whole team works like that. The people he chooses to work together have this sense that we're all here to do our job, and we all assume that we're all capable and deserve the respect to do our job until we prove otherwise. That sense that he hired you to do this job and he expects you to be good at it. So there's room for me to be good at it and for him to appreciate it. I know this sounds like maybe obvious stuff, but I've found that it's rare to come across it.

JEFF DASHNAW: Zöe Bell was an interesting situation because not only was she performing as a stuntperson, but also as an actress. I think she did a really great job doing both. Zöe is a breath of fresh air to work with. Very outgoing. Very physical.

BUDDY JOE HOOKER: Zöe Bell is like the Steve McQueen of female actresses. Steve used to do his own stuff. He actually did. A lot of guys said they did, but he really did. So she's getting to do all of her own stuff and can say it honestly. I'll be her witness.

JEFF DASHNAW: To ask someone to be on the hood of a car in a high-speed chase, while it's being banged into—it could get a little sketchy. So we did some tests down in Austin, put her on the hood. We had worked out a very nice safety system with John McLeod and Jamie Ryan, who is the stunt rigger for our company. We had her on a wire on the hood, which enabled

her to move around the hood. She did some stuff that even Quentin will admit scared him. At times, he yelled "cut" because what she was doing scared him and he thought, "Uh-oh, something went wrong." That's the luxury of having Zöe do her own stunts. You put an actress out there who's not in tune with doing her own stunts and you'd never be able to get that effect. The camera was right on Zöe and was on her all the time.

We did all of Zöe's performance portion of the movie, and then did all of the stunts. So we didn't necessarily do the movie in sequence. If I would have tried to put a stunt double on her, Zöe probably would have killed me. It wouldn't have been safe for me. You don't want to mess with Zöe. She's tough, but she's also a very sweet person. We all got to be kind of like family. It was a great experience for us.

TERRY LEONARD: If they make a mistake with Zöe on

ABOVE (CLOCKWISE FROM TOP LEFT): The crew offers to make it even *more* difficult for Buddy Joe Hooker to see out of his windshield. • Buddy Joe Hooker's dust and debris-covered Charger shortly after colliding with a movie marquee. • Zöe Bell holds on tight to the Challenger's hood; **OPPOSITE:** Buddy Joe Hooker and Tracy Dashnaw race down Highway 101; **UPCOMING SPREAD:** The cast and crew of *Death Proof* pose outside of Guero's Taco Bar.

the hood of that car, if they blow a tire, go off the road, she can't do anything. She's on that automobile and they're running a lot of speed. I wouldn't say it takes a lot of guts. It takes a lot of *intelligence* to do something like that because you have to lay it out in your mind, look at the safety rigging. That's what you do before you're on the hood of a car at 70 miles an hour.

If Tracy makes a mistake and gets that car off on the gravel shoulder and rolls a tire off a rim, what happens to Zöe? She can't get away from it. And even if she could, she's in trouble—you're locked in with the wreck. You need to think about the possibility of getting hurt and that's how you rig a stunt. You need to outsmart the act. You say, "Ok, I'm going to be safety'd here, I'm going to be safety'd there. If I roll off the hood here, I'm going to go there." So you use the possibility that something might go wrong as a way to find a way to circumvent it.

TRACY DASHNAW: Zöe was tied onto the car. She couldn't really go anywhere. So she was obviously at the mercy of Buddy Joe and me. We were moving pretty fast and I couldn't see over or around Zöe much of the time. I also couldn't see completely to my right, so I would either ask Rosario [Dawson] or her stuntdouble, Crystal Santos, to tell me what was coming up, a right or a left turn. They'd look out the window and tell me what to expect.

I think Zöe knows me well enough and felt comfortable enough with me that she knew if I truly couldn't see, we were slowing down or we were stopping. That was probably the biggest thing—for Zöe to be able to do her acting and not have to worry about whether or not she's safe on the hood of the car. I'm by nature a pretty calm person, so that probably helped her as well. Our personalities worked really well together. It was intense stuff every single day. In fact, I think Jeff mentioned once on a Friday, "Wow this was a helluva long week today." We're doing a week's worth of stunts each day. Often you'll do a few stunts a week, here and there. Maybe you'll do a car chase, they'll tow the actors around, but this was pretty much stunts all day long, day in, day out.

ZÖE BELL: Tracy Dashnaw is my new hero, without a doubt. Tracy is a mother, a dedicated mother, and she's a fucking *amazing* driver. There's just no two ways about it. She's amazing. And on top of that she pretty much had my life in her hands for a good three or four weeks. Being able to trust someone like that—I know we're all fallible, we all have the possibility of making mistakes at any given time, especially traveling the amount of miles we were. I can't imagine trusting anyone else the way I trusted her behind the wheel. It freed me up to be able to do whatever the hell I wanted on the front. I was free to really go to extremes and know that I was as safe as I possibly could be. Watching her and Buddy Joe drive, it was like watching people dance with big hunks of metal. It was unbelievable. A beautiful thing.

ROBERT RODRIGUEZ, Writer/Director: I thought of *Machete* around the time I was making *Desperado*. I remember shooting a trailer for it with Carlos Gallardo. I wrote a script for it after I finished *Desperado* and thought Danny Trejo would be great as Machete. I thought that we Mexicans should have our own action hero, like the kind of genre role that Charles Bronson would have played. The idea was from a story I heard that sometimes our government hires a federale from Mexico to do a job that was too dangerous to get their own FBI or DEA agents killed over. They'd get paid something like 25 grand. I thought that was a great concept for a movie, having this guy come to the States on a job like that, and he Mexicanizes all the expensive equipment. He ends up having a secret agenda where he wasn't really doing it for the money at all, but to get his revenge on someone who did him wrong. He ends up saving the day and getting the girl.

The original idea was that we'd make a straight to video *Machete* feature in time for the *Grindhouse* double disc release on DVD. I'm writing a script for it now, in my spare time, utilizing some of the script I wrote way back in '94. It's really fun and extremely liberating to write.

DANNY TREJO, Actor: Robert and I started talking about doing *Machete* back when we did *Desperado*. I don't know if Robert remembers, but we were talking about some badass that fights with machetes. A guy that was badder than Rambo. Rambo is like a girl compared with this guy. He's a character that I love. He kills the bad guys and gets their women—the wrong Mexican to fuck with.

CAYLAH EDDLEBLUTE, Production Designer: Some of the very first images we saw were drawings that [Troublemaker Digital Artist] Alex Toader had done of Machete—these phenomenal drawings of Danny Trejo with a chest full of knives. So we were presented with this beautiful art. But when you start to examine artwork like this, you see a huge sea of data where you have to figure out how everything will work together. How do you build it? How do you engineer it?

BELOW: Machete shows off his blades; **OPPOSITE (FROM TOP):** A fireball lights up the sky on the Troublemaker backlot as the crew (silhouetted in foreground) shields their eyes and ears. • Animatic version of Machete by Troublemaker Digital Artist Chris Olivia; **UPCOMING SPREAD:** Close-Up shot of Danny Trejo atop the motorcycle jump rig, firing the mini-gun.

THEY CALL HIM MACHETE

MAKING THE MACHETE TRAILER

Machete has six blades hanging from his waist. How can a person actually maneuver with all that material on them? So we built three separate belts, with two machetes hanging from each one. Robert wanted to make sure that all the blades were exposed, so that we would get the glint of the metal. He didn't want scabbards covering any of the blades, so we designed these open scabbards—perfect sleeves that the machetes could seat in. They would easily snap in and out for cool action.

ROBERT RODRIGUEZ: The machetes in his trenchcoat are real, Steve Joyner and Caylah Eddleblute did an amazing job on them. But the one he throws we did as an effect. I had him toss a real machete from one hand to the other, but when he swings the machete back to throw it at camera, I actually had him drop it and fake his throw. We then added a digital machete to fly at camera. It's a good slight of hand trick.

DANNY TREJO: Robert has a thing with me and knives. Even though my old parole officer said no sharp objects. In *Desperado*, when I opened my vest, I had a belt of knives. This time, I'm walking down the hallway, getting ready to kill about twenty guys. When I open my coat, it's lined with machetes. Robert's crew did a magnificent job. It looks just like a topcoat. It doesn't look like I have anything underneath there. But when you open it up, it's unbelievable.

STEVE JOYNER, Production Designer: Machete carried forty knives in that outfit. That was quite a load. So early on, our lead prop

fabricator, Jeff Poss, recommended creating them out of aluminum. He also recommended Mark McCord to us, who happens to be a knife maker. We were able to borrow him from John McLeod's special effects crew to design these knife blades out of aluminum for us, so everything was beautifully metallic and incredibly light weight.

CAYLAH EDDLEBLUTE: The thing about Mark is that he really understands how to make a prop so that it doesn't seem phony, so it seems like the real thing. It's important that props feel real to the actor. The balancing points need to be right, the handle needs to feel like the real thing. It has to seat in your hand properly. So when it swings, it's believable. All those things are key when you're making light weight versions of these weapons. Mark McCord hand cut and shaped every blade, every handle. We did use varying shapes and sizes of blades—not just the classic machete—to break things up visually.

We studied Toader's images for quite some time. Our Costume Designer Nina Proctor, along with Steve

and myself, worked out how to separate and how to build a knife harness that was separate from Danny's vest.

STEVE JOYNER: I learned a lot about gun holsters and gun leather from Mike Gibbons at Gibbons Entertainment in Hollywood. We have a 16 year relationship with Mike. He taught us a lot about the art of wearing guns and knives. That knowledge really helped us build the specialty leather parts to keep Machete's weapons all in order.

CAYLAH EDDLEBLUTE: Nina Proctor and her crew created a phenomenal vest. You can see all the detail in it, down to the rivet holes. They made sure to have a glint of light popping off of everything. Every detail is considered. They made the form pop out so each outline could be seen.

The inspiration for the small daggers on Danny's vest came from having drawn Salma Hayek's throwing knives for *Once Upon a Time in Mexico*. We were at Gibbons in Los Angeles—super busy day, lots

BELOW: Concept illustration by Trouble-maker Digital Artist Alex Toader; **OPPOSITE (CLOCKWISE FROM TOP):** Concept illustrations by Alex Toader. • Danny Trejo tries on his Machete jacket with help from Production Designer Caylah Eddleblute (L) and Costume Designer Nina Proctor (R). • Stunt Coordinator Jeff Dashnaw consults with Danny Trejo before shooting the motorcycle jump gag. • Production Designer Steve Joyner at work on Machete's *Escape From New York*-inspired table of weapons.

212

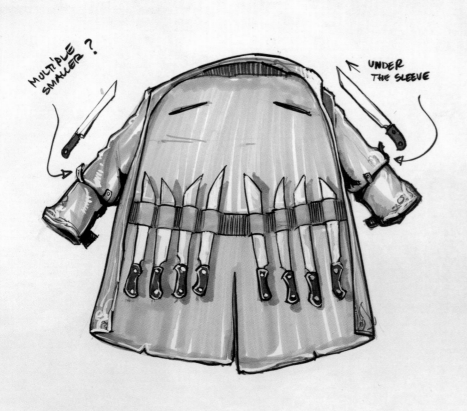

MULTIPLE SMALLER ?

UNDER THE SLEEVE

? PULL ON COLLAR BLADES DROP

of appointments. We had to get a reference to the knifemaker pronto, so I drew a freehand pattern for Salma's knives. It came out in one gesture. I was stunned.

So I applied that memory when drawing the pattern for Machete's vest full of throwing knives, all shaped like miniature machetes. Mark McCord cut and shaped them perfectly. We had the idea to add them late in the game, so more glints of light would play off of Danny as he moved. The costumers made them look elegant on the vest.

STEVE JOYNER: We added the knives as an homage to Danny's character, Navajas, from *Desperado*. All great storytelling involves a dagger, right back to "The Bard" himself. "Is this a dagger I see floating before me?" In Robert and Quentin's movies…yes it is!

After Machete is hired by the businessman to go out and get his target, the businessman takes him and shows him a long table of weapons he can choose from. The scene pays homage to the shot of Kurt Russell getting ready to go into Manhattan Island in *Escape from New York*.

CAYLAH EDDLEBLUTE: The scene was actually shot in our office. We pulled out all the work tables, set up all the weapons, brought in the dolly and the camera and boom, they did the shot. That was Robert Rodriguez, grindhouse style. He really wanted to use our facility here as the backdrop. We even used the hallway outside our office as the hospital corridor when Machete was on the gurney.

We even put three of our cool detonators from *Sin City* on the weapons table, for a cool little reference.

ROBERT RODRIGUEZ: The first big, wide shot of the motorcycle jump was done completely in the computer. I liked [Troublemaker Digital Artist] Chris Olivia's animatic so much, that I thought with just a little bit more finishing on it and lots of aging, you couldn't tell it was fake. Then, the close-up of Machete firing was done on a rig that John McLeod put together. The real motorcycle was on a high stand that would rock the bike down towards camera. We then blasted a real explosion behind him and had him firing blanks. The sky was clear so it served as a good blue screen in a way, and we added the passing telephone poles with the computer to give the illusion of movement. The

OPPOSITE: Concept illustration by Troublemaker Digital Artist Alex Toader; **BELOW:** Danny Trejo takes aim as Robert Rodriguez snaps some unit photography; **UPCOMING SPREAD:** *Machete* lobby cards. Photography by Robert Rodriguez, design by Kurt Volk.

DANNY TREJO IS
MACHETE

A RODRIGUEZ INTERNATIONAL PICTURES RELEASE STARRING DANNY TREJO · JEFF FAHEY
A TROUBLEMAKER STUDIOS PRODUCTION

DANNY TREJO IS
MACHETE

A RODRIGUEZ INTERNATIONAL PICTURES RELEASE STARRING DANNY TREJO · JEFF FAHEY
A TROUBLEMAKER STUDIOS PRODUCTION

DANNY TREJO IS
MACHETE

A RODRIGUEZ INTERNATIONAL PICTURES RELEASE STARRING DANNY TREJO · JEFF FAHEY
A TROUBLEMAKER STUDIOS PRODUCTION

DANNY TREJO IS
MACHETE

A RODRIGUEZ INTERNATIONAL PICTURES RELEASE STARRING DANNY TREJO · JEFF FAHEY
A TROUBLEMAKER STUDIOS PRODUCTION

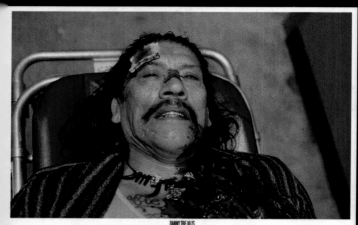

DANNY TREJO IS
MACHETE

A RODRIGUEZ INTERNATIONAL PICTURES RELEASE STARRING DANNY TREJO · JEFF FAHEY
A TROUBLEMAKER STUDIOS PRODUCTION

DANNY TREJO IS
MACHETE

A RODRIGUEZ INTERNATIONAL PICTURES RELEASE STARRING DANNY TREJO · JEFF FAHEY
A TROUBLEMAKER STUDIOS PRODUCTION

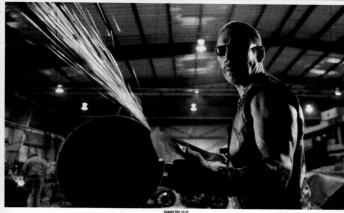

DANNY TREJO IS
MACHETE

A RODRIGUEZ INTERNATIONAL PICTURES RELEASE STARRING DANNY TREJO · JEFF FAHEY

A TROUBLEMAKER STUDIOS PRODUCTION

DANNY TREJO IS
MACHETE

A RODRIGUEZ INTERNATIONAL PICTURES RELEASE STARRING DANNY TREJO · JEFF FAHEY

A TROUBLEMAKER STUDIOS PRODUCTION

DANNY TREJO IS
MACHETE

A RODRIGUEZ INTERNATIONAL PICTURES RELEASE STARRING DANNY TREJO · JEFF FAHEY

A TROUBLEMAKER STUDIOS PRODUCTION

DANNY TREJO IS
MACHETE

A RODRIGUEZ INTERNATIONAL PICTURES RELEASE STARRING DANNY TREJO · JEFF FAHEY

A TROUBLEMAKER STUDIOS PRODUCTION

DANNY TREJO IS
MACHETE

A RODRIGUEZ INTERNATIONAL PICTURES RELEASE STARRING DANNY TREJO · JEFF FAHEY

A TROUBLEMAKER STUDIOS PRODUCTION

DANNY TREJO IS
MACHETE

A RODRIGUEZ INTERNATIONAL PICTURES RELEASE STARRING DANNY TREJO · JEFF FAHEY

A TROUBLEMAKER STUDIOS PRODUCTION

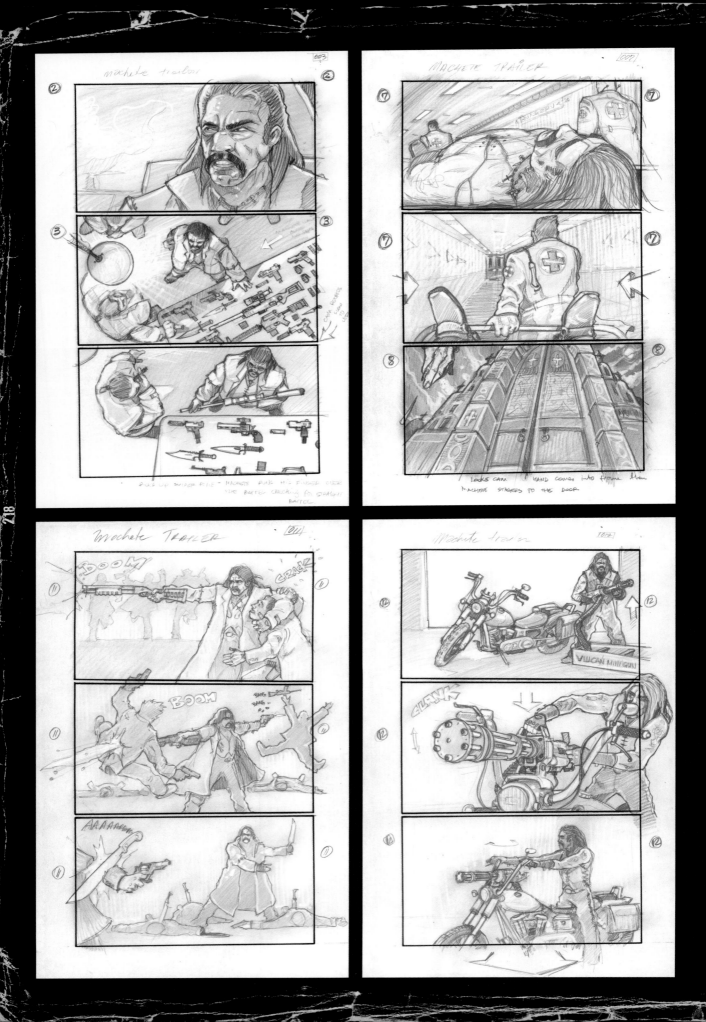

extreme aging also helps.

STEVE JOYNER: For Machete's mini-gun, we used a real one that uses specialty blanks. They come in belts of 500. You get just under a three second shot with a belt of 500 rounds. You sit there and click all these rounds together and *brap* they're gone. Robert was very efficient in his shooting, I think we only fired it five times.

For the closeup of Machete with the explosions behind him, we had a real Harley on a special gimble mount that John McLeod made. John set off a huge number of explosions behind Machete while the mini-gun tore through all those rounds.

DANNY TREJO: The motorcycle jump was very terrifying, but we did it. You know, Robert and his crew are probably the safest crew I've ever worked with. Every single member of Robert's crew is like Radar from M*A*S*H. They all know what he wants. Everybody knows their thing. Robert turns around and says, "Hey, give me that 5x9." And it's already there, it's been there. He doesn't even have to say it. He turns around and he sees a 5x9. He knows it's there. It's amazing to watch these guys. I was watching them while they were setting up all this stuff. I think they're all aliens and they all have some sort of mental telepathy thing going. I've never seen that on a set. It's like they all

know exactly what they're supposed to do. It's s
great to work with people who love what they're
doing. And I love what I do too. I have not lost the
enthusiasm for movie-making since I started in 1985

ROBERT RODRIGUEZ: I was just sort of getting into the
mindset of making a grindhouse movie, and *Machete*
helped put me in that headspace. For the scene in
the waterfall, I cast two different girls so in case one
didn't work out, I would have a backup. It wasn't until
got to the set that I realized, "Hey, this is a grindhouse
movie, he should be in the waterfall with *two* girls!" I
seems obvious now, but at the time I was only thinking
one. So for a grindhouse movie, just always think
"Where one will work, two is twice as good."

CAYLAH EDDLEBLUTE: The *Machete* trailer was probably
the most fun I've had since working on *From Dusk
till Dawn*. The shortness and the brevity of it had a
quality that was just really nimble. There was a rea
collaborative effort, we had to work with Nina Procto
and the costume department very closely and it was
a lot of fun. We were able to problem solve and
engineer stuff and have it look cool. There's nothing
like going out on the playground—just like when you
were a kid—and being able to rile it up.

STEVE JOYNER: The compressed shooting schedule of
Machete was truly grindhouse. It was fast, cheap and

out of control. Everybody got in there, everybody did everything, got rough and tumble, and we cranked it out.

ROBERT RODRIGUEZ: I really wish we could have shot *Planet Terror* the same way we did *Machete*. That would have been great, but probably would have killed the crew! We were so tired after those two days of shooting *Machete*. No one wanted to admit how fried they were, not even me! Finally someone broke the silence and everyone poured out how much it drained them. We had a small crew and were running from location to location to give the illusion that we had shot an entire movie. So, in a way, it was like shooting a mini feature in two days. We had such a small crew, I kept thinking we should keep the small crew and do *Planet Terror* that way, but it was just not going to happen with all the effects and the sheer size of the movie.

It's difficult shooting a trailer, but also in a way extremely fun to do. Since you're just getting the money shots, you're sort of crystallizing the movie with every shot and scene, and getting only the iconic images. So it's very gratifying at the end of the day. I shot the lobby cards for the movie, and if you look at all the images you can see how great it was to feel that sense of accomplishment in a few days.

DANNY TREJO: I'm so impressed with Robert. I'm a lot older than him, but he's my hero. Robert Rodriguez is to movie making what the automatic transmission was to car-building. Everybody had a stick shift before he came around. And then all of a sudden we're doing 80 or 90. If the technology isn't there, that sucker will invent it. It's amazing to watch him do this stuff. I remember way back when we were working on *Desperado*, we were staying in a hotel in Del Rio, Texas and I'm walking by his room. I hear Robert say, "Come here, I want you to see the trailer." And I'm like, "What are you talking about? We've only done one day of shooting!" And he already had the trailer cut. Amazing. Robert Rodriguez, the automatic transmission of movie-making.

ABOVE (FROM LEFT): *Machete* animatics by Troublemaker Digital Artist Chris Olivia; Animatic used to demonstrate the motorcycle jump rig by Chris Olivia; **OPPOSITE:** Danny Trejo sits atop the motorcycle jump rig.

EXT. STREET CORNER – DOWNTOWN

Sidewalk lined with Mexican laborers. Workers load up into the back of a truck.

The truck pulls away revealing MACHETE walking up.

      70's TRAILER GUY VOICE
HE CAME A STRANGER…

A fancy black car pulls up.

The window rolls down, revealing MACHETE'S FACE. Machete looks into the window. We see the driver.

      WELL DRESSED MAN
Get in.

INT. BLACK CAR – DAY

Machete is being driven. He explains his labor prices.

      MACHETE
70 dollars a day for yards and properties. 100 for roofing, 125 for septic…sewage.

      WELL DRESSED MAN
Have you ever killed anyone before?

Machete gives his a look.

      70's TRAILER GUY VOICE
HE WAS GIVEN AN OFFER HE COULDN'T REFUSE.

INT. WEAPONS ROOM – DAY

suit up scene in Escape From New York).

      WELL DRESSED MAN
As you know, illegal Americans are being forced out of our country at an alarming rate…For the good of both our people…Our new Senator…must die.

EXT. CAPITOL/STREET – DAY

Long lens shot of Machete walking in front of the Capitol.

      WELL DRESSED MAN (V.O.)
For that, we'll pay you $150,000. Cash.

INT. WELL DRESSED MAN'S OFFICE – DAY

Machete opens a suitcase. We see the cash.

EXT. ROOFTOP – DAY

He pieces a rifle together.

He aims his rifle at the Senator, then looks up and sees someone aiming at him.

Machete is shot several times. Multiple gunshots.

CUT TO BLACK

INT. HOSPITAL – TROUBLEMAKER HALLWAY – DAY

Machete on a gurney wheeled through hospital. (Close on his face. His POV of overhead

      70's TRAILER GUY VOICE
SET UP. DOUBLE CROSSED…AND LEFT FOR DEAD.

EXT. CHURCH – DOWNTOWN – DAY

MACHETE outside a giant church, looking battered.

INT. INSIDE CONFESSIONAL – OR CHURCH – DAY

      FATHER BENICIO DEL TORO
You want me to get a "confession" out of them?

      MACHETE
Yes, bro. I mean…Padre.

      FATHER BENICIO DEL TORO
          (shrugs)
I'll see what I can do.

We see Father Benicio with 2 pump action shotguns. KA-CHANK!

      70's TRAILER GUY VOICE
AND THEY SOON REALIZE…

INT. WELL DRESSED MAN'S OFFICE – DAY

Telefax comes in. Machete's picture all over it. Warning signs on the page.

      HENCHMAN
Ohhhhhh shit.

      70's TRAILER GUY VOICE
THEY JUST FUCKED WITH THE WRONG MEXICAN.

Henchman is showing the paper to

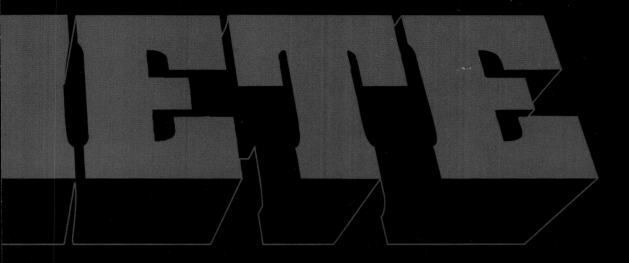

HENCHMAN
He's ex-Federale...That's DEA, FBI
and CIA all rolled into one!

•WELL DRESSED MAN
He's coming after us.

INT/EXT. ALL LOCATIONS – DAY/
NIGHT (SERIES)

*Various Shots of Machete locking
and loading, uncovering a stash
of weapons, etc...*

*Various shots of Machete
chopping Bad Guys at each
location...*

EXT. OLD AIRPORT AREA/HANGARS
– DAY

*We see Machete carrying a BIG
MACHINE GUN and mounting it to
the front of his MOTORCYCLE.*

HENCHMAN (V.O.)
And he's Mexican.

EXT. DOWNTOWN – ROOFTOP – DAY

*We see Machete raise his machete
over his head. An entire crowd
of workers behind him all raise
their own machetes. He's got an
army.*

WELL DRESSED MAN (V.O.)
God help us.
            (alternate)
Fuck.
            (alternate)
He's coming after us.

EXT. OLD AIRPORT AREA/HANGARS
– DAY

Machete kick starts the bike.

70's TRAILER GUY VOICE
HE KNOWS THE SCORE...
            (alt)
ACTION. SUSPENSE. EMOTION...

INT. WELL DRESSED MAN'S OFFICE
– DAY

*Shaky cam as Well Dressed Man is
on the phone.*

WELL DRESSED MAN
Where's my wife and daughter!

70's TRAILER GUY VOICE
HE GETS THE WOMEN.

EXT. WATERFALL – DAY

*We see Machete in waterfall
making out with a gorgeous babe.*

70's TRAILER GUY VOICE
IF YOU'RE GOING TO HIRE
MACHETE...

TO KILL THE BAD GUY...

INT. HALLWAY #2 – NIGHT

*See Machete opening his
trenchcoat in slow motion. It's
full of MACHETES.*

70's TRAILER GUY VOICE
...YOU BETTER MAKE DAMN SURE...

*He uses his machetes like
throwing knives. Bad guys
getting pegged and screaming.*

70's TRAILER GUY VOICE (cont'd)
...THE BAD GUY...

EXT. STREET – DAY

*Machete's motorcycle leaps over
a car-laden barricade.*

*Long lens like in FIRST BLOOD as
motorcycle comes flying over...
Explosions behind him...*

*We see WELL DRESSED MAN looking
up into lens as it flies toward him.*

70's TRAILER GUY VOICE
...Isn't YOU...

*Closer on Machete as he's
airborne, firing his machine
gun that's mounted to the cycle's
handlebars.*

FREEZE FRAME that image.

70's TRAILER GUY VOICE (cont'd)
MACHETE. Pray he isn't out there.

EXT. TBD – DAY

*Father Benicio making the sign
of the cross...*

FATHER BENICIO DEL TORO
En el nombre de padre, hijo,
espiritu santo...

*And then with the same hand he
squeezes a small detonator he
was holding.*

EXT. OLD AIRPORT – DAY

*HELICOPTER EXPLODES and ND BAD
GUYS fly off every direction.*

*This same shot is used in ALL the
trailers.•*

THE END.

IT'LL SCARE THE STUFFING OUT OF YOU

MAKING THE THANKSGIVING TRAILER WITH ELI ROTH

ELI ROTH, Director: Growing up in the 80s, it seemed like every holiday had its own horror film. It started with *Black Christmas*, then came *Halloween*, followed by a slew of low-budget gems such as *Mother's Day*, *My Bloody Valentine*, and *Silent Night, Deadly Night*. So many holiday-themed slasher films were made that they even came out with *April Fool's Day*. Clearly they were running out of holidays, so it was only a matter of time until the Thanksgiving horror film would come out. Or so it seemed...

My friend Jeff Rendell and I saw every single film the day they came out and often had to drag our parents with us because the films were R-rated (as all slasher films should be). I have wonderful memories of the usher at the Dedham, Massachusetts movie theater telling Jeff's father that he didn't think it was appropriate for two twelve year olds to be seeing *Silent Night, Deadly Night* to which Jeff's dad replied "I don't give a goddamn fuck what you think—I don't pay you to think! Just gimme those goddamn

tickets!" Ah, sweet memories. But year after year each holiday passed without that one slasher film we were waiting for—*Thanksgiving*. Growing up in Massachusetts, Thanksgiving was a big fucking deal. We had not just one but two full-time reenactment villages where you could go and see how the Pilgrims lived—or fuck with them when they claimed to have no idea what television was and ask them if they watched the Celtics game. That always got them. To us it was so obvious—how could someone not make a Thanksgiving slasher film? By the time we were teenagers, we decided it was our purpose in life to take this problem into our own hands and create the horror film of our dreams. So in November of 2006, we got to fulfill our destiny and shoot the trailer for our dream project, *Thanksgiving*.

I remember back in 2005 when Quentin and Robert first started talking about *Grindhouse*. I had been watching a lot of films at Quentin's house, and he always started the night with a good round of

ABOVE: Thanksgiving dinner courtesy of KNB. • **OPPOSITE:** Co-Writer/Actor Jeff Rendell (L) and Director Eli Roth (R) pose with the Kladno Majorettes before shooting the slaughter.

exploitation trailers. When they asked me if I wanted to direct a faux exploitation trailer, it was not just the chance of a lifetime, it was the perfect way to shoot some scenes from *Thanksgiving*. I had been wanting to make the film in the style of an 80s movie, and now I had the perfect format. I called up Jeff and told him about *Grindhouse* and how we were going to shoot the trailer and that it would be part of Quentin and Robert's movie. He couldn't believe it was real—it seemed too good to be true. We had written so many ideas for the film over the years that we just culled our favorite ones and wrote them into a four-page script. We refined the voice over and narrowed it down to something we could shoot in two days. The only question was: how in the hell was I going to shoot this, act in *Grindhouse*, and direct *Hostel: Part II* all at the same time?

After some consulting with Elizabeth Avellán, my brother [and 2nd Unit Director] Gabe, and my *Hostel: Part II* co-producer Dan Frisch, I decided that the best way to do it was to tack on two days to the end of the *Hostel: Part II* shoot. I was already in Prague so I wouldn't have to travel any crew members, and I'd just cast the trailer with whoever was shooting with us at the time. It just so happened that we were shooting scenes with Jay Hernandez and Jordan Ladd, so I wrote in parts for them. They changed their flights back to the U.S. and stayed for two extra days just to be in the trailer. I needed all the Americans I could get, so I cast my co-producer Dan Frisch (who has a great Indiana drawl), the KNB effects guys Mike McCarty and Kevin Wasner, myself, and our Production Accountant Mark Bakunas, who comes from St. Louis and has amazing hair.

Greg Nicotero and Howard Berger from KNB did the effects, and our on-set team of Kevin and Mike would handle the gore during shooting. Michael Biehn was also in Prague shooting a film, and he heard about the trailer and asked if he could be in it. It was perfect. Since he was in *Planet Terror* and Jordan Ladd was in *Death Proof*, it would be perfect grindhouse crossover between the two films. I couldn't believe it—the star of *Aliens* and *The Terminator* was asking me if he could be in *Thanksgiving*. It was too fucking cool.

The real challenge was how to fake Prague for small town America, specifically, Plymouth Massachusetts. My brother Gabe produced the trailer with me, and while I was finishing shooting *Hostel: Part II* he was location scouting all over the Czech Republic and putting the production together with Dan Frisch and our production manager, Pavlina Zipkova. Gabe found a great gym for the high school scene, as well as some possible parade locations. Ironically, we were scheduled to shoot the trailer for *Thanksgiving* over Thanksgiving weekend. Explaining this concept proved to be exceedingly difficult. Most of my conversations went something like this:

"Yeah, I'm shooting this trailer for *Grindhouse*. It's called *Thanksgiving*. We're shooting *Thanksgiving*."

"Wait, you're shooting the *Grindhouse* trailer? Didn't I just see that on the internet?"

"No, this is a trailer for *Grindhouse*. But it's not the *Grindhouse* trailer. It's *Thanksgiving*."

"That's when you're shooting it?"

"No, well, yeah, I mean, it's called *Thanksgiving*, but we're shooting it over Thanksgiving. It's for *Grindhouse*, but it's not the *Grindhouse* trailer. Wanna do it for free?"

Now try translating that into Czech.

We hired a costume designer named Tereza Dvorakova to make the Turkey Pilgrim mascot. Tereza worked with Mike McCarty and Kevin Wasner from KNB to rig it for the decapitation. I knew the key to making the trailer work was successfully pulling off the parade, and Gabe, Jeff and I were adamant that we had to have a Mayflower float. If we spent money on anything—and almost everyone was either doing it for free or a fraction of their rate—it would be on that float.

We scouted a bunch of locations around Prague, until our location manager, Honza, suggested the town of Kladno. Kladno's about half an hour outside of Prague, and amazingly they had a street that could double for the town center in small town America. And even if the Czech signage got in there, who cared? It's grindhouse—it's supposed to look low budget. We found both the parade location and the gym there, and Honza worked wonders with the city council to get them to approve us on such short notice. The only question was how to fill the street with extras, since we couldn't really afford to hire enough extras to make a convincing parade. Gabe and Pavlina talked to a local radio station, who agreed to do promotions saying, "Come be in a Quentin Tarantino/Robert Rodriguez film!" I mean, I hate to namedrop, but in this case, I made an exception. Not to sell myself short, but "Come be in a new splatter film from the director of *Hostel* for free" doesn't exactly get people lining up around the block in the Czech Republic.

Chris Rosewarne, who did some great conceptual illustrations on *Hostel: Part II*, did some killer designs for us of the Mayflower float, and we hired a construction team to build it. Through some clever promoting and the help of our sound recordist Tomas Belohradsky, Pavlina and Gabe and I were able to pull together not only a marching band, but the Kladno majorettes. These majorettes, aged 5-10, said they would be in the parade in full uniform, twirling batons at 7:00 in the morning on a Wednesday at no charge. I asked Pavlina if the girls had any idea what we were going to shoot, and she said they were told

it would be bloody, and the girls still wanted to do it. I thought this is either going to be the greatest scene I've ever filmed or a total fucking disaster. Either way we'll get it on film.

Jeff Rendell flew into Prague the day before we began shooting, and brought a ton of cheesy Thanksgiving decorations with him. Once Jeff got to his hotel, I broke the news to him—he was going to play the Pilgrim. I knew that nobody would understand how to play the killer like Jeff would. He's got the right look for it, and even though he'd never acted a day in his life, I knew that he'd be brilliant. And he was. As soon as he put on the jumpsuit, hat and driving gloves, he smiled and said "This outfit just makes me want to kill people." I've never seen him look so happy.

My Director of Photography, Milan Chadima, who shot both *Hostel* films with me, dug up lenses from Prague Panavision that hadn't been used since the 70s. We said it was going to be like film school where you get a camera for two days and you just have to cram as much as you possibly can into the shoot. We'd only do one or two takes at most, and if there was a focus problem or a crew member in the shot, too bad. This was grindhouse and things like continuity and razor sharp focus were out the window. The first night of shooting was awesome. When I saw the first

BELOW (CLOCKWISE FRO
Co-Producer Dan Frisch and
Wasner with the Dan Frisch/T
hybrid courtesy of KNB. • Mi
and Kevin Wasner of KNB mak
minute touchups to decapitat
Eli Roth sets up a shot; **OPPO**
Rendell takes a swing at Kevin
the turkey suit) as Eli Roth obs

kids who did a great job of not laughing. However, I felt too guilty to have them there when Jeff fucked the Dan Frisch turkey body, so we shot that as a split screen and composited the shot later.

By 11:30 we moved outside, and thanks to global warming, I was able to shoot a sex scene in a convertible with the top down at the end of November in Prague. Our art director found a 1950s cherry red convertible—probably the only one in the Czech Republic—and we were able to use it just so long as we didn't stain it with fake blood. This was certainly a challenge since we were filming a decapitation scene, but I figured that even if people notice the plastic lining the seats, it'll make it more authentically low budget. We filmed the scene in the woods with Jordan Ladd and Jay Hernandez. Jordan came out of the makeup trailer with this awesome side ponytail, and Jay came out of the wardrobe trailer in acid washed 80's jeans and a letterman's jacket. It was pretty genius. I'd never seen Jay do that kind of comedy before, and both he and Jordan were hysterical. We got back to Prague at probably 2:30 in the morning, which of course did not stop us from going out. I crashed around 4:30, but I think everyone else's evening ended, yet again, at 7:00 in the morning at the Darling Club with Helen the Midget giving everyone lapdances. I'm not kidding.

We slept all day the next day to get back onto a day schedule and to prepare for what would be the greatest day of filming in my life.

POV shot through the window of the grandmother making the turkey, I got chills. It really looked like an 80s-style slasher film. Milan and I kept banging out shots, and the crew was pleasantly shocked at how fast we were moving. It was really freeing to not have to worry about continuity or to have any real story to tell. Every shot had to be a gore shot or a slasher movie shot.

We filmed the dinner scene with the Dan Frisch turkey body. I don't know why, but I just had this image of Dan Frisch showing up to a Thanksgiving dinner and then seeing his decapitated head on the body of a cooked turkey. He was a great sport about it and even wore a fanny pack just for the shot. Tereza dressed everyone in the absolute worst holiday sweaters we'd ever seen, including my *Hostel* producer Chris Briggs, who vomits at the dinner table. We were all laughing during the turkey dinner, except Lilian Malkina who played the grandmother. Lilian is a wonderful soul and has a great sense of humor. I had directed her in *Hostel: Part II* and she was kind enough to do this as a favor to me. However, I suspect the meat thermometer in the ass was a bit much for her because she looked genuinely shocked. My *Hostel* prop master Karel Vanasek played the grandfather, and we hired some

The day began at about 7:00 in the morning in Kladno. The majorettes and band members started showing up at crew call, and, as soon as we had people, we began filming. It got light enough around 7:55, and we did shots of the sign raising up and of Kevin Wasner dressing in the turkey Pilgrim costume. It was pretty cold out so we kept the majorettes in a heated tent nearby, and only called them to set once camera was ready. The power went out in the wardrobe trailer, yet Tereza and her crew managed to dress every single pilgrim, Indian, and marching band member in the dark on time. I still don't know how they did it, but by 8:15 we had the Mayflower filled with pilgrims waving to the crowd. We shot most of the parade hand-held, and got as many different angles of the parade "clean," because once the blood started I knew we'd lose people. The majorettes were a gift from the movie gods—these adorable, sparkly, clean girls all showed up in matching uniforms, twirling their batons in their little white boots. We tried to shoot quickly so they wouldn't get cold, and they were troopers. These girls loved being on camera, and you can tell because so many of them were staring directly into the lens in every shot.

Around 11:00 I looked at Milan and we nodded to each other, smiling with evil grins. It was time. Time for

blood. When Kevin came out dressed in the turkey outfit, all the majorettes burst out laughing. They loved him. I looked at Gabe and Jeff and we just shook our heads. This was going to be a mess. We warned the kids that there was going to be blood, and the kids nodded as if they understood. Yes, we told them in Czech. We all knew we'd pretty much get one take at the decapitation because once the blood squirted then the costume would be ruined, the street would be a mess, and we'd probably get kicked out of Kladno. We got our set-up shots of Jeff stepping out with the axe, and then got Kevin in position for the decapitation. Mike McCarty rigged the outfit and filled a small pump with pressurized blood, and Kevin would be inside running around pumping the blood with one hand, while staggering around like a turkey with its head cut off. We'd keep going until the blood ran out, and no matter what happened, we'd keep shooting. Gabe got dressed up in our "Injun" puppet, which was a recycled puppet from *Hostel: Part II* that we decorated like an offensive stereotypical Native American. I felt that if the film was going to feel like it was early 80's we couldn't be politically correct. Then I looked at photos online of current Thanksgiving parades around America and realized that I couldn't hold a candle to what most American parades were doing that very weekend. Gabe would be there to help steer the girls, and hopefully they wouldn't trample him. Milan put the camera on his shoulder, Jeff raised the axe, and we rolled.

I can honestly say I've never heard girls scream so loud in my life. They needed no direction whatsoever once that Turkey head came flying off. Jeff nailed it perfectly. Blood spouted everywhere. The girls bolted, screaming at the top of their lungs, knocking into each other, crying. Kevin chased after the girls, knocking into barricades and then into Gabe before falling into the street. Mike McCarty played our "parade rioter" and kicked over the barricades and ran through the crowd screaming, "Get the fuck out of the way!" Pilgrim women screamed, running in a panic. Pilgrim men shoved people out of the way. It was total chaos, yet as soon as we yelled cut, everyone stopped and went right back into place, ready for another take. We did take after take after take of people running around screaming, and no one got hurt. Physically, that is. Mentally I'm sure some of these kids are scarred for life, like the four year old who burst into tears when a giant decapitated yellow turkey charged after her spouting blood, waving his arms like a lunatic. There were a few of those, and any time a kid cried, we ran over with the camera, trying to film them, which most of the time made them run away, crying even harder.

Tomas Belohradsky, my sound recordist on both *Hostel* films, had worked all night on another film the night before, but still came out just to play the tuba player. We were laughing so hard we could barely breathe. Nearly every shot had Mike McCarty running through

ABOVE (CLOCKWISE FROM LEF...
KNB's Kevin Wasner (in the turkey ...
leads the Thanksgiving festivities ...
The Kladno Majorettes and the blee...
turkey carcass. • The cast and crew...
Thanksgiving (first row from left) Produ...
Gabriel Roth, Base Camp Guy Coo...
Co-Writer/Actor Jeff Rendell, KNB's M...
McCarty, KNB's Kevin Wasner (in tur...
suit), Eli Roth and the Kladno Majoret...
OPPOSITE (CLOCKWISE FROM LEF...
Vendula Kristek shows some skin as ...
Cheerleader. • KNB's Mike McCarty ...
Kevin Wasner add the finishing touche...
Eli Roth's decapitated head. • (from l...
Director Eli Roth, Actress Jordan La...
Producer Gabriel Roth and Co-Wri...
Actor Jeff Rendell prepare to shoot ...
make-out scene. • KNB's bleeding turk...

screaming "Get the fuck out of the way!" as he bounced through the majorettes. After about an hour of shooting the decapitation, Milan and I felt we had gotten enough, and by that point the girls were totally into it. It was really fun to watch these girls go from being horrified to actually getting the joke, and then all vying to get in every shot either jumping over the decapitated body or kicking around the severed head. Kevin Wasner was great and kept talking to the girls between takes, showing them he was still alive, so that by the end they were posing for pictures with the decapitated turkey. A number of them had blood stains all over their white boots which probably won't ever come out, and for that I'm sorry, but I can honestly say that the fans around the world will thank them. And it was worth it. At least for us.

The sublime moment of the morning was when we were shooting the dead turkey pilgrim lying in the street, and Kevin was getting himself into position, so he could flop back and squirt the blood. Kevin was lying down and the girls were gathered around the body. Milan asked Kevin to reposition himself, and, as soon as Kevin sat up, all the girls jumped back screaming and ran away. We were so pissed we didn't get it on film, but sure enough, the next take, they did the exact same thing, and we got it. We let most of the extras go and filmed the "aftermath" scene with Michael Biehn and Mark Bakunas. Biehn was hilarious and nailed it on the first take, as did our production accountant Mark Bakunas, who played the deputy. Michael was really cool and posed for pictures with everyone, and then we got the hell out of there before anyone realized what had happened.

The only thing that could top a parade full of screaming five year old majorettes was one hot stripping cheerleader on a trampoline. The whole crew was super adrenaline-charged after the parade, and we were all laughing through lunch at the various moments we'd witnessed. The total absurdity of 60 year old men dressed as pilgrims kicking around a decapitated turkey head with five year old majorettes just made everyone smile. Vendula, the cheerleader showed up, and she pretty much stopped the room. She spoke no English, and through a translator I double checked that she understood what the scene was about. She totally got it, as did Petr, who had played a part in *Hostel: Part II* and came in for free to be the boyfriend. I must confess that I broke the "one or two take only" rule when it came time to film Vendula stripping on the trampoline. I heard that David Lean shot a lot of footage during *Lawrence of Arabia*. I also heard that Kubrick did about fifty takes minimum for every single shot. And I remember being on the set of *Meet Joe Black* when Martin Brest took sixty seven takes of Brad Pitt drinking a glass of champagne. And now I finally understood why. We probably shot more footage of that girl's tits bouncing around than all the other scenes combined. Take after take after take, over and over, up and down they went. I mean, Vendula's a pro, she got it perfect on the first take, but you know what? It's grindhouse. It's an exploitation film. What's the point in shooting an exploitation trailer if you don't get to exploit anybody? I was simply doing my job. And if asked, I'd do it again in a heartbeat.

GRINDHOUSE TRAILER
"THANKSGIVING"

by
Eli Roth
&
Jeff Rendell

EXT. HOUSE IN THE WOODS - NIGHT

A hand-held SLASHER POV of a secluded house in the woods. A light is on in the kitchen, where A GRANDMOTHER cooks a turkey. The POV creeps towards the woman in the house, peeking through the window first, then coming through the front door, slowly creeping up on her.

An 80's-style ultra-serious voice over begins:

NARRATOR
This holiday season...

The killer picks up a carving knife and raises it behind the woman, who's bent over the oven. She turns around and seeing the camera SCREAMS

NARRATOR
Prepare to have the stuffing scared out of you.

We freeze frame on the screaming woman's face.

CLOSE UP - A beautifully roasted turkey on a silver platter in front of an empty black background. A black gloved hand STABS A CARVING KNIFE into the Turkey, which bleeds thick, red blood. A cheaply animated title splashes over black in red letters:

NARRATOR
Thanksgiving.

The word "Thanksgiving" splashes across the screen in a gory, bloody animated type face that slowly drips blood down the screen.

EXT. PARADE - DAY

A Thanksgiving parade is in progress, complete with floats,

banners, a marching band, and a Turkey Mascot in a man-sized costume, spinning a baton bringing up the rear. People watch from risers as the parade passes through Main Street. They are mostly focused on the floats and marching band.

NARRATOR
In the town of Plymouth Massachusetts, the fourth Thursday in November is the most celebrated day of the year.

INSERTS - DARK ROOM

Quick cuts: A killer wearing a Pilgrim hat zips up a black jumpsuit, slips on black 'Torso'-style fingerless driving gloves, and flips up an axe.

NARRATOR
But an uninvited guest has arrived. And this year, there will be... NO LEFTOVERS.

THE PILGRIM KILLER steps out into the parade and LOPS OFF MASCOT'S HEAD WITH AN AXE. Chaos ensues. The marching band's music notes turn sour. People scream, panicking, running everywhere, including the fat tuba player. The fat tuba player and the other band members kick the mascot's head around as they run through the streets.

The decapitated turkey lays in the street, blood spewing out of its neck like a fire hydrant. The killer's black boots step through the blood as people run around, panicking and screaming.

CLOSE UP - BLACK ROOM - the carving knife stabbing into the turkey. Blood leaking. (Our title page - same shot as before.)

NARRATOR
Thanksgiving.

INT. HIGH SCHOOL GYM - DAY

It's dark. Two teens are alone in the gymnasium. The guy wears a high school letterman's jacket, the girl wears a cheerlead-

ing uniform. The girl leads him out from the bleachers, up to a trampoline. The guy looks a little hesitant.

VARSITY GUY
If we get caught in here before the big game, coach'll have my neck!

The cheerleader shushes him and starts to dance around on the trampoline in a cheerleader uniform. She slowly starts to strip, taking off her top. The girl turns around and takes off her panties, showing her ass to her boyfriend. His eyes are nearly bursting out of his head as THE KILLER grabs him from behind, yanking him out of frame.

The girl turns and bounces, doing a half-naked split in the air. As she lands down on the trampoline, a CARVING KNIFE stabs UPWARD THROUGH THE TRAMPOLINE, just as she's landing.

Just at the moment of impact, we hear a scream and cut to our:

TITLE SHOT - the knife stabbing into the turkey.

NARRATOR
Thanksgiving.

EXT. CAR - NIGHT

A car parked at make out point. Probably a convertible, depending on weather. A high school couple (played by people in their early 30's) kiss gratuitously, ripping each other's clothes off. The girl breaks the kiss. The guy looks around, annoyed.

MAKEOUT GUY
Come on, Judy, you gave me one for my birthday.

JUDY
Tucker, no! I don't feel like it.

MAKEOUT GUY
Come on, quit clownin' around, willya?

JUDY

I said no.

Tucker looks in her eyes.

MAKEOUT GUY

I love you Judy.

Judy looks up, all smiles. She spits out her gum.

JUDY

Happy Thanksgiving, baby.

Judy shoves the guy back, pulling his pants down.

NARRATOR

You'll come home for the holidays... in a body bag.

The guy leans his head back, out the driver's side window, positioning himself so she can go down on him. The girl starts to perform oral sex on the guy, holding one hand on his chest.

THE GUY'S UPSIDE DOWN POV - sees the killer approaching him, swinging an AXE. The killer CHOPS THE GUY'S HEAD OFF. The girl in the car does not notice, assuming he's having an orgasm. She reaches up to touch his face, and is met by a BLEEDING STUMP. She screams as the blood hits her face and turns around. We see the killer outside the passenger side window. He swings the axe and we cut to:

THE TITLE - "Thanksgiving." The knife stabbing into the bloody turkey.

EXT. WOODS - NIGHT

Judy cries in the arms of Bobby, a high school jock in a letterman's jacket and very tight acid washed jeans.

JUDY

Bobby, Bobby, it was terrible, he killed Tucker! He -

BOBBY
(interrupting)

Cool it, Judy!

She shuts up. Looks in his eyes.

BOBBY

Relax. Bobby's here.

Bobby gives her a reassuring look. Judy nods, wipes away the tears, and starts making out with Bobby. She put her hands on his cheeks and pulls her head away only to discover BOBBY'S DECAPITATED HEAD IN HER HANDS. She drops the head - screaming - to reveal THE PILGRIM, holding the bloody axe right in front of her. He chases after her.

NARRATOR

Thanksgiving.

INT. HOUSE IN THE WOODS - NIGHT

The same house from the opening credits. A grandmother answers the door, revealing a young couple holding baked goods and bottles of wine. They all hug and kiss hello.

The guy wears a holiday sweater.

NARRATOR

Arrive hungry...

An entire family is tied up in chairs at a Norman Rockwell-style dinner table. They have obviously been beaten up and look around at each other terrified. The killer, wearing a pilgrim hat to hide his face, dramatically pulls a cloth which unveils the sweater guy's body prepared as if it were an actual Thanksgiving turkey. (Headless, on its back, arms severed at elbows, knees up towards mid-section, legs bound with string, tiny chef's hat accoutrements on the feet.) The guy's decapitated head is filled with stuffing.

NARRATOR

...leave stuffed.

TITLE: the knife stabbing into the turkey. THANKSGIVING.

NARRATOR

Thanksgiving. Coming, this February.

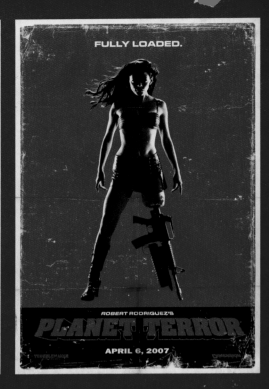

BLOOD, LUST & BRUTALITY

THE POSTER ART OF GRINDHOUSE

STEVEN GOLD, BLT & Associates: In motion picture advertising, there are those rare occasions when a film comes along that truly excites art directors and account executives alike. *Grindhouse* is that kind of movie. After an amazing collaboration with Robert Rodriguez on *Sin City*, we couldn't wait for his next movie. We never anticipated that we'd not only be allowed full access to Robert but to Quentin Tarantino as well. To say that our *Grindhouse* team at BLT was psyched beyond belief would be a gross understatement. The reality is that this project quickly became the true highlight of the year for all of us.

KURT VOLK, Troublemaker Studios Graphic Designer: In the fall of 2005, Robert handed me a few double feature movie posters and asked me to come up with some *Grindhouse* artwork that was in the same vein. We were preparing a small booklet for the AFM [American Film Market] at the time and needed to convey to distributors what the film would look and feel like, months before anything was shot. We don't normally create much of the promotional artwork inhouse, so this was something new for us—a new challenge. So Robert, Quentin and I tossed the art

back and forth for a few weeks, fine-tuning it, until we settled on two double feature posters that featured an illustration of Cherry on one side and the *Death Proof* car on the other, blasting off the page.

During the fall of 2005, we also shot a trailer for *Machete* with Danny Trejo. Robert took an amazing photo of Danny standing on top of a limousine in front of the Texas capital. The image is totally iconic, really amazing. Troublemaker Digital Artist Chris Olivia took the image and transformed it into a Frank Frazetta-inspired masterpiece. The sky is opening up, breathing fire and Danny is about to crush some skulls. I honestly think it's one of the coolest images I've ever seen. I slapped some text on it and that became the *Machete* poster.

When it came time to create the artwork for the 2006 San Diego ComiCon, we ended up polishing some of the AFM art to use as promotional posters. We made the *Planet Terror* posters into miniature one-sheets, complete with folds and scuff marks, and made the *Death Proof* and *Grindhouse* double feature posters into "window cards." One sheets are the big posters

ABOVE: *Death Proof* and *Planet Terror* Teaser posters created for the 2006 San Diego ComiCon. Design by Kurt Volk.
OPPOSITE: *Machete* one sheet. Design by Kurt Volk, photo montage by Chris Olivia.

YESTERDAY HE WAS A DECENT MAN LIVING A DECENT LIFE
NOW HE IS A BRUTAL SAVAGE
WHO MUST SLAUGHTER TO STAY ALIVE

DANNY TREJO IS

MACHETE

AN **RIP** PRODUCTION

a RODRIGUEZ INTERNATIONAL PICTURES release starring **DANNY TREJO / JEFF FAHEY**
screenplay by Robert Rodriguez / produced by Elizabeth Avellán/Robert Rodriguez and Quentin Tarantino/Written and Directed by Robert Rodriguez

TROUBLEMAKER STUDIOS   BACK BACK

[27" x 41"] that we're familiar with today. These posters have been around forever, but prior to 1982 they were shipped to theaters flat, folded into eight sections. That's the reason for all the tiny horizontal and vertical fold lines.

Window cards, on the other hand, we don't see too much of these days. At least not ones that advertise movies. Window cards were smaller [14" x 22"], cheaply made two or three color posters that were silk-screened onto cardboard and usually posted outside in the elements—you could find them on everything from telephone poles to barbershop windows. Because these cards were so cheap to produce, and because they didn't require the approval or distribution of the NSS [National Screen Service], they became very popular on the grindhouse circuit.

Sometimes window cards are also called "Benton Cards," since the Benton Card Company was responsible for a great deal of this amazing art. The fine folks at Benton were extremely supportive of our project and we certainly owe them a big debt of gratitude for their help.

Window cards would also be shipped with a blank spot at the top for theaters to stamp the time and date of the showing. So for the *Death Proof* ComiCon poster, Graphic Artist Ellen Lampl designed a beautiful stamp for us, featuring Austin's now-defunct Burnet Road Drive-In. Our Production Designer, Steve Joyner, used our laser-cutter to etch Ellen's design into a piece of wood, which we inked and used like a letterpress. The results were pretty stunning and didn't require any Photoshop hocus pocus.

STEVEN GOLD: It began for us in June of 2006. We saw our first glimpse of the ComiCon posters. From an art point, they were quite authentic looking, harking back to the 1970s with expert precision. On the "cool meter," however, they were off the charts. Like some kind of Pavlovian signal, we all began salivating. We were eager and ready to begin this campaign.

In mid-August, through the direction of David Pearson, Dimension's creative executive, we began researching 70s B-horror movies and lobby cards and posters and overall campaigns. David asked us to create some teaser looks that we could send to Robert and Quentin as a way to begin the process. Two days later we had a presentation ready to go. We waited for the one call that would really begin this campaign. That call happened on or about October 20th. David Pearson called me and said to get Rick Lynch, the "L" in BLT, and myself down to Austin to meet with Robert and Kurt Volk, one of Robert's creative geniuses at Troublemaker Studios. A week later we were at Troublemaker Studios, meeting with Robert and Kurt. The best way for a firm like ours to create campaigns is to be given access to the filmmakers so we can hear their thoughts and ideas from the onset. Sitting with Robert and watching some footage and seeing the

work already done, gave us an amazing starting point. Kurt showed us his research, which was amazing and flooded us with an infinite number of ideas.

Robert is always great at letting us know what he doesn't want, which is equally important. We left Austin with solid direction from Robert's camp. Fully equipped to begin the *Planet Terror* one sheet looks. Next, we had to meet with Quentin to get his take on the campaign.

Like Robert, Quentin Tarantino is involved in every aspect of his films. His eye for detail and authenticity is legend in this industry. He is arguably one of the most detail-oriented filmmakers in the world. Meeting with him to discuss his visions for the advertising was one of the many highlights of this or any project. After he carefully educated us on the history of the

OPPOSITE: *Grindhouse* Combo posters created for the 2006 San Diego ComiCon. Design by Kurt Volk; **BELOW:** *Grindhouse* standee. Design by BLT; **UPCOMING SPREAD:** *Planet Terror* character teasers. Design by Kurt Volk and BLT. • *Death Proof* character teasers. Design by BLT.

FULLY LOADED.

ROBERT RODRIGUEZ'S

PLANET TERROR

APRIL 6, 2007

EL WRAY IS GONNA MAKE 'EM PAY.

ROBERT RODRIGUEZ'S

PLANET TERROR

APRIL 6, 2007

YOU MIGHT FEEL A LITTLE PRICK.

ROBERT RODRIGUEZ'S

PLANET TERROR

APRIL 6, 2007

HIS PERSONALITY CAN BE INFECTIOUS.

ROBERT RODRIGUEZ'S

PLANET TERROR

APRIL 6, 2007

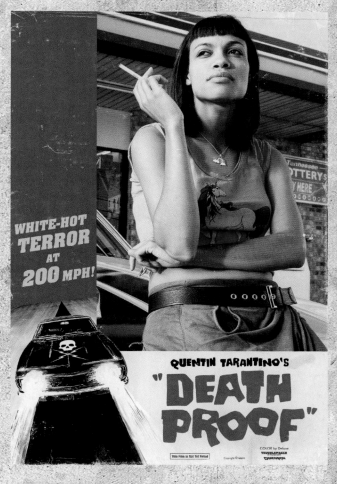

WHITE-HOT TERROR AT 200 MPH!

QUENTIN TARANTINO'S
"DEATH PROOF"

WHITE-HOT TERROR AT 200 MPH!

QUENTIN TARANTINO'S
"DEATH PROOF"

WHITE-HOT TERROR AT 200 MPH!

QUENTIN TARANTINO'S
"DEATH PROOF"

WHITE-HOT TERROR AT 200 MPH!

QUENTIN TARANTINO'S
"DEATH PROOF"

grindhouse style of motion pictures and advertising art, we took our direction and began the arduous task of revising and reinventing.

KURT VOLK: Along the way, Robert and I also made a bunch of lobby cards for the movies. Lobby cards were traditionally 11" x 14" stills from the movie that were printed on cardstock and distributed to theaters. They would be posted out front or in the theater lobby with the intention of telling the story visually, through pictures. A passerby could get a feel for what the movie was about, just by looking at a few images. For this reason, lobby cards usually featured the most over-the-top imagery—the most blood, lust and brutality that the film had to offer.

So while shooting *Grindhouse*, we made a ton of these lobby cards. Robert would shoot a scene, send me a few stills, and, by the end of the day, the actors could see printed lobby cards of the scenes they just shot. I think it was kind of a cool way to get the actors excited and to very simply convey the look and feel of the movie *while* it was being made.

STEVEN GOLD: The first project for us was to realize a sketch of the *Grindhouse* in-theater standee. We were told to make it grand and jaw dropping. Given the parameters that most theaters allow, we did our best. We created a façade of an old 70s style theater complete with box office and walls filled with lobby cards. One wall was dedicated to *Death Proof* and one to *Planet Terror*. On the *Planet Terror* side, Robert had opted for taking select shots from the unit photography and having us lay them into a retro-looking shell. The result was varied images, distressed so they felt like they'd been weathered. The *Death Proof* side proved a bit more challenging for us because Quentin wanted every detail to be authentic. He supplied us with several different looks at which point we laid in photos of his choice in the exact order he wanted and, after some minor tweaking, finished the *Death Proof* side. Using JJ & A, a local company that specializes in this type of work, we had a mock-up created and showed to all the powers that be in the form of jpegs. Once approved, a full size (12' x 9') standee was created. It was everything we hoped it would be. Once in theaters, it was truly the one

ABOVE: *Grindhouse* banner artwork. Design by Kurt Volk and BLT; **UPCOMING SPREADS:** Lobby cards for *Planet Terror* and *Death Proof*. Design by Kurt Volk & BLT.

standee that stood out in a pool of many during the busy holiday season.

Next, our task was to create a banner that could be a companion to the standee. Once again, Robert and his team gave us their ideas and we executed. With input from Quentin and several rounds of exploration, a banner was created which captures the very essence of the movie. It's big and bold and in your face.

The last phase of our work was to create a final one sheet for both *Planet Terror* and *Death Proof* as well as a combo poster similar to what Robert had previously created. Robert had already pretty much mapped out what he wanted while Quentin had his own ideas. After many rounds of back and forth, a consensus was taken from Quentin's, Robert's and the Weinstein's camps and a couple one sheets were born.

To the average person, the day-to-day challenges of motion picture advertising may seem dull, even hum drum. They may not truly understand or even know the effort it takes to get to a final one sheet.

To those of us in the industry, however, a project like *Grindhouse* allows us a rare opportunity to get inside the filmmakers minds and really explore all that is exciting about movie marketing. The effort is mammoth and the following people lent their expertise to the process: From the Dimension Films, David Pearson; from BLT and Associates: Rick Lynch, Ronnie Blumenberg, Chris St. George, Chris Davidson, Noah Witlin, Edwin Alvarenga, Eddie Nunez, Jeff Barnett, Kevin Ramos, Jose Perez, Jorge Diaz, Bud Lam and Danny Escandon, Jr.

PLANET TERROR

A RODRIGUEZ INTERNATIONAL PICTURES RELEASE STARRING ROSE McGOWAN · FREDDY RODRIGUEZ · MICHAEL BIEHN SCREENPLAY BY ROBERT RODRIGUEZ PRODUCED BY ELIZABETH AVELLÁN, ROBERT RODRIGUEZ AND QUENTIN TARANTINO DIRECTED BY ROBERT RODRIGUEZ
ALSO STARRING JEFF FAHEY · JOSH BROLIN · MARLEY SHELTON A TROUBLEMAKER STUDIOS PRODUCTION
TROUBLEMAKER STUDIOS DIMENSION FILMS 07/03

PLANET TERROR

A RODRIGUEZ INTERNATIONAL PICTURES RELEASE STARRING ROSE McGOWAN · FREDDY RODRIGUEZ · MICHAEL BIEHN SCREENPLAY BY ROBERT RODRIGUEZ PRODUCED BY ELIZABETH AVELLÁN, ROBERT RODRIGUEZ AND QUENTIN TARANTINO DIRECTED BY ROBERT RODRIGUEZ
ALSO STARRING JEFF FAHEY · JOSH BROLIN · MARLEY SHELTON A TROUBLEMAKER STUDIOS PRODUCTION
TROUBLEMAKER STUDIOS DIMENSION FILMS 07/03

PLANET TERROR

A RODRIGUEZ INTERNATIONAL PICTURES RELEASE STARRING ROSE McGOWAN · FREDDY RODRIGUEZ · MICHAEL BIEHN SCREENPLAY BY ROBERT RODRIGUEZ PRODUCED BY ELIZABETH AVELLÁN, ROBERT RODRIGUEZ AND QUENTIN TARANTINO DIRECTED BY ROBERT RODRIGUEZ ALSO STARRING JEFF FAHEY · JOSH BROLIN · MARLEY SHELTON A TROUBLEMAKER STUDIOS PRODUCTION

TROUBLEMAKER STUDIOS · DIMENSION · 07/03

PLANET TERROR

A RODRIGUEZ INTERNATIONAL PICTURES RELEASE STARRING ROSE McGOWAN · FREDDY RODRIGUEZ · MICHAEL BIEHN SCREENPLAY BY ROBERT RODRIGUEZ PRODUCED BY ELIZABETH AVELLÁN, ROBERT RODRIGUEZ AND QUENTIN TARANTINO DIRECTED BY ROBERT RODRIGUEZ ALSO STARRING JEFF FAHEY · JOSH BROLIN · MARLEY SHELTON A TROUBLEMAKER STUDIOS PRODUCTION

TROUBLEMAKER STUDIOS · DIMENSION · 07/03

PLANET TERROR

A RODRIGUEZ INTERNATIONAL PICTURES RELEASE STARRING ROSE McGOWAN · FREDDY RODRIGUEZ · MICHAEL BIEHN SCREENPLAY BY ROBERT RODRIGUEZ PRODUCED BY ELIZABETH AVELLÁN, ROBERT RODRIGUEZ AND QUENTIN TARANTINO DIRECTED BY ROBERT RODRIGUEZ
ALSO STARRING JEFF FAHEY · JOSH BROLIN · MARLEY SHELTON A TROUBLEMAKER STUDIOS PRODUCTION
TROUBLEMAKER STUDIOS DIMENSION FILMS 07/03

PLANET TERROR

A RODRIGUEZ INTERNATIONAL PICTURES RELEASE STARRING ROSE McGOWAN · FREDDY RODRIGUEZ · MICHAEL BIEHN SCREENPLAY BY ROBERT RODRIGUEZ PRODUCED BY ELIZABETH AVELLÁN, ROBERT RODRIGUEZ AND QUENTIN TARANTINO DIRECTED BY ROBERT RODRIGUEZ
ALSO STARRING JEFF FAHEY · JOSH BROLIN · MARLEY SHELTON A TROUBLEMAKER STUDIOS PRODUCTION
TROUBLEMAKER STUDIOS DIMENSION FILMS 07/03

PLANET TERROR

A RODRIGUEZ INTERNATIONAL PICTURES RELEASE STARRING ROSE McGOWAN · FREDDY RODRIGUEZ · MICHAEL BIEHN SCREENPLAY BY ROBERT RODRIGUEZ PRODUCED BY ELIZABETH AVELLÁN, ROBERT RODRIGUEZ AND QUENTIN TARANTINO DIRECTED BY ROBERT RODRIGUEZ ALSO STARRING JEFF FAHEY · JOSH BROLIN · MARLEY SHELTON A TROUBLEMAKER STUDIOS PRODUCTION

TROUBLEMAKER STUDIOS   DIMENSION FILMS   07/93

PLANET TERROR

A RODRIGUEZ INTERNATIONAL PICTURES RELEASE STARRING ROSE McGOWAN · FREDDY RODRIGUEZ · MICHAEL BIEHN SCREENPLAY BY ROBERT RODRIGUEZ PRODUCED BY ELIZABETH AVELLÁN, ROBERT RODRIGUEZ AND QUENTIN TARANTINO DIRECTED BY ROBERT RODRIGUEZ ALSO STARRING JEFF FAHEY · JOSH BROLIN · MARLEY SHELTON A TROUBLEMAKER STUDIOS PRODUCTION

TROUBLEMAKER STUDIOS   DIMENSION FILMS   07/93

PLANET TERROR

A RODRIGUEZ INTERNATIONAL PICTURES RELEASE STARRING ROSE McGOWAN · FREDDY RODRIGUEZ · MICHAEL BIEHN WRITTEN BY ROBERT RODRIGUEZ PRODUCED BY ELIZABETH AVELLÁN ROBERT RODRIGUEZ AND QUENTIN TARANTINO DIRECTED BY ROBERT RODRIGUEZ
ALSO STARRING JEFF FAHEY · JOSH BROLIN · MARLEY SHELTON   A TROUBLEMAKER STUDIOS PRODUCTION

TROUBLEMAKER STUDIOS   DIMENSION   07/03

244

PLANET TERROR

A RODRIGUEZ INTERNATIONAL PICTURES RELEASE STARRING ROSE McGOWAN · FREDDY RODRIGUEZ · MICHAEL BIEHN WRITTEN BY ROBERT RODRIGUEZ PRODUCED BY ELIZABETH AVELLÁN ROBERT RODRIGUEZ AND QUENTIN TARANTINO DIRECTED BY ROBERT RODRIGUEZ
ALSO STARRING JEFF FAHEY · JOSH BROLIN · MARLEY SHELTON   A TROUBLEMAKER STUDIOS PRODUCTION

TROUBLEMAKER STUDIOS   DIMENSION

PLANET TERROR

A RODRIGUEZ INTERNATIONAL PICTURES RELEASE STARRING ROSE McGOWAN · FREDDY RODRIGUEZ · MICHAEL BIEHN SCREENPLAY BY ROBERT RODRIGUEZ PRODUCED BY ELIZABETH AVELLÁN ROBERT RODRIGUEZ AND QUENTIN TARANTINO DIRECTED BY ROBERT RODRIGUEZ
ALSO STARRING JEFF FAHEY · JOSH BROLIN · MARLEY SHELTON A TROUBLEMAKER STUDIOS PRODUCTION
TROUBLEMAKER STUDIOS DIMENSION 07/03

PLANET TERROR

A RODRIGUEZ INTERNATIONAL PICTURES RELEASE STARRING ROSE McGOWAN · FREDDY RODRIGUEZ · MICHAEL BIEHN SCREENPLAY BY ROBERT RODRIGUEZ PRODUCED BY ELIZABETH AVELLÁN ROBERT RODRIGUEZ AND QUENTIN TARANTINO DIRECTED BY ROBERT RODRIGUEZ
ALSO STARRING JEFF FAHEY · JOSH BROLIN · MARLEY SHELTON A TROUBLEMAKER STUDIOS PRODUCTION
TROUBLEMAKER STUDIOS DIMENSION

WHITE-HOT TERROR AT 200 MPH!

QUENTIN TARANTINO'S
"DEATH PROOF"

COLOR by Deluxe

TROUBLEMAKER STUDIOS

DIMENSION FILMS

This Film is Not Yet Rated

Copyright © MMVII

246

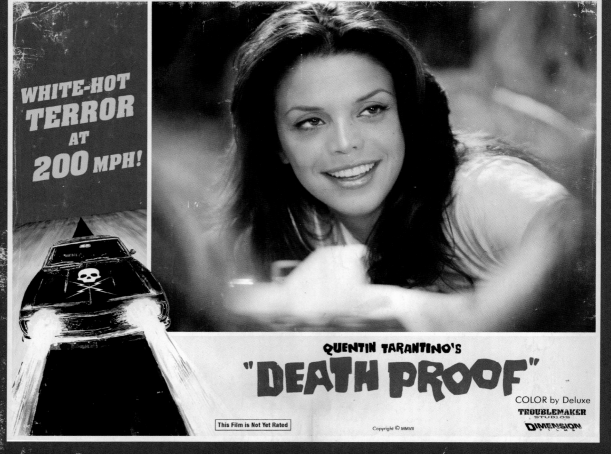

WHITE-HOT TERROR AT 200 MPH!

QUENTIN TARANTINO'S
"DEATH PROOF"

COLOR by Deluxe

TROUBLEMAKER STUDIOS

DIMENSION FILMS

This Film is Not Yet Rated

Copyright © MMVII

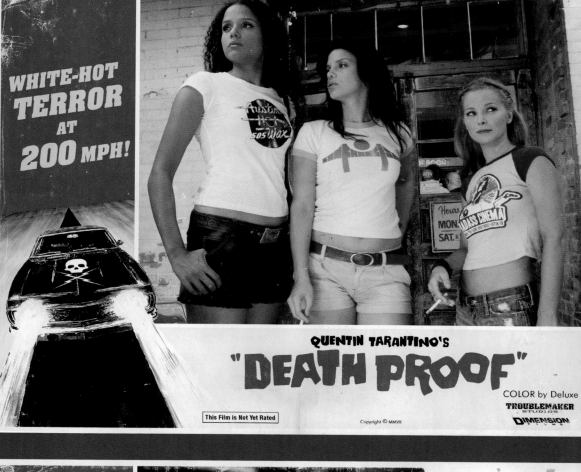

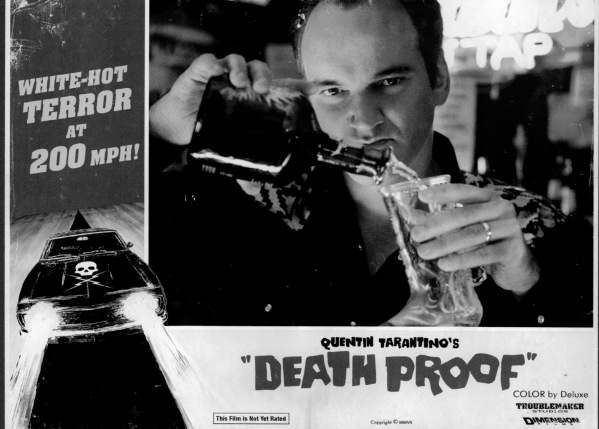

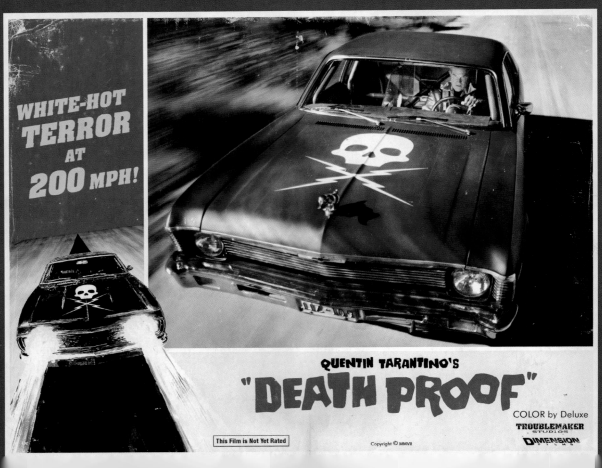

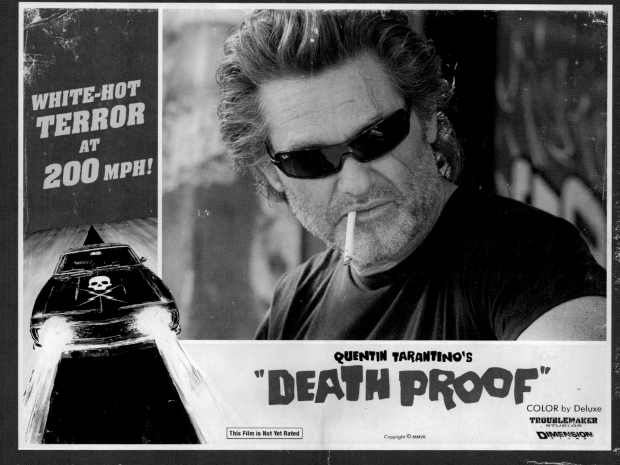

Photos on pages 6, 16-25, 27-32, 35-44, 46-49, 51-53, 55-72, 74-78, 80, 95-96, 98-101, 104-111, 113-114, 116, 118-120, 122-124, 127, 129-137, 139, 141, 143, 146, 150 & 253 by Rico Torres.

Photos on pages 8, 152, 154, 156, 159, 162, 165, 167-169, 171-172, 174, 176, 182, 190, 193, 195-197 & 206 by Andrew Cooper.

Photos on pages 2, 26, 34, 45, 50, 54, 109, 208, 210 & 216-217 by Robert Rodriguez. · Photos on pages 119, 122, 191 & 209 by Kurt Volk. · Photos on pages 200 & 205 by Brian Bettwy. · Photos on pages 224-229 courtesy of Eli Roth. · Photos on pages 102-104 & 113 courtesy of KNB. · Artwork on pages 1, 11, 15 & 256 courtesy of the Benton Card Company. · Photos on pages 142, 147 & 149 by Aaron Burns. · Photos on pages 93-99, 120-121, 125-126, 128, 136-137, 138, 140-141, 163-164, 166, 169, 171, 173, 183, 191-192 courtesy of the Grindhouse Property Department. · Photos on pages 144-145 by Eleonora Avellán. · Photos on pages 33, 73 & 112 courtesy of Dimension Films. · Artwork on pages 82-92, 115, 126, 209, 212-214, 218 & 220 courtesy of Troublemaker Digital. · Photos on pages 194-195, 198-199, 200-204, 213, 215 & 221 by John Sandau. · Photos on pages 142, 147 & 149 by Chris Jack. · Photo on page 91 by Christopher Zaleski. · Photo on page 10 courtesy of Getty Images. · Photo on page 140 by Ofer Zidon.

The editor wishes to thank Robert Rodriguez, Quentin Tarantino and Elizabeth Avellán as well as the tireless cast and crew of "Grindhouse." Your generosity and willingness to make time for that kid with the tape recorder and legal pad is not taken for granted. Thank you.

This book would also not have been possible without the absurd generosity, support and tolerance of Meredith Volk.

THE TWO MOST HELLISH HORROR HITS THAT EVER TURNED BLOOD TO ICE!!!

IT WILL SCARE THE LIVING YELL OUT OF YOU!

HAIR RAISING!
SEE — THE MADMAN'S GRUESOME CHAMBER OF HORRORS!

See the ghastly ghouls...IN FLAMING COLOR!

NOTHING LIKE THIS IN ALL THE HISTORY OF HORROR!

THE TWIN TERROR SHOW THAT TOPS THEM ALL

TOGETHER IN ONE SMASH EXPLOSIVE SHOW

TERROR FLOODS THE SCREEN

LIKE NOTHING YOUR EYES HAVE EVER SEEN BEFORE

and Directed by JACQUES MARQUETTE
Screenplay by RAY BUFFUM • Music by WALTER GREENE
A MARQUETTE Production · Released by HOWCO International

FABULOUS! FANTASTIC! TERRIFYING

TWO GIRLS! — TWO PICTURES!

One Girl Bad ... One Girl ? ?

DOUBLE SPECTACLE-TERROR!

FIENDISH FRENZIED BLOOD-CHILLING